BELTZHOOVER

BELTZHOOVER

Gayle O. Kamp

Deanna Thomas Oklepek

AuthorHouse™
1663 Liberty Drive, Suite 200
Bloomington, IN 47403
www.authorhouse.com
Phone: 1-800-839-8640

AuthorHouse™ UK Ltd.
500 Avebury Boulevard
Central Milton Keynes, MK9 2BE
www.authorhouse.co.uk
Phone: 08001974150

First published by AuthorHouse 08/01/06

ISBN: 1-4259-4965-7 (sc)

Printed in the United States of America
Bloomington, Indiana

This book is printed on acid-free paper.

Text compiled and indexed by Gayle O. Kamp along with additional researching.

Orders are to be sent to AuthorHouse. Other questions or inquires, such as genealogical in nature, may be sent to Gayle O. Kamp gokamp@aol.com *or to Deanna Oklepek* d.oklepek@att.net

FOREWORD

Who was Christian Melchior Beltzhuber? Where did he come from? Why did he come to America?

In beginning our quest for more information fifteen years ago all we had to start with was an old family Bible with a publication date of 1814. The names were vaguely familiar, but our curiosity to find out more was overwhelming. Fifteen years ago we traveled to Pennsylvania, Maryland, Mississippi, Salt Lake City and Tennessee and in doing so have found a great deal of information about the Beltzhoover family. We have met new cousins and made new friends.

The first record of the Beltzhoover (Beltzhuber) family in America is their immigration record found in the <u>Passenger and Immigration Lists Index, Volume 1, A - G</u>, by P. William Filby with Dorothy M. Lower, Gale Research Co. Here we found Christian Melchior Beltzhuber listed with his wife and five children. Going further into the source material we found in <u>Neue Beitraege zur Auswanderung nach Amerika im 18, Jahrhundert aus Altwuerttembergischen Kirchenbuechem unter Hinzuziehung anderer Quellen</u> by Adolf Gerber, Stuttgart : J.F. Steinkopf, 1929 (Lancour 134), on page 23, that they immigrated from a little town in Germany called Metterzimmern, north of Stuttgart. This book tells us that Melchior and his wife were actually married in Schnaitheim, Germany (near Heidenheim), the birth dates of the five children, that they left Germany with permission and that they were all living on April 21, 1752.

In <u>Meyers Orts=und Derkehrs=Lexicon des Deutshcen Reich , Volume 2</u> by Dr. E. Uetrecht, Leipzig and Wien Bibliographisches Institut, 1913, we find Metterzimmem listed as a village on the Metter River, in the state of Wuerttemburg, province of Neckarkreis, 4 kilometers (about two and one-half miles) from the town of Bietigheim.

What was going on in Germany and other countries at that time? Why did Melchior want to leave Germany with his family?

Germany in the 17th and 18th centuries was not one country as we know it today, but rather a large group of small states each being governed by a different ruler. The rulers were mainly interested in themselves and the taxes that they could exact from their subjects. It was also expected that their subjects would practice the religion of their rule, being mainly Catholic or Lutheran at that time. The Thirty Years War (from 1618 - 1648) devastated the German economy. Farms were often ruined beyond repair. Trade and industry came to a standstill. A succession of later wars and invasions prevented any substantial recovery.

Meanwhile, colonization was beginning to take place in America. A few Germans had come to Jamestown as early as 1607 and others had helped the Puritans construct the town of Boston, but the first real beginning of German settlement in the English colonies was made by Franz Daniel Pastorius when in 1683 he settled a large group of Germans about 6 miles from Philadelphia and named the town Germantown. Other Germans slowly began to arrive and settle in Germantown. Additional settlement was delayed due to the outbreak of the War of the League in Augsburg and the War of the Spanish Succession in 1701. Then the winter of 1708 - 1709 was very cold with a great deal of snow, one of the worst winters on record. Many fruit trees and vines were killed by the deep frost and heavy snow.

v

During the Spanish Succession War the German area known as the Palatine (along the Rhine River) was ravaged by the French armies and about 15,000 Germans were admitted into England. The English economy was unable to absorb a group this size so the English government encouraged the Palatines to sail to America. A small group did go to America, founding a settlement at Newburgh, New York in 1708. This group was followed by another group about two years later. Other German settlements started in New Jersey and Maryland, but Pennsylvania was the most attractive colony to the German immigrants. The majority of the Germans who settled in PA were Lutherans or German Reformed Lutherans, all of whom were happy just to be able to farm the fertile land of the colony on their own land.

By 1747, the Governor of Pennsylvania estimated that Germans accounted for more than three-fifths of the total population of 200,000 in the colony. He praised the Germans for their hard work in helping Pennsylvania become a flourishing colony. The peak years of German immigration into Philadelphia were 1749 - 1754 when more than 37,000 Germans arrived.

Other colonists, however, were not so happy, including Benjamin Franklin. They feared that the Germans would soon outnumber the English.

During the Revolutionary War the German-Americans played a very important part in fighting and helping to supply goods and food for the troops. The German-Americans actually manufactured the Kentucky rifle which was lighter than the guns being used by the English-Americans. They built the Conestoga wagon which was the wagon used in later years by the Pioneers traveling westward. During the war the German-Americans were able to get many of the Hessians (paid mercenary soldiers from Germany) to leave the Tory troops and to join the Americans. Many of the Hessians stayed on in America after the Revolutionary War as they saw what the Germans had been able to do in America - land was free or either very cheap. Though English was the official language of the government, many laws and rulings were routinely translated into German by Maryland and Pennsylvania for this important group in their population.

During the 1700's the shipping companies wanted to fill their ships from Europe to America so they paid men to travel to Europe and to pass out brochures on the "New Land". The men were always well dressed and often told exaggerated stories about life in the colonies, thus influencing many to travel. These men became known as "Newlanders".

Melchior and his family all seemed to attend Lutheran Churches in America after their arrival and Metterzimmern was a Lutheran (Evangelische) state, so he did not leave because of religious persecution. More than likely he left because he wanted to make a better life for himself and his family.

How did the Beltzhuber family travel to America? It is not know exactly when they left their home in Metterzimmern, Germany, but it is possible that they left on April 12, 1752 or soon thereafter as indicated in the Adolf Gerber book that they were all living on that date. If so, then it took the family a little over 6 months to complete their trip to Philadelphia. It is most likely that they traveled on the Rhine River to Rotterdam and according to The Adolf Gerber Lists they traveled to America with Hans Jerg (Georg)

Printzighofer (Brenzighofer) who was born in 1698, a cartwright by trade, and his wife, Anna Maria Rieger (they were married July 9, 1737) from a neighboring village called Sersheim. These journeys to the "new land" could take from two to six months. Along the Rhine River many tollgates had been set up and the tolls had to be paid along the way. After arriving in the port of Rotterdam, there were many thieves and conmen preying upon the unsuspecting immigrants, stealing from them, charging inflated prices, etc. Some immigrants ran out of money at this point. However, even with little or no money immigrants could still travel on the ships on the "Redemption System". This allowed passengers to pay a portion of their fare at the time of boarding the ship with the remainder to be paid by family or friends upon their arrival, or, they could "redeem" their fare in labor once the ship docked in Philadelphia, similar to being an indentured servant. When the ship arrived in Philadelphia with redemptioners on board, a doctor would come first to examine them and to determine whether anyone carried a contagious disease. After the male heads of households swore to the Oath of Allegiance to the British king, the interested citizens would board the ship and determine which of the redemptioners suited their needs. Upon reaching an agreement, the citizens would pay the ship's captain for the remaining passage due. Sometimes the family was divided up among different purchasers, or one member (often a son or daughter) was indentured to pay for the others' passages. After 1750 nearly half of all the arriving immigrants were redemptioners. In our research we have not been able to determine whether of not the Beltzhuber family were redemptioners or if they had the means to pay their passages in full.

The Beltzhubers traveled from Rotterdam to England and on to America on a ship named "President" and under the leadership of Captain Dunlop, arriving in Philadelphia on Wednesday, September 27, 1752. Upon the arrival of the ship, Melchior Beltzhuber subscribed and swore to the Oath of Allegiance to the King of Britain. It is not yet known where they went at this point, but it is believed that the family stayed in Pennsylvania, probably near York in York Co. Pennsylvania. The next public record that has been found of them was a church record of baptisms from the personal records of Pastor Jacob Goering from York County dated November 11, 1760, where Anna Maria, widow of Melchior Beltzhuber was holding up (lifted) the infant, Catharine Barbara Schartel for her baptism. The parents of the infant were George Frederick and Maria Schartel. It is then presumed that the original adult immigrant, Christian Melchior, had died by that time. It is interesting to note that Pastor Jacob Goering performed pastoral duties not only in the vicinity of York, PA, but also Hagerstown, MD where we find children of Christian and Melchior Beltzhuber living.

The German-Americans have played an important role in the development of this nation and in 1989 it was estimated that one in every five US Citizens had some German ancestry. The Germans are second only to the British in sending immigrants to America. The contributions the Germans have made are many, such as the Christmas tree, the Easter bunny, hamburgers, frankfurters, tootsie rolls, Hershey bars, the Kentucky rifle and the Conestoga wagon, just to name a few. The Germans were hard working, organized, industrious people and all of us who are descended from this family can be proud of them and what they, and ourselves, have accomplished.

Deanna Thomas Oklepek

Abbreviations

Adm., administrator of estate
acct., account, exec. of adm.
anc., ancestry, ancestors
b., born, brother
bap., bpt., baptized
bur., buried
c., ca., cir., circa., (about) used
    in connection with dates
cf., confer, compare
ch., chn., child, children
C.S.A., Confederate States Army
co., county
CW., Civil War
d., died.
dau., daughter
d.s.p., died without issue
DAR., Daughter of the American
    Revolution
da., dau., dt., daughter
dec., dec d., deceased
d.i., died in infancy
div., divorced, dissolution
d/o., daughter of
d.y., died young
ead., eadem., in the same way
est., estate
ex., exec., executor, executrix
f., father
fgs., family group sheets
gdn., guardian
gen., genealogy; genealogical
g., gr., grave
gg., great-grand
G. A. R., Grand Old Army of the
    Republic (CW veteran)
hist., history; historical

i., infant, infancy, issue
Ibid., same
Illus., Illustrated
Intestate., died without a will
Is., issue
J.P., Justice of Peace
LDS., Latter Day Saints
M. G., Minister of Gospell
m. , married
m\1., married first
MM., Monthly Meeting, Soc.
    of Quakers/Friends
M/M., Mr. & Mrs.
n.d., no date
n. i., no issue
n.p., no place, no publisher
ob., obit., died, obituary
p.. pp., page, pages
prob., pro., probated
RW., Revolutionary War
S.A.R., Sons of the
    American Revolution
soc., society
s/o., son of
sp., sps., sponsor, sponsors
tp., twp., township
unm., unmarried
U.S.A., United States Army
V.D.M., Voluns deus; minister
vol., volume
V. R. , vital records
wd., wid., widow
wf., wife
w., i., without issue
w/o., without
y., young

Introduction

Having a life-long love of the research of family histories, beginning at the age of 12 with a first pedigree chart, it seemed natural to me that the study of Beltzhoover would consume such a large amount of research.

At retirement in 1981, I began the compilation of the numerous files collected over the many years of research of my own families and then of my wife's families. This resulted in The Kamp Papers, Vol. I pp. 503 (1984) and Mrs. Kamps families, The Kamp Papers, Vol II pp. 883 (1986).

One of the unsolved ancestoral lines of Thelma (Thelma Cass Kamp) was an Eva Beltzhoover.

With my membership in Western Pennsylvania Genealogical Society, I found a Beltzhoover researcher, Deanna Thomas Oklepek and quickly I became hooked on Beltzhoover.

HOW TO USE THIS BOOK:

The superscript number following a family members name is the generation number. The numbering begins with the emigrant as number 1- and the numbering continues throughout the text. The number inside the parenthesis ( ) refers back to the parents number. Therefore, one can find the latest name in the index and go backwards on their line to the emigrant.

Example:

20-GEORGE PETER BELTZHUBER/BELTZHOFER, SR.[3] (3)

Footnote numbers such as [3], a superscript number at the end of a paragraph or sentence, is a footnote number and is the reference or source which is on the bottom of the same page.

<u>Maiden names are cross-referenced in the index.</u> If you know the spouses name, a quick check of the index should show you their place in the Beltzhoover family.

Gayle O. Kamp

ACKNOWLEDGMENTS

Much of the Beltzhoover information is a result of the considerable and able research of Deanna Oklepek along with the additional research by your compiler.

Others that we thank for their help are: George Beltzhoover, Joan Moore, Edward Beltzhoover, Elizabeth Peach and Jerri Burket. Don Lerew, Patty Coates, Vivian Krecker Beltzhoover, Virginia Lee Beltzhoover Morrison, Jane Beltzhoover Ziegenfelder, Joe Cannon, William Beltzhoover Conner, Mrs. William Butzner, Jr., Rhea J. Beltzhoover Hughes, Donald and David Hall, Norman Schwotzer, Ruth Coy, Russell Darrell Meridith, Craig Devor, Peter Romeika.

There are, no doubt, those that we have missed naming. Please excuse us for that. Many are so listed in the footnotes. We are in debt to all those named and unnamed that contributed.

PREFACE

Those of us who are dedicated to the research of the Beltzhoover family welcome Beltzhoover cousins ever where, in moving this research forward. We have diverse backgrounds but a common interest in the heritage.

For whatever reasons the family left Germany to sail to American in 1752 on the ship President and traversed the challenging seas to the Colonies, to an unknown future. They became tavern and hotel owners, farmers, river-boat captains, owners/managers of metal furnaces, sound business people and solid citizens.

The Beltzhoovers have their share of heroes. such as those who served in the wars. There may be others that we did not discover in the searches.

2. Melchior Beltzhuber (Melcher Belsheever), Rev. War in Capt. Peter Bell's/Beall's Co. Baltimore, MD.

5. Johann Jacob Jacob Beltshoover, Rev. War in Capt. William Heyser's Co. A. Washington Co., MD.

7. Thomas Beltzhoover, Rev. War, Pvt. in Capt. Christopher Lowman's Co., York Co., PA

10. Ludwig Beltzhoover, Rev. War, Pvt. in Capt. Philip Albright's Co., York Co., PA

20. George Peter Beltzhoover, served in the War of 1812

48. Daniel Beltzhoover, served CW

53. Elizabeth Mary Beltzhoover Cox Norris, a Civil War nurse

70. Daniel M. Beltzhoover, Col. graduated West Point, served Union Army then Confederate Officer in the Civil War.

102. George Stacker, Col. Confederate Army

124. Melchor M. Beltzhoover, Civil War in Col. Black's Co A. 62nd PA.

151. Samuel G. Beltzhoover, CW, Confederate Adjutant, G. S. O.

222. William Beltzhoover, served in Civil War

298. Thomas Husler Beltzhoover, Emergency Fleet Commission WWI

326. Mary Beltzhoover Dacy Jenkins, served in France in WWI

352. George Morris Beltzhoover, served in CW, PA Reg t.

475. Eric Dewitt Thomas, served in WWII, Korea

483. Geoffrey Montgomery Talbot Jones, served in OSS, WWII

492. George Morris Beltzhoover, Jr. served in WWI

539. Creedon Beltzhoover, served in WWII

558. Harry Zea, served WWI

559. William J. Zea, served WWI

627. Woodrow Allison Al Rowland, Battle of the Bulge, WWII

639. Lawrence M. Jackson, Jr. M.D. Col. served WWII, g. Arlington Cem.

696. Russell Darrell Meridith, served in WWII

725. Luther Linwood Leidigh, served in WWI

These ancestors, generally, practiced high moral standards, integrity, goodness, fair dealings, upright demeanor, caring for their families and respecting their neighbors and friends. Ancestors that one can be proud of. Families are people, not just dry statistics in some archive. We hope that you come away with a greater appreciation of your Beltzhoover heritage.

xv

CONTENTS

BELTZHUBER S IN GERMANY

The origins of the Beltzhoover family in Germany are only shown in-so-far as Deanna Oklepek has discovered in her research. The numbering system begins with the immigrant.

The records are from the Evangelical Church Records, Metterzimmern,, p. 95 showing the parents as Hans Jerg and Anna Barbara Beltzhuber.

HANS JERG BELTZHUBER, wf., Anna Barbara STAIGERS.

All children were born Metterzimmern, Neckarkreis, Wuerttremberg, Germany.

Children: (BELTZHUBER)

(1) Maria Magdalene Beltzhuber, b. 16 Jan. 1698, m; 17 Nov. 1716,
Germany, Hanns Jacob Fackler
(2) Justina Barbara Beltzhuber, b. 17 Feb. 1699, Germany; m. 10
Nov. 1722, Hans Jerg Mack.
(3) Johannes Beltzhuber, b. 18 Feb. 1700
(4) Jacob Beltzhuber, b. 28 Mar. 1701
(5) Hans Martin Beltzhuber, b. 11 May 1703, Germany
(6) Hans Jerg Beltzhuber, b. 1705
(7) Agnes Susanna Beltzhuber, b. 7 Feb. 1707
(8) Matthais Beltzhuber, b. 22 Aug. 1709; 15 Aug. 1733, Anna
Catherine Goehring.
(9) Anna Jacobina Beltzhuber, b. 16 Mar. 1711
(10) Jacobina Margretha Beltzhuber, b. 19 May 1712
(11) Christian Melchior Beltzhuber, b. 7 Aug. 1713, d. before Nov.
1760; m. 21 July 1739, Anna Maria ? Beltzhuber.

1-CHRISTIAN MELCHIOR/MELCHOR BELTZHUBER[1], (1713-1760), b. 7 Aug. 1713, Metterzimmern, Neckarkreis, Wuertemberg; d. before Nov. 1760, in York Co., PA; m. 21 July, 1739, at Schnaitheim, Jagsjreis, Germany, Ann Maria --?--; d. Sept. 1786, York Co., PA. [1] [2] [3]

Regarding the variations of the spelling of the surname Beltzhoover. Many records were found to have different spellings. The immigrants of Beltzhuber were soon known as Beltzhoover. Even those family members that came to Pittsburgh establishing the suburb that is known as Beltzhoover, to this day. Generally, your compiler used the names of Beltzhuber and Beltzhoover to simplify the text.

Spellings: Belzhuber, Beltzhuber, Betzhoover, Betzhuber, Beltzhover, Beltzhoffer, Belsheever, Belshoover, Belshover, Belshuber, Beltshuber, Belzhoover, Beltshoover, Belthouser, Beltzhoober, and even Weltzhoffer, Wentzhafer and Peltzhuber.

The name Melchior was seen spelled several ways in the records. Some of those spellings are Melchior, Melcheor, Melcher, Melchor.

Christian Melchior BELTZHUBER left Germany and came to America 4-12-1752, "Venia Emigrandi" (with permission) on the ship "President", Capt. Dunlop, Rotterdam, Holland to Philadelphia, and took the oath of Allegiance on Wed. 27 Sept. 1752. He came from Metterzimmern, Germany, with his wife, A. Marie. They were not Hollanders. The "President" orginated in England and went to Rotterdam and thence to Philadelphia, PA. [4]

Passenger and Immigrations Lists. Index 1st. Ed. Vol. I, A-G with the source shown as 2464. This source lists his first six children and his wife, A. Maria. Melchor and Ann Maria were married in Schnaitheim. [5]
Metterzimmern is a burgh in the area of Bietigheim-Bissinger,

----

1. Oath of Allegiance, Court House, Philadelphia, PA. Genealogical Dept. Pennsylvania State Library, Harrisburg, PA

2. US Fed. Archives Center, Chicago, IL Book-Passenger & Immigations Lists Index, First Ed. Vol. I A-G Courtesy Deanna Oklepek

3. German Pennsylvania Pioneers   Ralph B. Strassburger Vol. I (1772-1775) p. 489-490 List 185 C. Courtesy Ruth C. Coy

4. Oklepek, Deanna Westmont, IL 10/95

5. Gerber, Adolph list p. 23 #2464

just north of the city of Stuttgart. [1]

   In The History of Pittsburgh and Environs, 1902, pp.155, a biographical sketch of Silas Pryor Beltzhoover, it states, "The Beltzhoover family dates back to very early times in American history, the pioneer members of this family came in 1645. In early generations they settled in Western Pennsylvania, taking up land in the infant colony before the grant of Charles II to William Penn." As researchers we are not sure of these statements. [2]

   Melchior BELTZHUBER in Feb., Mar., and Apr. 1807 was involved in property sales in Hagerstown, MD., 'valuable town property' for sale. His wife Maria had letters at the post office in July of 1807. Those letters for Maria were from F. Clements, and Benjamin Cogle. Were they gone to Pittsburgh by July of 1807? When Melchior was in Hagerstown it is believed that he owned Tavern(s).

   Elizabethtown was named by Jacob Hager for his wife. It was also called "Elizabeth Hundred" for the number of acres in a plot or the number of men of military age available. From it's beginning, though, the residents referred to it as 'Hager's Town." [3]

   Deanna Oklepek found records at the Pennsylvania State Library to substantiate that Anna Maria 'widow Beltzhuber' was in York Co., Tax records from 1757-1769. In 1779 she is shown living in York Town. There is also a record of bpt. Catharine Barbara Schartel, showing that Anna Maria, widow Melchior held the infant. [4] [5]

   Pastor Jacob Goering of Chirst Lutheran Church, York, PA. performed the baptism. Pastor Goering also performed baptisms and marriages in the vicinity of Hagerstown, MD.

   The estate/probate of Anna Maria (Mary) Beltzhuber was

----

1. Ibid., Oklepek, Deanna. Melchior & Anna
Maria marriage record shown in Evangelical Church records.,
Metterzimmern, BK 1., p. 174

2. The History of Pittsburgh & Environs, 1922
pp. 155, biographical sketch of Silas Pryor Beltzhoover

3. Marsden, Mindy Exec. Dir. Washington County Historical Soc., Hagerstown, MD. 5/2002. Courtesy Ruth C. Coy.

4. Penna. State Library Film Roll 5220

5. York Co., PA., Church Records, Vol.9 p. 109,
Penn. State Library

begun with the filing of the Administrator's Bond, Sept. 6, 1786 and settled, partially, on 29 Nov. 1787 and finally on 7 Sept. 1788 at York Town, York Co., PA. The administrator was Jacob Beltzhuber of Hagerstown, Washington Co., MD, age 41, her son.

The children that were born in Germany from George Conrad Beltzhuber, on, were born at Metterzimmern, Neckarkreis, Wuerttemberg, Germany. [1]

Your researchers are not sure that Ludwig and Theobald are in this line, but there are many indications that they were in the same places, churches, etc.

WILL OF MELCHEOR BELTZHOOVER, No. 201
CARNEGIE LIBRARY, FILM # 407, Wills of Allegheny County
VOLUME I, PAGES 278-279

In the Name of God Amen. I, Melcheor Beltzhoover of the County of Allegheny & State of Pennsylvania being very weak of Body but of sound mind, memory and understanding, blessed be God for the same, do make and publish this my last will and Testament in manner & form following to wit.- First of all I Command my immortal soul unto the hands of God who gave it, and my body to the earth to be buried in a decent Christian like manner at the discretion of my Executors herin after named and as to the worldly estate wherewith it has pleased God to bless me in this life, I wish to have Sold to the best advantages and to the highest bidder, out of which I give & devise unto my dear wife, <u>Elizabeth</u>, the part which the Law of this Commonwealth has provided for. To my son <u>Jacob</u> five shillings who has allready received a full Compensation and equal Share of my estate. And the remainder I Give & devise unto my children, <u>Henry, George, Elizabeth, Daniel, Samuel,</u> and <u>William</u> to be equally divided amongst them, whoever it is understand that the said Henry has received two hundred and twenty seven acres of land Situate in St. Clair Township, on the saw mill run, and one horse valued at five hundred and ninety three pounds, fifteen shillings money of the Commonwealth aforesaid- & further the said George hase received houses, lots & horse, furniture belonging to me and did remain at Hagerstown, valued at four hundred pound money Aforesaid, and Also that the said Daniel hase received from me from time to time the sum of two hundred and Seventy five pounds like many-which amount received by the said Henry, George, and Daniel is to be considered in part of their share, And in Case any of the amount aforesaid Should exceed an equal devidant it is to be repaid to my Executors.- And Lastly I nominate Constitute & appoint my two sons Henry and Daniel Beltzhoover to

----

1. Evangelisch (Evangelial) Church Records, Metterzimmern, Neckarkreis, Germany, pages 180-181, year 1741.
Courtesy Deanna Oklepek.

be the executors of this my will hereby revoking all other wills legacies and bequests by me heretofore made and declaring this and no other to be my last will and Testament. In witness whereof I have hereunto set my hand and seal this eight day of April in the year of our Lord one thousand eight hundred and six. Before signing I have requested to insert between the twelth and thirteenth line the worths to the best advantage.

Signed, sealed, published produced
& declared by the said person to be   Melchor Beltzhoover
his last will and testament in the   seal
presence of us   William Musthoff, John Johnston, William M. Belch Allegheny County   On the 29th May AD 1809. Before me Sam Jones, Regt of wills personally appeared John Johnston & William Wusthoff two of the subscribing witnessess to the within will & being duly sworn according to Law depose & say that they were present & did see Melchor Beltzhoover sign, seal publish pronounce & declare the within Instrument of Writing to be his Last will & Testament & that he was of sound mind & memory at the time. Witness my hand and seal
Letters Granted May 29 - 1809   For Sam Jones Regr   Seal

> Recorded 29th May 1809   Wm Jones
> Issue: (Order of children is not known)
>> 2-Melchior Beltzhuber[2], b. 27 Jan. 1740, Germany
>> 3-George Conrad Beltzhuber, b. 8 Nov. 1741, Germany
>> 4-Daniel Beltzhuber, b. 18 Mar. 1744, Germany; died the same day.
>> 5-Johann Jacob Beltzhuber, b. 8 Feb. 1746, Germany
>> 6-Johann Martin Beltzhuber, b. 3 Nov. 1747, Germany
>> 7-Thomas Beltzhuber, b. 27 Sept. 1749, Germany
>> 8-Anna Maria Dorothea Beltzhuber, b. 3 Oct. 1751, Germany.
>> 8a-Theobald Beltzhoover b. ca. 1753; d. (date and place not known); m. Anna Maria ---?---. Church records show the following, "Michael Beltzhoover (1773-1843) son of Theobalt Beltzhoover and wf. Anna Maria ---?----. [1]
>> It appears that Michael was in York Co., PA., and that his gandmother was also there. There is a reference to "Anna Maria held a child Catherine Barbara Schartel on 11 Nov. 1760, during a baptism, and refers to her as a widow of Melchior. (widow of Melchior, original immigrant), so possible grandmother of this Michael, **if** Theobalt is a son of the original immigrant.
>> Michael Beltzhoover, b. 9 June 1773; bpt. 11 July 1773, sp. Michael Deubel and wf. Margretta. Tombstone inscription reads that Michael was

----

1. <u>Washington Co., MD. Church Records</u>   , Family Line Publications

4

born 9 June 1773.

There is a land record of Michael Beltzhoover, p.
18 of Pennsylvania Original Land Records, North
Codorus Twp., York Co., PA. [1]

Michael BELTZHOOVER, d., 22 Oct. 1843, grave-
stone, First Lutheran Burial ground, Carlisle,
PA. Family Bible. Michael Beltzhoover married
Anna Maria Cornman, b. 6 May 1782, Lebanon
Twp., Lancaster Co., PA.; chr. 6 June 1782. She
was the daughter of James (John?) and Elizabeth
Cornman. (Genealogy of Cornman/Corman/Korman
Families in America 1712-1916, The Sentinel,
Carlisle, PA., 1916, Internet-Cornman: Robin L.
W. Petersen). [2]

Robin Petersen advises that there is also a
record of "Mary Cornman, b. 1790, m. David
Braught. Anna Maria Braught's headstone reads
that she was born 6 May 1782. Anna Maria and
David Braught's first child was born in 1810.
Robin Petersen concludes that Anna Maria had
two husbands. Michael Beltzhoover was still
living, therefore, if Anna Maria married second, there must have been a divorce (rare) of
Michael Beltzhoover and Anna Maria Corman.

9-Catherina Beltzhuber, no birth date, b. USA

10-Ludwig Beltzhuber, b. 1756, USA. Not mentioned in
his father's will. May be that he was dec'd.
by then or he may belong to some other Beltzhoover family?

11-Margaretha Beltzhuber, b. ca. 1755; m. George
Troxel [3]
Margaretha's baby, Elizabetha Troxel, b. bpt.
1771, Zion Reformed Lutheran Church, Hagerstown, MD.

Second Generation

2-**MELCHIOR/MELCHEOR BELTZHUBER**[2] (1), b. 27 Jan. 1740, at
Schnaitheim, Germany, d. 26 May 1809, Pittsburgh, PA., g. Allegheny Cemetery Sect 20 Lot 14. occupation, butcher; m.,
Elizabeth SCHUNK/SHUNK, b. ca. 1739; d. 22 Aug. 1816 (ca. 77);
g. Allegheny Cemetery, Pittsburgh, PA. She died at "Hatfield,
the seat of her son, Daniel Beltzhoover, near this city."

----

1. Colonial Name Index

2. Petersen, Robin L.

3. Ibid., Mrs. Nimick "Surmised as a sister because the baby's baptism was sponsored by Melchior and
Elizabeth Beltzhoover."

In a pamphlet "A Town of the Past...Beltzhoover...a link to the Future" it is written, "In 1794, Melchior Beltzhoover paid 10 shillings (c. $100.) for 248 acres of sloping farmland on a hillside south of Pittsburgh. He was buying a farm, a place to raise his large family, but he was also creating the roots of a community that bears his name today. Beltzhoover passed from a farm to a German Community and then in the 1860's, streets were laid out and neighborhood began to assume the shape it retains today". [4]

Since according to records and written information, both Captain John Beltzhoover was the first Beltzhoover to Allegheny County and his son, Jacob, according to some accounts, say, Melchior Beltshoover and his son, Jacob. Could it be that Capt. John and Melchior Beltzhoover are one and the same? Just using different first names?

"It is 1.7 miles from downtown Pittsburgh; McKinley Park is a wooded delight...etc." [5]

The Pittsburgh Reporter, BiCen(tennial). date unknown, states that, "Allentown, originally was part of St. Clair Township, one of the original townships in Allegheny County. The property was bought by an early settler, John Ormsby, from the William Penn family and Ormsby sold a slice of it to Melchior Beltzhoover in 1794."

"Beltzhoover (Melchior) and his son Jacob operated a farm, tavern and tan yard on the property, and in 1827 sold 124-acre section to Joseph Allen, a butcher."

"According to historian, C. A. Weslager, the Allen and Beltzhoover farms were turned into subdivisions in the 1850's."

Immigration lists show Melchior as age 12 in 1752. There is no stone for Melchior in the cemetery, only for his wife. He and Elizabeth are buried in a common grave, having been moved there from another location. His will dated April 8,
----

1. Pittsburgh Gazette 27 Aug. 1816 Courtesy Deanna Oklepek

2. Cramer's   Pittsburgh Magazine Almanac   1817, p. 72 Courtesy Norman Schwotzer.

3. Family Bible. published 1814, by M. Carey, Phila., PA.,   Courtesy Deanna Oklepek

4. The Pittsburgh Reporter, BiCentennial   issue, date unknown

5. A Touch of the Past...Beltzhoover....a link to the Future..   by Neighborhoods for Living Center, Pittsburgh, PA. No date. Richard S. Caliguirwas Mayor which would give an approximate year.

1806, shows his wife, Elizabeth, and children: Jacob, Henry, George, Samuel, Elizabeth, Daniel and William. [1] [2] [3]

Melchior lived in Hagerstown, MD., before he moved to Pittsburgh. He purchased a lot on Mt. Washington.

Found in the Western MD., Genealogical Magazine the following transactions by Melchor in Hagerstown: Washington Co., MD (Hagerstown), Melchior sold lot 83 on 2 Aug. 1782 to Michael Stover. Elizabeth Beltzhuber rel. dower (p. 116); Jonathan Hager sold land to Rosannah Heester and he appointed three attorneys on it, one being Melchor Beltzhuber, 28 July 1783; Melchor purchased from Thomas Worley, acting for Isaac Baker, of NC., 25 acres. The Wagon Ford on the west side of Conococheague Creek adj. Hopewell, 28 Aug. 1783; Melchor, tavernkeeper, bought from Frederick Stidinger 2 x 80' of his lot in Elizabeth Town, which adjoins Melchior's lot 105, 27 May 1783; Melchor purchased from Jonahan Hager, Jr., lots 377, 378, 379 and 380 in Elizabeth Town, 25 Aug. 1784. [4]

In 1797.Melchior Beltzhoover was proprietor of a tavern on the corner of the public square, near the court house (Hagerstown). The Tavern was called "Beltzhoover Tavern" and then "The Globe." Later the Tavern name was changed to "Sign of the General Washington." [5]

It is thought that Catherine Beltzhoover, the first child, died before 1806, since she is not mentioned in the will.

Concerning Elizabeth SHUNK BELTZHUBER, b. ca., 1739; d. 21 Aug. 1816, Pittsburgh, PA. It is not known where they were married or where she was born. Tradition has it that she was a relation of Gov. Francis Rawn SHUNK, son of John SHUNK who married Elizabeth RAWN, daughter of emigrants Caspar and Barbara RAHN/RAWN. It has never been proven that John SHUNK, the emigrant had a daughter, Elizabeth. Gov. Francis Rawn Shunk married a sister to Archibald LINDSAY. Was Elizabeth SHUNK BELTZHOOVER a sister to Francis SHUNK? Melchior lived

----

1. Ibid., Oklepek, Deanna

2. Index of Estates Upper Ohio Valley, Vol. 68. New York Genealogical and Bio. 1937 p. 150

4. Will of Melcheor Beltzhoover, recorded 29 May 1809, p. 278, no. 201, Allegheny Co., PA., Courtesy Deanna Oklepek

4. Western Maryland Genealogical Magazine, Vol. 3 1987, p. 126; Vol. 4 1988, p. 78; Vol. 4 1988, p. 79; Vol. 4 1988; Vol. 5 1989. Courtesy Deanna Oklepek

5. Scharf, Thomas J. History of Western Maryland and Biographical Sketches Regional Publishing Co. Baltimoe 1968 Vol. II, Illus. p. 1166 Washington Co., MD. Free Library 9\22\97

first Hagerstown, MD., and later moved to Pittsburgh.   [1]   [2]

Gov. Francis Rawn Shunk, b. 7 Aug. 1788, d. 20 July 1848, g. August Lutheran Cem., Trappe, PA. (Gov. from 1/21/1845-7/09/1848), m. --?-- Findlay, a daughter of Gov. William Findlay (1768-1846, b. Mercerburgs, PA., member Penn. House 1797, PA State Treasure 1807-1817, Gov. 1817-1820; Senator 1817-1827, g. Harrisburg Cem., Harrisburg, PA.).
Francis Shunk was the father-in-law of Charles Brown (member PA House 1841-1845; U. S. Rep. 1847-1849) and grandfather of Francis Shunk Brown (b, 1858, Philadelphia PA., an Att'y., Attorney General PA. 1915-1919).

Gov. Shunk was a farmer's son from Trap/Trappe. PA, Montgomery Co., PA. of Palatine German descent.

There is another source of the possible relationship of Schunk. (1) Wilhelm Schunk of Walsheim (Germany) and wife Catherine Schwartz emigrated to America 1771 and had children, John, Catharine, Elizabeth, Maria, and Simon. (PA Dutchman, Winter 1954) from Monocacy and Catoetin Vol. II p. 92. (2) Children of Wilhelm Schunk of Walsheim, district of Hamburg, Saar, and his wife Catharina Schwartz namely Johannes, Catharina, Elizabeth, Maria, Simon, have been in America the past nine or ten years: Record 18 Oct. 1781 New World Immigrants p. 28 Annotations to Pennsylvania German Pioneers.

There is information that indicates that Melchior was in Baltimore, Hagerstown and then to Pittsburgh. In 1790 Wash. Co. MD., Melchior and his family are shown and that they held five slaves. In 1800 he was in St. Clair Twp., Allegheny Co., PA.   [3]

On 11 June 1790, Melcher Beltzhuber of the State of Maryland for 50 pounds bought 3 acres, 2 perches from John Ormsby, a tract of land on the Monongahela River in Manor of Pittsburgh, called "Coal Hill", in the area formerly in Washington Co., but now Allegheny Co.   [4]

Beltzhoover Borough was in Lower St. Clair Township, Allegheny Co., PA. and was incorporated 9 June 1875, had been
----

1. Ibid., Nimick, Mrs. Francis B.

2. Williams, Thomas J. C. A History of Washington County Maryland including a History of Hagerstown
Illus. John M. Runk and L. R. Titsworth, publishers 1906 p. 335

3. The Washington Spy. An Index of Hagerstown Newspapers. 1790-1797 Washington Co. Free Library
Hagerstown. Courtesy Deanna Oklepek

4. Abstracts Allegheny Co. PA. Deed Books I and II, p 35 (page 111 in original deed book)
Deanna Oklepek

separated from Lower St. Clair Township in 1869 to form part of Allentown Boro. The name was for the prominent BELTZHOOVER family in the neighborood. The post ofice was established in 1882. [1]

Melchior BELTZHUBER (Melcher Belsheever) served in Capt. Peter Bell's/Beall's Company, taken from Revolutionary War lists. He met the battalion at Baltimore, MD. [2] [3]

Melchior's will dated 8 April 1806, listed wife, Elizabeth and all of these children, except Catherine. (Might Catherine, have died before 1806 and without issue?). He owned land in St. Clair Township on Saw Mill Road. Witnesses were William Musthoff, John Johnston, William M. Belch. On the abstracts of wills, Jacob Beltzhuber was omitted as a child of Melchior, but he is shown in the original will. [4]

Mrs. Deanna Oklepek is a member of DAR on Melchior Beltzhoover [5]

Issue: (the children are not in proper order)
12-Jacob Beltzhoover[3], b. 16 May 1770, Hagerstown, MD. "Came to Pittsburgh with his father. Melchior, from Maryland."
13-Catharina Beltzhoover, b. 11 July 1772, Hagerstown, MD., d. ca. before 1806; chr. 26 July 1772, Zion Ref. Luth. Church, Hagerstown, Washington Co., MD., m. 9 Nov. 1804, Hagerstown, George Stout
14-George Beltzhoover, b. 1774, stayed in Hagerstown, a Tavern Keeper; d. 25 Nov. 1848, Baltimore, MD. Married 10 Dec. 1799, Catherine GOLL.
15-Henry Beltzhoover, b. 10 Jan. 1776, Hagerstown, Washington Co., MD; chr. 14 Jan 1776, St. John Ev. Luth. Church, Hagerstown, Washington Co., MD. "Came to Pittsburgh with his father, Melchior, from Hagerstown, MD.

----

1. Ibid., Warner & Co.   History of Allegheny Co., A____ (1889) p. 53

2. Browne, William Hand, Ed.   Archives of Maryland. Journal and   Correspondence of the Council of Safety 1777-1778 Baltimore, Maryland Historical Society 1897 Volume 16 Courtesy Deanna Oklepek

3. Ibid., Mrs. Francis B. Nimick

4. Harriss, Helen L. and Elizabeth J. Wall   Will Abstracts of Allegheny Co., PA_____ Will books I through V 1986 pp. 201, 278 Courtesy of Deanna Oklepeck.

5. Ibid., Oklepek, Deanna

16-Samuel Beltzhoover, b. 3 April 1785; m. Mary
    Bausman
17-Elizabeth Beltzhoover. b. 23 Feb. 1781; m. John
    Thompson Mason
18-Daniel Beltzhoover, b. 3 April 1783; d. 4 Oct.
    1839, Natchez, MS; m/1, 24 Sept. 1812, Pitts-
    burgh, PA., Arabella Wallace; m/2 Jane Harris
    Stockman. [2]
19-William Beltzhoover, b. ca. 1785, he owned a
    Tavern in Hagerstown. Nothing further known.

3-GEORGE CONRAD "Conrad" BELTZHUBER[2] (1), (1741-1815), b.
8 Nov. 1741, Germany, d. intestate, 8 Dec. 1815, Dover Twp.,
York Co., PA. His wife wrote a will in June of 1823, so it
was presumed that he died prior to that date. [3] [4]

George Conrad Beltzhuber went by the name of Conrad. He
was in the census under that name and died intestate 8 Dec.
1815, as evidenced by this Administration and Inventory.
George and Michael his sons were named administrators. The
inventory is written in German.

Conrad Beltzhoover, d., 8 Dec. 1815, Dover Twp., York
Co., PA. intestate; Feb. 17, 1817, Adm. of Conrad Beltzhuber,
Dover Township, York Co., PA. Payments in return for services
included the names of Geo. Beltzhuber, Michael Beltzhuber,
Jacob Witman, Rudolph Miller, Israel --?--, John --?--, Thos.
McKinney, John Nesbit, Jacob C--?--, John W--?--, Andrew
Strayer, William Urich, Jacob Hake (may have been the father
of Conrad Hake who married Catherine/Rebecca Witman), George
Belshouyer, Patrick McDouagh, Christina Beltzhuber (for board-
ing threshers?), Christian Linderman.

Inventory of Goods and Chattel, Conrad Beltzhuber late,
of Dover Twp., York Co., PA., deceased December 8, 1815. Adam
Rubert and Christian Hamm. L.? George Beltzhuber, Michael
Beltzhaber, Jacob Witman, Rudolph Miller, Michael Beltzhuber.
Filed Dec. 23, 1815.

There was a place called 'Conrad's Crossing' in Chance-
----

1. History of Allegheny County, PA., (1889)   Warner & Co., p. 237 Sketch of Thomas Varner family.
"Thomas Varner m., in 1824, Mary Beltzhoover, dau. of Henry Beltzhoover. Henry Beltzhoover came with his
father, Melchior, from Hagerstown, MD., to Pittsburgh about the beginning of this century."

2. Pittsburgh Gazette , A. A. A. 11 Nov. 1839, Courtesy Norman Schwotzer

3. Ibid., Oklepek, Deanna. Immigration & LDS records show George Eduard, but close exam church
records est. name as George Conrad.

4. Beers. History of Cumberland and Adams Co.'s PA   Bio. Chapter LIL, Monroe Township, p. 506

ford Twp., York Co., PA., and members of the descendants of

Eva Beltzhoover Witman were married at that location. Named after Conrad Beltzhoover or Conrad Hake?

George Beltzhuber/Beltshoover resided, in 1779, at Dover, Dover Township, York Co., PA., wife, Christena Sophia ZINN Beltzhuber/Beltzhoover. [1] [2] [3] [4]

A deed selling Conrad's land (by the heirs) to George Beltzhuber of Allen Twp., Cumberland Co., PA., shows heirs as, Michael Beltzhuber; John Knisely & Eve, his wife; Rudolph Miller & Christina, his wife; and Mary Beltzhoover.

Christena Sophia ZINN Beltzhuber, wrote her last will and testament, 26 June 1823, which was witnessed by George Neiler and Wm. Caldwell. Her will was probated 9 Sept. 1823, Reg. J. Barnitz. In her will she mentions her children, George, Michael, Polly, Christena and Eva. The estate consisted of her house and lots in Dover, PA. The properties were to have been disposed of and share and share alike, except Eva Beltz-huber was to get fifty cents "and that is to be her full share of my estate." George and Michael Beltzhuber were named as excecutors.

Issue: (BELTZHUBER/BELTZHOOVER)

20-George Peter Beltzhuber[3], b. 12 Feb. 1768, York Co., PA., chr. 27 Mar. 1768. Sponsors were Peter Lent & wife. [5]

21-John Michael Beltzhuber, b. 18 June 1772, chr. 9 Aug. 1772 [6]

22-Margreth/Mary "Polly" Beltzhoover, b. ca. 1773. (Polly is often used for Mary, Margaret, Martha)

23-Christina Beltzhoover, b. ca. 1774: m. 10 Jan 1805, York Co., PA., Rudolph "Rudy' Miller? Married by Rev. Geisweit. Christina's name appears as

----

1. Last Will and Testament of Christene Beltzhuber, York, PA., courtesy of Deanna Oklepek, 1/96

2. George Conrad Beltzhoover found in LDS records. Courtesy of Deanna Oklepek

3. Bates, Marlene Strawser and F. Edward Wright   York County , PA., Church Records of the 18th Century   p. 194, 199, 228 Family Line Publication, Westminster, MD., Maryland Gen. Soc., Library, Balt., MD. Courtesy Deanna Oklepek

4. York Co., PA. Historical Society, based on Deeds 2 p.56 1791 (maiden name ZINN) Deanna Oklepek

5. Ibid., Bates, M. Christ Evangelical Lutheran Church City of York., p. 194

6. Bates, M. & F. Edw. White, York Co., (PA) Church Records of the 18th Century   1991, Vol. I and II, Christ Evangelical Lutheran Church, City of York., p. 199

Beltzheber but other records show Beltzhuber.

24-Eva Beltzhoover, b. 12 Feb. 1775, Cumberland Co.,
     d. 9 June 1850, m. c. 1799, PA., Jacob WITMAN
24a-Margreth Betzhuber, b. 10 Feb. 1778, d/o Conrad
     and Xtina (Christina) Betzhuber. [3]

5-JOHANN JACOB BELTZHOOVER[2] (1), b. 8 Feb. 1746, Germany; m. Anna Maria _____. Was his wife Anna Maria Magdalena or might Johann Jacob have married second a Magdalena?

Johann Jacob Beltzhoover in the 1776 Census in Frederick Co., MD, Elizabeth Hundred as age 27. Jacob purchased land from Jonathan Hager, Jr., lot 57, Elizabeth Town (Hagerstown) 16 June 1784. Also purchased land from Isaac Baker of NC through his friend Thomas Worley of Washington Co., MD., 25 acres, Waggon Ford on Conococheague Creek. [4]

Johann Jacob served as "Jacob" in the Revolutionary War in Capt. William Heyser's Company. A Company formed from Washington Co., MD. His pension applications were not approved. [5] [6]

    Issue: (BELTZHOOVER)
      25-Jacob Beltzhoover[3], b. 23 Dec. 1773, Hagerstown,
         Washington Co., MD., He was christened 25
         Dec. 1773, Zion Reformed Lutheran Church,
         Hagerstown, MD., parents were Jacob Beltzhuber
         and wf. Anna Maria. Sponsors were Melcher
         Beltzhuber and wf. Elizabeth.
      26-Elisabeth Beltzhoover, christened 20 Sept. 1776,
         St. John Evangelical Lutheran Church, Hagers-
         stown, MD., sponsors were Jacob and Magdalena
         Beltzhuber. Your compilers believe that this
         Elisabeth married as Elisabeth Kelhoover, 28
         January 1797, George Doyl.

6-JOHANN MARTIN BELTZHOOVER[2] (1), b. 3 Nov. 1747, Germany. A Tavern-Keeper in Hagerstown. He purchased land from

----

1. Marriages and Marriage Evidence in Pennsylvania German Churches from First (Trinity) Reformed Church, 1744-1853, p. 481. Courtesy Elizabeth Peach

2. York County Deed Book 3-F p. 3-6. Deanna Oklepek

3. Records of Strayer's Lutheran Church, Dover Twp., York Co., PA. (also known as Salem Union Church) Courtesy Elizabeth Peach 5/27/00

4. Western Maryland Genealogy Magazine _____ Vol. 4 1988, p. 177; p. 41

5. History of Washington Co., MD. _____ Vol. 4, 1988, page 171

6. Ibid., History of Washington Co., MD. _____ Thos. Scharf p. 1190

Jonathan Hager, Jr., on 4 Mar. 1784, lots 31 and 135 in Elizabeth Town. [1]
    Issue:

    7-**THOMAS BELTZHOOVER**[2] (1), b. 27 Sept. 1749, Germany. Served in the Revolutionary War as a Pvt. under Capt. Christopher Lowman, York Co., PA. [2] [3]
    Issue:

    8-**ANNA MARIA DOROTHEA BELTZHOOVER**[2] (1), b. 3 Oct. 1751, Germany; m. Nicholas Hachen. She was six months old when immigration to Philadelphia in 1752. [4]
    Issue: (HACHEN)
        27-Johannes Hachen[3], b. 2 Feb. 1791, Hagerstown, MD
        28-Daniel Hachen, b. 16 June 1796, Hagerstown, MD
        29-William Hachen, b. 1 Oct. 1797, Hagerstown, MD
        30-Anna Maria Hachen, b. 12 April 1799, Hagerstown, MD. [5]
        31-Abraham Hachen, b. 15 April 1800, Hagerstown, MD

    10-**LUDWIG BELTZHOVER/BELTZHOOVER**[2] (1), b. 1756, USA. Confirmed in 1773, at the age of 17, in a church in York Co., PA. Melchior's will dated April 8, 1806 mentions all the children, but does not mention Ludwig. Ludwig Beltzhoover is listed as a taxable inhabitant of City of York in 1783, locksmith, 3 persons, valuation 40 pounds.

    Ludwig Baltzhoover is shown as having served in the Revolutinary War as a Pvt. in Capt. Philip Albright's Co., on a list dated Sept. 1, 1776, states that Ludwig was from York Co. PA and was German. The roll of the Captain, taken in camp near King's Bridge, NY., 1 Sept. 1776, after the Battle of Long Island. Shown as a Private is Ludwig Beltzhoover. [6]

    Part of the regiment was present at Battle of Fort Washington, Nov. 16, 1776; the remainder of the regiment accompanied Washington in the retreat across New Jersey and took part in the Battles of Trenton and Princeton.

    Presumed to be the son of Melchior as there is no further

---

1. Ibid., <u>Western Maryland Gen. Magazine</u> pp. 615-621

2. Ibid., Oklepek, Deanna

3. <u>History of York Co., PA</u> Vol. I, p. 266

4. Ibid., Oklepek, Deanna

5. Zion Reformed Lutheran Church, Hagerstown, MD, baptismal record. "AnaMaria Belzhuber, sponsor."

6. Ibid., <u>History of York Co., PA.</u>, Vol. I p. 173

proof. Married? Unknown.
    Issue: (BELTZHOVER/BELTZHOOVER)
        32-Anna Maria Beltzhover/Beltzhoover[3], b. 8 Oct.
            1784, York Co., PA; chr. Christ Ev. Luth.
            Church, York, PA. Sponsors were Ludwig and wf.,
            the parents. [1]

    11-MARGARETHA BELTZHOOVER[2] (1), at Pittsburgh, m. George
TROXEL. At the baptism the baby was sponsored by Melchior and
Elizabeth Beltzhoover. Melchior was believed to be her older
brother and his wife Elizabetha. Margaretha may have also
married, Christoph. Hess as Eliz. Belshuber and may she have
also married Michael Deubel?
    Issue: (TROXEL)
        33-Elizabetha Troxel, b. 1771, bpt. Zion Reformed
            Luth. Church, Hagerstown.

<u>Third Generation</u>

    12-JACOB BELTZHOOVER[3] (2), b. 16 May 1770, Maryland; d. 7
Aug. 1835, g. Allegheny Cemetery, Sect 16 Lot 135. Jacob
Beltzhoover is listed as a single man in the Tax Records in
1791. Jacob Beltzhoover was in Upper St. Clair Township,
Allegheny Co., PA., in 1798, as was Jacob Witman. Jacob Beltz-
hoover came to Pittsbugh with his father, Melchior, from
Maryland before the opening of the century. [2] [3]

    It is thought that Jacob Beltzhoover went ahead of his
father Melchior, from Hagerstown to the Pittsburgh area and
the others followed. [4]

    Jacob and his brother, Daniel prospered the most in this
family. Their brother, Samuel did not do as well. [5]

    Jacob BELTZHOOVER married Elizabeth SAAM BAUSMAN. From
the History of Allegheny Co., Vol. II, 1889, p. 42, " Elizabeth's first husband, Jacob Bausman, had accumulated a large
amount of property in Pittsburgh, had a thriving tavern and
ferry boat system when he died. When Jacob Beltzhoover
married Elizabeth he took over all these properties and in-
----

1. Ibid., Bates, M. & F. Edw. White   <u>York County (PA) Church Records of the 18th Century</u>   p. 228
Her name and dates also found in the LDS records.

2. Ibid., Warner & Co.,   <u>History of Allegheny Co.,</u>   Vol. II, 1889. p. 42

3. Will of Jacob Beltzhoover, recorded 30 Oct. 1835, p. 242, no. 158, Allegheny Co., PA.,
Courtsey Deanna Oklepek

4. Ibid., Oklepek, Deanna

5. Ibid., Oklepek, Deanna Jan, 1996

stantly became wealthy." She died Pittsburgh, 1841. It is shown that her maiden name was SAAM as records Mrs. Nimick and Deanna Oklepek found in the Greensburg Courthouse, Westmoreland Co., PA., that Adam SAAM Jr. and Jacob and Elizabeth BELTZHOOVER signed papers in an agreement giving Adam SAAM what was to be Elizabeth's share of her father's property. [1]

Elizabeth SAAM, b. 20 Dec. 1767, d. 11 Dec. 1841, Pittsburgh, PA.; g. Allegheny Cem., Pittsburgh, was the daughter of Adam SAAM b. Jan. 1735; d. 22 Sept. 1809, and wf. Mary Magdalena BUHL, b. 1731; d. 28 Feb. 1815.

Jacob Philip BAUSMAN came to America 10 November 1764, traveling with Andreas Bausman on the Ship "Boston". Jacob Bausman owned a vast amount of land in the Pittsburgh area, a farmer, and operated a ferry service from his house on the south side of the Monongahela River and Fort Dunmore. He was one of the original trustees of Allegheny Co. and along with Jacob Haymaker/Haymacher, was truestee of the land deeded by the Penn's to the German Church. [2] [3] [4]

Jacob Philip Bausman, b. 25 Sept. 1740, Frelaubersheim, Rhnhssm Hessen; died in Pittsburgh 12 August 1797. Jacob Bausman had children :(Bausman) Jacob; Elizabeth 1782-bef. 1813) who married James Hilliard; William (1785-1785); John (1786-1787); Mary (1790-1835), d. Stewart Co. TN who married, 10 Dec. 1807, Samuel Beltzhoover; and Adam, b. 1795, whose wife was Caroline. [5]

In 1812 on the 9th Sept. there was a deed by Jacob Beltzhoover and wf. Elizabeth Bausman, widow of Jacob Bausman, selling 409 acres to John Bausman. The children of Jacob Bausman are also listed.

The third U. S. Census 1810 report shows Jacob Beltzhoover in St. Clair Township.

Jacob Beltzhoover's will probated 30 Oct. 1835 named children and grandchildren as well as son-in-laws. Servants were named Frank, Tom and Ann and children indentured to me; Amy (black woman) There is a record of Negroes in Allegheny County (PA) that Jacob Beltzhoover held slaves. Precisely, "a

----

1. Ibid., Mrs. Nimick

2. History of Washington Co., PA., by Boyd Cumrine pp., 148, 152, 153, 167, 638 Deanna Oklepek

3. Pittsburgh, The Story of a City by Leland D. Baldwin, pp. 102, 162 Deanna Oklepek

4. Pittsburgh Gazette, August 27, 1797, Sale of Estate, Deanna Oklepek

5. Ibid., Mrs. Francis L. Deanne

mulato male, Frank, born 6 Sept 1811, a child of Negro woman, Amy, his slave S/Jacob Beltzhoover, 3 Feb. 1812." [1]

The will lists properties, which appeared to be extensive. [2]

Issue: (BELTZHOOVER)

34-Margaret Beltzhoover[4], b. 11 Sept. 1798; d. 2 June 1832; m. Samuel STACKER.

35-Sarah Beltzhoover, b. 22 April 1800; d. 24 May 1851; m. Dr. Frederick BAUSMAN. Sarah m.\2, Rev. Jeremiah Knox.

36-Mary Ann Beltzhoover, b. 1 May 1803; d. 25 July 1880; m. Francis BAILEY.

37-Harriett Beltzhoover, b. 25 Mar. 1806; d. 4 May 1877; m. John MURRAY.

38-Eliza Beltzhoover, b.8 Mar. 1809; d. 9 April 1832, m. Rody PATTERSON.

13-**CATHERINA BELTZHOOVER**[3] (2), b. 11 July 1772, d. ca. before 1806 (d. ca. 34); chr. 26 July 1772, Zion Ref. Luth. Church, Hagerstown, Washington Co., MD.; m. 2 Nov. 1804, Hagerstown, George STOUT. Since Catherina is not mentioned in Melchior's will which was dated 1806, it is possible that she died in childbirth or shortly thereafter.

Issue: (STOUT)

38a-William Stout[4], b. 16 Aug. 1805, Hagerstown, Chr. 30 Mar. 1806, Zion Ref. Church, Hagerstown, MD.

14-**GEORGE BELTZHOOVER**[3] (2), b. 1774, stayed in Hagerstown, Md., and became a Tavern Keeper. He died 25 Nov. 1848, Baltimore, MD. George Beltzhoover married at Hagerstown, 10 Dec. 1799, Catherine Garehart GOLL, b. 1767, Hagerstown, d. 27 Sept. 1845, Hagerstown, widow of Baltzer/Balthazar GOLL. They were married by Rev. Bower(s). [3] [4]

There are records that indicate that George Beltzhoover m., 10 Dec. 1799, Catherine Gearhart/Garehart, Wash. Co., MD. [5] [6]

----

1. Schenkel, Edwin N., *Negroes in Allegheny County, PA. 1780-1813*, Historical Soc. of PA., Western Pennsylvania Genealogical Soc. Quart., 29/1 2002, p. 43

2. Will Jacob Beltzhoover, recorded 10 Oct. 1835, p. 242, no. 158, Allegheny Co., PA.

3. Index to Hagerstown, MD. Newspapers 1797-1804   Maryland Herald and Elizabeth-town Advertiser

4. Morrow, Dale W. compiler   Marriages of Washington County Maryland Vol. I 1799-1830   #B70 "Cath. Colb"

5. Chcp.Lewisco@WestVirginia's.com

6. Newspaper, MD. Herald & Elizabethtown Advertiser Friday 9 Nov. 1804 Deanna Oklepek

A distribution of Estates of Wash. Co., MD., 1817-1818 include Catherine Gearhart, daughter of Christian Gearhart.

Catherine Goll could have been reported married using the name COLB/GOLB/GOLL/GULL. [1]

Baltzer/Balthazar Goll/GALL (his name was shown as Baker Gale, Baker Gole and even Golb), b. c. 1745, Germany, d. 7 Apr. 1799, Haggerstown, was not only a leading merchant, but a prominent and public spirited citizen of the county for many years. He m.\1, Mary Elizabeth --?-- and they had a daughter, Mary Elizabeth Goll, b. 10 June 1775; m.\2, 1 June 1784, Catherine Garehart (Rebecca?). He died April, 1799, leaving a young widow and six children. [2] [3]

Baltzer Goll was the son of George Balthazar Goll and wf., Anna Maria Goll.
Children of Baltzer & Catherine Goll were: [4]
    Balthazar George Goll (1787-1849) m. Mercy Stull
        Beall
    Christian Frederick Goll (1789-1823), m. Maria
        Sophia Stull
    Infant Goll, (1792-1799)
    Unnamed Goll (1792-1792)
    Catharine Anna Maria Goll (1793-   )
    John Goering Goll (1795-1820) m. Barbara Kendal
    Rebecca Goll (1797-   )
    William Goll (1798-1851), m. Elizabeth Hook

George Beltzhoover was named guardian of these surviving children. [5]

George Beltzhoover went to Hagerstown. He owned "The Globe", a tavern that attained wide-spread celebrity. "The Globe" was a great rendezvous for the huge wagons in which in those days the produce from the surrounding countryside was transported. "The Globe" sometimes it was called The Beltz-hoover Inn) was kept for many years by George Beltzhoover, a brother of William Beltzhoover, who was the proprietor of "The

----

1. Baltimore   "American"   4 June 1823 and 27 Nov. 1849.

2. Ibid., Williams, Thomas C.   Hist. of Washington Co., MD.   p. 99

3. Ev. Lutheran Church Records, Hagerstown, MD. Deanna Oklepek

4. Family Search 2/26/00

5. Western Maryland Genealogical Magazine   ,Vol. 5, 1989, p. 66

Fountain Inn" in Baltimore.   [1]   [2]

George Beltzhoover, in 1823, took over the "Columbian Inn" on Market St., in Baltimore, MD.

On Aug. 7., 1843, Chancery Court (Chancery Papers) #9018, John R. Jones and Rebecca Jones vs. William Goll, George Beltzhoover, John Glenn, William B. Norris, James Moir, William J. Cole, Alexander Baltzell and Catherine Baltzell. BA Injunction against sale of Indian Queen Hotel in BC.

On October 12, 1803, Catherine Beltzhoover advertised to sell houses, lots, and land in Washington Co., PA., her life estate. Some letters being held at the Beltzhoover Tavern for Mrs. Beltzhoover were sent by John Massey Newman, James Nowell.

Ellis in his History of Fayette Co., PA., has this to say about early taverns, "For the acomodations of the public, taverns were established at an early date. Soon after 1800 these houses of entertainment had increased considerably." T. Fleming in his "Liberty Taverns" has this to say. "In the decade of the Revolution and a good many preceeding (sic) decades....the owners of the American Tavern was one of the most influential and respected members of the community. His access to money made him a kind of banker with numerous and outstanding loans. Circuit Court Judges presided there. In the public rooms, gentlemen and ladies had lively music, witty converstation, and balls."   [3]

"The Tavern was a polling place on election day. Mail was distributed there. The militia performed in the front yard on Training Day and got drunk. A well run tavern would clear a thousand pounds a year....more than a lawyer, maybe three times a doctors income or a clergyman."   [4]

Melchior Beltzhoover owned and managed the Beltzhoover Tavern and GEORGE WASHINGTON REALLY DID SLEEP HERE! That is, General Washington and entourage came to Hagerstown, MD., on Oct. 20, 1790.   [5]

----

1. Ibid., Scharf, J. Thomas   History of Western Maryland   pp. 1002, 1166

2. History of Baltimore City and County of Maryland   by J. Thomas Scharf, pp. 513-517

3. Ellis, Franklin   History of Fayette Co., PA.,   Illus. 1882 p. 559

4. Fleming, Thomas   Liberty Taverns   , Doubleday & Co., 1976

5. An Index to Hagerstown Newspapers 'The Washington Spy', Aug. 26, 1790-Feb. 1 1797, Washington Co., Free Library, Linda B. Clark

From Hagerstown, MD., Newspaper Information, The Washington Spy Elizabeth-Town dated Oct. 21, 1790. "Yesterday afternoon, at 2 o'clock, the approach of the President of the United States was announced in this Town, when (to the great honor of the Troop) the Company of Light Horse, under the command of Captain Davis, paraded, splendidly equipped, in a few minutes, and with the principal Gentlemen, met the Illustrious Strager three miles from Town, and escorted him to its environs, where they were met by the beautiful and martial-like Company of Infantry, commanded by Captain Orr. He was then conducted through the main Street (he bells ringing) amidst the welcome Applause of its grateful inhabitants, to Mr. Beltzhoover's Tavern."

"In the evening, the Town was illuminated, Bonfires appeared in all quarters, and every public demonstration of joy was exhibited on the happy occasion."

"An elegant Supper was prepared by direction, of which the President and principal Inhabitants partook; at the close of which the following Toasts were drank, accompanied with a discharge of Artillery and volley of Musq....to each."
"1. To the President of the United States (Here the President was pleased, so gave the following toasts.

"1. Property to the Inhabitants of Elizabethtown."
"2. The Legislature of the United States."
"3. The Land we live in,"
"4. The River Patownnack."
"5. May the Residence Law be perpetuated, and Patownack
        View the Federal City."
"6. An increase in American manufactories."
"7. May Commerce and Agriculture flourish."
"8. The National ---bly of France."
"9. The Marquise De la Fayette."
"10. May the Spirit of Liberty light the World."
"11. The Memory of those who fell in the defense of
        American Liberty."
"12. The Memory of Doctor Franklin."
"13. May America never want virtous Citizens to Defend
        her Liberty."
"The whole scene of perfect pleasure, good-humor, satisfaction and hilarity terminated before 10 o'clock in the greatest composure, order and quietude."

At 7 A. M. the next day, Pres. Washington departed and set out for Williams-port in order to make his passage down the noble River (The American Thames) which will waft him home.

Mr. Beltzhoover must have been a very influential man as the activities at his Tavern indicate. The newspapers of the times in Hagerstown have so many things recorded, as having taken place at Beltzhoover Tavern, it is too long to name them

19

all. A Dancing School; Masonic Procession meetings; horse racing with one thousand dollar prizes and horses at stud at the Tavern with names like 'North Star' 'Nimrod' 'Sir Solomon' 'Jupiter' 'Little Johnny' 'Bolivar'; selling stock in the local banks; collecting the taxes on property in other counties, e. g. Allegheny Co., PA.; Volunteer Troop of Cavalry Officers meeting; Celebration of 4th of July at Beltzhoover's Tavern. George Beltzhoover must have owned and managed several taverns. On the 20th Mar. 1821 he took over the Globe Tavern from Otho Stull, on the 4th of Mar. 1823 the Globe was taken over by Mrs. Kendall. The furniture etc., of the Globe had been sold in the meantime. The same thing may have happened wih the Indian King Tavern also known as The Hagerstown Hotel. There are records that indicate that he had loaned money and was offering items for sale unless the debts were paid immmediately. [1]

In one of the records from Hagerstown newspapers it says " Beltzhoover Tavern, see Indian King Tavern." It is thought that Melchior, Daniel, George and William Beltzhoover all had taverns at one time or another in Hagerstown. In 1791, Peter Schaffner, took over Beltzhoover's Tavern and changed it's name to the 'Sign of the General Washington.' Beltzhoover lived in a large brick house next door to the tavern, probably the old Dorsey house. He afterward resumed the tavern business in 1793. In 1814 the tavern was back being called 'The Globe' [2]

It is most difficult to sort out which Taverns the Beltzhoover family owned and managed. Your compiler believes that the Beltzhoover's also brokeraged the sale of other Taverns and properties.

"In 1841 Bernard de Bruyn wrote that Capt. Robt. Barclay of England did an agricultural tour of George Beltzhoover's and that his cattle are the best I had yet seen in the States."
Issue: (Could it be that George and Catherine had no children of their own?)

15-**HENRY B. BELTZHOOVER**[3] (2), b. 10 Jan. 1776, Hagerstown, Washington Co., MD., chr. 14 Jan. 1776, St. John Ev. Luth. Church, Hagerstown, Washington Co., MD; d. 19 Nov. 1842; m. ca. 1802, Elizabeth Bell (1780-   ).

Elizabeth Bell was the daughter of John Bell and wf., Ellener/Ellen/Elander Blackmore, b. ca. 1759, Frederick Co., MD., d. 5 May 1849, Allegheny Co., PA. John Bell was the son

----

1. Index to Hagerstown Newspapers   . Jan. 1820-Dec. 1824 Maryland Historical Trust. Linda Clark.

2. Ibid., Williams, Thomas J. C.   Hist. of West. MD.   , p. 99

of Robert Bell of Romney, WV. and before that from Ireland. Robert Bell's wife was Agnes Fleming of Edinburg.

Henry Beltzhoover came with his father, Melchior, to Pittsburgh from Hagerstown, MD.   [1]   [2]   [3]

From Hagerstown newspapers, 5 July 1793, Henry Beltzhoover, letters at the Post Office, not claimed.   Letters were from George Bender and Peter Burket.   [4]

Henry Beltzhoover is shown as being in Fayette Township, Allegheny Co., PA., in 1810.   [5]   [6]

Henry Beltzhoover is shown as an early settler in Lower St. Clair Township, Allegheny Co., PA.. along with his sons, Melchior, John, William, Henry. Samuel and Daniel.   [7]

In his will Henry Beltzhoover names daughters, Maria, Ellen, Catherine, Elizabeth and Nancy Cooley. His will was dated 15 June 1841; recorded 30 Nov. 1842, names his wife Elizabeth (BELL) and states that a graveyard to be established on the property in Upper St. Clair Township, Allegheny Co., PA. [8] [9]

The Bell's were from Romney, WV. Robert Bell came to Western Pennsylvania. He had eight sons and two remained in PA., James and John, settling on Chartiers Creek. James married Mary Newkirk and John married Elander/Ellender/Ellen Blackmore (c. 1759-5 May 1849), b. Frederick Co., MD., d. Robinson Twp., Allegheny Co., PA. Ellen Blackmore was the d/o Samuel Blackmore from MD. Ellen and John Bell are bur. Chartiers Cemetery, Noblestown Rd., Allegheny Co., PA. John and

----

1. Ibid., Warner & Co.   History of Allegheny Co., PA   1889 p.237

2. Pittsburgh Post Death Notices   , Dec. 3, 1842. Henry Beltzhoover died 19 Nov. 1842,
Microfilm notices of Death 1786-1910, film #p 359 Roll One, Carnegie Library, Courtesy Norman Schwotzer.

3. St. John's Lutheran Church, Hagerstown, MD

4. Ibid.,   Index of Hagerstown Newspapers

5. Ibid.,   Hist. of Allegheny Co.   , p. 17

6. Ibid.,   History of Allegheny Co.   , p. 54 Sketch of Lower St. Clair Township, mother of Baldwin Township, Early Settlers.

7. Ibid.,   History of Allegheny Co., PA   p. 54

8. Ibid.,   Abstracts of Allegheny Co., PA   Will Books. No.283 pp. 348 Courtesy Deanna Oklepek

9. Will of Henry B. Beltzhoover, recorded 30 Nov. 1842, p. 348, no. 283, Allegheny Co., PA.

Ellen had a daughter who married Henry Beltzhoover. [1]

    Issue: (BELTZHOOVER) (not in order of birth)

39-Melchior Beltzhoover[4], b. 1810, m. Mary Hughey

40-John Beltzhoover, wf. Anne _____

41-William Beltzhoover, b. c. 1817, d. before 1867;
    m. Mary McGibbney. [2]

42-Mary (Maria) Beltzhoover, (1803-1831); m. 23 Mar.
    1824, Thomas A. Varner (1799-1883).

43-Ellen Beltzhoover; m. Cooley

44-Henry G. Beltzhoover, b. 13 Jan. 1819; d. 1892
    (74), Pittsburgh, m. Hettie Talcott Pryor
    (1821-1892)

45-Catherine Beltzhoover

46-Samuel Beltzhoover, M.D., b. 17 Mar. 1823, d. 10
    April 1890. "Dr. Sam"

47-Elizabeth Beltzhoover

48-Daniel Beltzhoover, 19 Jan. 1825. PA; d. 29 July
    1886, g. Union Dale Cem., Pittsburgh in the lot
    owned by Thomas Alderson. Daniel m. Jane
    Alderson, who died in 12 Nov. 1882 (50), g.
    Union Dale Cem. Daniel served in the Civil War
    in Co. A. 18 P.V.I. He lived in the 32nd Ward
    of Pittsburgh.

49-Nancy Beltzhoover (-1883), res. near Castle
    Shannon; m.\1, Samuel Kennedy, m.\2, Samuel
    Cooley

16-SAMUEL BELTZHOOVER[3] (2) b. 19 Sept. 1785; d. 3 Dec. 1817/1819 Pittsburgh, PA. Samuel Beltzhoover was in St. Clair Township, Allegheny Co., PA., census 1800. Who was Mesha BELTZHOOVER in St. Clair Township in 1800 census? Samuel Beltzhoover married 10 Dec. 1807, Mary Bausman. Mary Bausman was the daughter of Jacob Bausman. [3]

    On 26 Aug. 1814, Samuel Beltzhoover, of Coal Hill, St. Clair Township, Allegheny Co., PA., advertised in the Pittsburgh Gazette with a reward for a runaway indentured negro boy named, Oliver.

    Issue: (BELTZHOOVER)

50-Matilda Beltzhoover[4] (1808-1809), b. 20 Apr. 1808;
    25 April 1809

51-Jacob Beltzhoover, Capt. (1809-1846), d. 3 Oct.
    1846 (37), St. Louis. Capt. of 'St. Louis
    Reveille', a riverboat Capt. in New Orleans.
    unm.

52-Frederick William Beltzhoover, b. 2 July 1811,

---

1. Cushing, Thos. History of Allegheny Co., PA.,_____ Courtesy of Elizabeth Peach

2. Peach, Elizabeth

3. Family Bible, published by M. Carey Philadelphia 1814. pp. 677, 678, 679. 680. Deanna Oklepek

Pittsburgh; d. 4 Aug. 1843; g. Calvary cem.,
St. Louis, MO; m. 24 July 1834, St. Louis King
Fr., St. Louis, MO., Frances Theresa Knapp
(1812-1856).
53-Elizabeth Mary Beltzhoover, (1813-1877), m. William Mason Cox; m./2, 16 Mar. 1846, at Stewart
Co., TN., Alfred B. Norris. [1] [2]
54-Arrabella Beltzhoover (1815-1816), b. 18 June
1815. She drowned, 25 July 1816. Family Bible
55-Samuel S. Beltzhoover (1818-1851), b. 31 Oct.
1818; d. April 1851, (33-6-25), St. Louis, MO.
Family Bible

17-ELIZABETH BELTZHOOVER[3] (2), b. 23 Feb. 1781; d. 29
June 1836. Washington Co., MD; m. 1797, John Thomson MASON. b.
Chopawamsic, VA. 15 Mar. 1765, of Frederick Co., Baltimore
City, MD.; d. Wash. Co., MD., 10 Dec. 1824. Letters held at
Beltzhoover Tavern, Hagerstown, MD., for Elizabeth 1808 were
from Andrew Baughman, Philip Boyers, Jr., Francis Breathel,
and Martin Baechtel. [3]

John Thomson MASON was the son of Thomson MASON of Raspberry Plain and wf. Mary King Barnes (Episcopalian). John
Thomson MASON was the nephew of George MASON of Gunston Hall.
John Thomson MASON and his wife, Elizabeth, owned "The Montpelier" outside Hagerstown, MD. [4]
Issue: (MASON)
56-Mary Barnes Mason[4], m. John Winter, 9 April 1833,
Montpelier
57-Elizabeth Ann Armistead Thomson Mason, b. 7 April
1803; d. 20 Jan. 1857; m. 9 April 1829, John A.
Wharton
58-Abram Barnes Mason, b. 21 Oct. 1807; d. 10 April
1863; m. Margaret St. Clair Clarke Patterson,
29 Nov. 1831
59-Melchor Beltzhoover Mason, b. 3 Oct. 1812; m. Mary
Daily
60-John Thomson Junior Mason, b. 15 July 1818; d.
1848
61-Thomas Mason, b. 15 July 1818; d. 1848
62-Virginia Wallace Mason, b. 16 April 1820; d. 6
Oct. 1858

18-DANIEL BELTZHOOVER[3] (2), b. 3 Apr. 1783, Hagerstown,

----

1. Ibid., Family Bible pub. 1814

2. Sistler, Byron and Barbara   Early Middle Tennessee Marriages   Nashville, TN 1988

3. Archives of Maryland, Attorney General's Office

4. Curator of Gunston Hall in Maryland, 1991 Courtesy of Deanna Oklepek

MD; he owned a Tavern in Hagerstown, MD., d. 4 Oct. 1839, at
The City Hotel, Natchez, MS, of yellow fever; g. Natchez City
Cem., Natchez, MS; (Daniel was attended by Dr. Lloyd Beltzhoover Henry, he was referred to as Dr. Lloyd. Your compiler
is not sure if he was named Henry or not. Daniel, m./1, 24
Sept. 1812, at Braddock's Field, PA., Arabella WALLACE, (he
was 29 and she was 19), Arabella was the daughter of George
Riley Wallace; m./2 16 Sept. 1824, by Rev. Stockton, at Bassenheim Furnace, Beaver Co., PA., Miss Jane Harris STOCKMAN
(he was 47 and she was 17), b. 5 April 1807, Beaver Co., PA;
d. 2 Feb. 1888, Pittsburgh, PA.

Jane Harris Stockmans' parents were Nathan STOCKMAN
(1763-1812), b. Ireland; came to American in 1765 with his
parents to Chester Co., PA., after he married he moved to
Buffalo Valley and then to Beaver Falls, PA.; d., Beaver
Falls, PA; m. 10 Oct. 1789, wf. Mary ROAN (1764-1847), she
was born Derry Two., Lancaster Co., PA., now Dauphin Co. PA;
d., Sharpsburg, PA. Mary Roan was the d/o Rev. John Roan and
wf. Anne Cochran. [1]

Nathan Stockman and wf. Mary Roan had the following
children: James (1791-1844), d. San Antonio, TX, when he died
he had one daughter living who m., Reeve Lewis and res. Lake
Providence, LA.; Annie (1793-1878), m. Mark Clark of Beaver
Co., PA. and they had 12 chldren; John Roan (1796-1842), d.
Natchez, MS, he had 8 children, 5 living when he died, 3 dau.
in New Orleans, LA and a sons, S. Dryden Stockman in NOL and
John R. Stockman res. San Francisco; Isabella (1798-1873), m.
James Sharpe; Joseph (1800-1835), un.m. NOL., ; Samuel (1802-
); Laird Harris (1804-   ); and Jane Harris (1807-1888) m.
Daniel Beltzhoover. [2]

Mrs. Jane H. Beltzhoover, bur. 9 Feb. 1888, Natchez, MS.
in the Koontz lot. (body brought from Pittsburgh). [3]

"Daniel Beltzhoover was the best known tavern owner
(Hagerstown)" [4] [5]

There is confusion about whether Daniel remained in
Baltimore and came to Hagerstown later. William Beltzhoover
----

1. Ibid., Deanna Oklepek

2. Ibid., Deanna Oklepek

3. Pittsburgh Gazette   24 Sept. 1824

4. Williams, Thomas J. C.   History and Biographical Record of Washington Co., MD. 1968   p. 235

5. Dickens   History of Washingto Co., MD.,   Index Family Line Publications 1992,
Allen Co., Fort Wayne, IN Library

owned "The Fontain Inn", in Baltimore and may be the one that owned a farm about four miles out of town. Where he raised wheat, corn, a head of cows and heifers. "The Fountain Inn" was for years one of the most popular inns in Baltimore. [1]

Daniel returned to Hagerstown. In April and December 1833-1834 he was in Hagerstown and managed the "Globe Inn." In October 1834 records show he was in Wheeling, VA/WV running "The Virginia House." In January 11-25, 1835 his daughter Anna Isabella died in Hagerstown.

Daniel's son, Daniel (age 11) remained in Hagerstown and attended The Hagerstown Academy, run by Wm. R. Abbott. There is a letter in possesion of the Beltzhoovers' of Natchez. 6 April 1837. in which Mr. Abbott wrote To Daniel Beltzhoover in Wheeling, VA/WV to the effect that "Daniel had an "itch" and was treated by Dr. Frederick Dorsey. That he (Daniel) had been isolated, etc." Dr. Frederick Dorsey lived in the house that had belonged to the Beltzhoover's and was directly across the street from the "Globe Inn."

Daniel moved around considerably. Sometime, probably 1837 the family moved to Wheeling, Ohio Co., VA (later WV) and he operated the well known, Virginia Hotel. Excerpts from the History of Wheeling City, "Up to 1837 and even much later, the old Virginia House\Hotel, though often changing proprietors, maintained its postion as the best house in Wheeling." [2]

"Daniel Webster, his wife and daughter, Kate....they came by coach to Pittsburgh and then by chartered boat to Wheeling."

"Beltzhoover, who kept the house and kept a good one...(was host)." (Henry Clay was believed to have been there at the same time.) "Beltzhoover kept his house for a year after...." Beltzhoover moved from Wheeling to Natchez, MS. His wife's brother was a Mayor of Natchez at one time. In Natchez "The City Hotel, with 120 rooms, was built." [3]

Arrabella/Arabella WALLACE BELTZHOOVER, d. 13 May 1823, Bassenheim, Zelienople, Butler Co. PA (30). Mrs. Beltzhoover is buried on the Bassenheim mansion estate. The obituary in the Pittsburgh Gazette 23 May 1823, says, she leaves her husband with four children. Several children must have died in infancy, as the oldest would have been about ten years old. The Sexton Records Adams Co., MS. includes an infant son, Wm.

----

1. Ibid., Williams Thomas C.   History of Washington Co., MD   . p. 91

2.   History of Wheeling City and Ohio Co. VA

3.   Classic Natchez   , p. 29 Courtesy Ruth Audley Coy

Beltzhoover, b. 25 Nov. 1840.   [1]

The family lived near Bassenheim Furnace in Beaver Co., PA., which was near Zelinople, Butler Co., PA. Dr. Detmar Basse built both the home and the furnace. Dr. Basse was also known as Dr. Detmar Basse Muller (for miller as he also owned a grist mill). Zelienople is named after his daughter, Ziele Basse (Mrs. P. L. Passavant). Daniel B. purchased Bassenheim Farm and Furnace and home in 1818. The furnace was closed in 1824 and by 1826, Daniel Beltzhoover was the proprietor of the farm on which the ruins of the furnace stood. There is nothing in the records of Zelienople Historical Socity of neighboring Beaver Co., PA. indicating a place called "Hatfield." The Passavants did visit the Beltzhoover's when they lived in Wheeling, WV. The Pittsburgh Gazette on Aug. 27 1816, reported the death of Eliz. Beltzhoover, consort of Melchor, "at Hatfield, the seat of her son, Daniel Beltzhoover, near this city."   [2]

Virginia Lee Beltzhoover Morrison has gone into Colonial Dames on her grandmother's, Jane Harris Stockman's line.

The second, third and fourth children born at a place called Hatfield, PA. Hatfield was referred to several times in records of Pittsburgh as a place "near Pittsburg."
  Issue: (BELTZHOOVER)
    63-George Wallace Beltzhoover[4], b. 10 July 1813, Pittsburgh, d. 19 April 1895, at his residence in East End, Pittsburgh, PA., g. Allegheny Cem. He was with Singer Nimick & Co. unm. In the 1880 census Pittsburgh, George W. Beltzhoover (66) was head of household and his stepmother, Jane H. (72) was in the household along with sisters, Arabella and Zara and servants named Mary and Debra O'Connell.
    64-Melchior Wallace Beltzhoover, b. 23 Mar. 1815, Hatfield, PA., d. 12 Nov. 1879, Pittsburgh. He never married and lived in the Monogahela Hotel for forty years. The owners of "Lady Gay' (1865), the second largest tonnage steamer to 'Miss Kate', were Capt. J. A. Williamson, Cincinnati, OH, J. D. Isham and Capt. M. W. Beltzhoover. The 'Lady Gay' cost $120,000 and was launched in Cincinnati and was placed in the service with St. Louis and New Orleans Packet Co. It was destroyed in 1870 near Chester, IL., when an obstruction in the river punctured the hull. No lives were lost.
----

1. Bessor, Joyce M. Ex. Dir. Zelienople Historical Soc. Mar. 2003

2. Ciam, Ron. Beaver Co. Historical Research and Landmarks Foundation Mr. 2003

65-Henry Wallace Beltzhoover, b. 19 July 1816, Hat-
        field; d. 10 Dec. 1844, Natchez, MS., g.
        Natchez City Cem.
66-Jane Wallace Beltzhoover, b. 4 Mar. 1818, Hat-
        field, PA., d. 18 Mar. 1821, Hatfield.
67-Eliza Wallace Beltzhoover, b. 14 Mar. 1820, Bassen-
        heim, Beaver Co., PA., d. May 1854, Natchez,
        MS., g. Kingston, Adams Co., MS., m. 31 May
        1849, Natchez, MS., David B. Swayze, s/o Nathan
        (1815-1853) & wf., Catharine Swayze. Private
        Cem. records of a cem. between Hutchings Land-
        ing and Sammy Creek, Natchez, MS., shows child-
        ren: George Wallace Swayze (1850-1853, and
        Eliza W. Swayze 1820-1843. [1]
68-Catherine Wallace Beltzhoover, 11 Mar. 1821, Bas-
        senheim Furnace, Zelienople, PA., d. 26 Sept.
        1821, PA.
69-Arabella Beltzhoover, b. 11 July 1822, MD; d 3 May
        1823.
Children from the second marriage
70-Daniel Beltzhoover Col., b. 11 April 1826; d. 31
        Oct. 1870, Mobile, AL., g. Old Mt. St. Mary's
        Cem. on Anthony's road in Emmitsburg, MD.;
        grad. West Point; Col. in Confederate Army.
        Married 7 Jan. 1850, Elizabeth Miles, b. 25
        Dec. 1826; d. 18 Nov. 1858.
71-Mary Roane Beltzhoover, b. 24 Sept 1827, Zieleno-
        ple; d. 25 June 1895. Natchez. Virginia's
        great-grandmother, m. Washington Koontz.
72-Katherine Mason Beltzhoover, 27 Jan. 1830; d. 17
        Feb. 1895, g. Natchez City Cem., "Aunt Kate",
        m. 13 Dec. 1855, Presbyterian Church in
        Natchez, Dr. Alexander C. Ferguson, b. 5 Aug.
        1819, d. 17 Feb. 1895, g. Natchez City Cem.
        Sexton records, Adams Co., MS., refers to her
        as Mrs. Kate M. Beltshover, bur. 17 Feb. 1895
        (W) 65 years. A married name of Ferguson is
        not mentioned. n.i. [2]
73-Anna Isabella Beltzhoover, b. 21 April 1832,
        Baltimore, MD; d. 25 Jan. 1835, Hagerstown, MD.
74-Jane Caston/Coston Zara Beltzhoover, b. 1 Feb.
        1837, Wheeling, VA/WV; bpt. 13 Sept. 1840,
        Trinity Episcopal Church: d. 8 Mar. 1903,
        Atlantic City, NJ., she was identified as Miss
        Zara, bur. 13 Mar. 1903, the body brought to
        Natchez for burial from Altantic City, accord-
        ing to the Sexton Records, Adams Co., MS., g.
        Natchez City Cem. From "Social Mirror" by

----

1. Archives & History, Jackson, MS; Private Cemeteries of Natchez and Adams Co., MS.

2. Beltzhoover, Ruth Audley

Adelaide Meller Never, 1888, p. 12, under "Beauty" lists, "Miss Zara Beltzhoover of Penn Ave., was formerly a geat belle and beauty. Possessing a classic face, with jetty eyebrows, hair and eyes, and dark rich coloring. She might have sat for a portrait of Walter Scott's lovely "Rebecca." Even now her soft white hair shades a most attractive face. Literary pursuits are her delights. The old home in which she lives is interesting to a degree, filled as it is with elegant old-fashioned furniture and many heirlooms. She is quoted as worth $100,000 ($1,923,000 in 2002 dollars)."

75-Arrabella Wallace Beltzhoover, b. 21 Feb. 1837, Hagerstown, MD., bpt. 13 Sept 1840, Trinity Episcopal Church; d. 4 Sept. 1909, Washington, DC., g. Mt. St. Mary's Cemetery Emmitsburg, , Frederick Co., MD., under the name of Beltzhoover: m. 13 June 1852, Evangelical Lutheran Church, Waynesboro, Franklin Co., PA, Ezra HEARD, n.i.

76-Abraham Barnes "Little Major" Beltzhoover, b. 17 May 1839, Natchez, Adams Co., MS. bpt. 13 Sept. 1840, Trinity Episcopal Church; d. 25 Nov. 1840, g. Natchez City Cem.

20-GEORGE PETER BELTZHUBER/BELZHOFER, SR[3] (3), (1768-1846) b. 12 Feb. 1768, chr. 27 Mar. 1768, Christ Ev. Luth. Church, York, PA. (sponsors at baptism were Peter Lent and his wf.); d. 27 April 1846 (80-2-15), Monroe Twp., g. Old Graveyard, Churchtown or Allen, (the same as Mt. Zion), Cumberland Co., PA.; m./1 Catherine 'Regina' MICHAELS. b. 5 Oct. 1767; d. 12 Jun. 1825, g. Old Churchtown, Cem. [1]

In The Allenberry Story by Kathleen A. Heinze it says, "He (George) married Catherine MICHAELS and they had six (actually eight according to the records and History of Cumberland and Adams Counties) children. After Catherine's death, George married secondly, Ann Maria Gross of East Pennsborough Township, 18 Jan. 1827." George would have been 59 at the time of the second marriage. Daniel's cem. records state, "son of George and Mary." Other records show the name George and Polly as parents at the death of Daniel. Anna

----

1. PA Genealogical Magazine, III, 1983 p. 248. Inscriptions from Old Graveyard, Allen Twp., Cumberland Co., PA

Maria GROSS Beltzhoover was called Mary/Polly. [1]   [2]   [3]   [4]

Might her name have been Catherine Regina and she went by
the name of Regina? Regina b. 1767; d., 12/15 June 1825 (57-
8-7). A Brandt family Bible lists George M. Beltzhoover d.
above dates, Regina Beltzhoover, d. 12/15 June 1825, (57-8-7)
and Daniel d. 23 Apr. 1847, (17-2-12). George Peter was
called George in his mother's will. George Peter Beltzhoover
was referred to as Belshuber/Belzhofer/Balsuver/Belshoover as
well as Beltzhuber. [5]

George died from drowning in the Yellow Breeches Creek,
near his home which was near Boiling Springs, PA., and is now
known as Allenberry-on-the-Breeches,-- a well known Resort Inn
and Playhouse. He served in the War of 1812. The History
of Cumberland Co., PA., indicates that George Beltzhoover,
Sr., moved about 1798 from York Co., PA., having bought the
farm (now contained within the grounds of Allenberry).
[6] [7] [8] [9]

Yellow Breeches Creek was the site of an iron works, next
to the Crocketts. Boiling Springs was laid out in 1845 on
former Dickey land. James Crockett's land on YBC was sold to
George Beltzhoover by exec's in 1798, the area is still called
Allenbury/Allenberry, according to Crockett family information.

The ownership of Allenberry moved through the following
hands from George Peter Beltzhoover to Michael Beltshoover and
wf. Anna Maria HERMAN, to Helen Beltzhoover, Mary Elizabeth
BOSLER and to Dewitt Clinton Bosler and then back into the
possession of Helen Beltzhoover BOSLER. See further information at BOSLER'S. The Beltzhoovers, the Boslers, and the

----

1. Cumberland Register   (newspaper), Harrisburg Genealogical Library

2. Daniel, son of George and Mary Beltzhoover, Harrisburg State Library

3. Beers,   History of Cumberland and Adams Counties, A   Bio. Chapter LIL, Monroe Township p.506

4. Ibid.,   Cumberland Co., PA Church Records   p. 218

5. Hoover Histories   Vol. 8 No. 4, 1991

6. Pennsylvania Vital Records   , Vol. III, Index by Eleanor Antioiak. From Penna. Gen. Magazine
and PA. Magazine of History and Bio. Wheaton Public Library, Il., Courtsey Deanna Oklepek

7. Cumberland Register.   Harrisburg, PA

8. Ibid., Cumberland Co. PA., Church Records p. 218

9. Bates, Marlene Strawser and F. Edward Wright   York County Church Records of the 18th Century.

Sadlers were all related by marriage, and through these relationships their land holdings were consolidated. (see Herman)

In 1944, the Heinze family purchased the Allenberry property. Further articles about the Allenberry can be found in the writings of Charles Heinze, "April Fool on the Yellow Breeches" and "Building and Developing Allenberry."

Regina Beltzhoover may be the Regina, b. 5 Oct. 1767; d. 12 June 1825 (57-8-7), South Middleton Twp., Cumberland Co., PA., g. Old Churchtown Cem. [1] [2]

At the baptism of Michael Leydig, 17 Mar. 1793 the sponsors were George and Regina Beltzhuber.

"in A Place Called Boiling Springs" booklet p.196 when discussing Atterbery it refers to George Beltzhoover as, "He was married to Catherine Michael and they had six children. After Catherine's death he married Anna Maria Gross of East Pennsborough in 1827. They had a son, Daniel, born in 1830. Daniel died in 1847 (17)

George Beltzhoover m./2 18 Jan. 1827, Mrs. Anna (An) Maria GROSS of E. Pennsboro Township, Cumberland Co., PA. Anna Maria GROSS Beltzhoover is probably Mary (Mrs.), relic of George, who died 16 Mar. 1867 (70-11-14) near Churchtown, b. 2 April 1786; g. Old Churchtown Cem. Monroe Township, Cumberland Co., PA. Church records say she (Mary) d. 16 Mar. 1867 (70-2-12). [3]

Anna Maria Gross (1786-1867) (81), would have been age 41, when Daniel was born. [4]

In Boiling Springs, PA., there is currently an Allenberry Resort Inn and Playhouse "on the Yellow Breeches Creek". The history of this property dates back to the mid-1770's when the Crockett family lived and worked on two large tracts of land which included what is now known as the Fairfield and the Allenberry tracts. The Crocketts built the first limestone structure, and the large bank barn which is now Fairfield Hall, both by 1785. In 1798, George (Balsuver) Beltzhoover purchased the land from Johann Peter Leidig, son of Leonard Michael Leidigh and father of Rebecca, when Peter was in

----

1. Quickel's Zion Lutheran & Reformed Church

2. Ibid., Marriages & Deaths in Cumberland Co., PA._____, 1821-1830, Democrat Repblican issue held in the Library of Congress p. 48

3. American Volunteers____, Carlisle, PA., 1 Feb. 1827; 30 April 1846

4. Bates, Marlene Strawser and F. Edward Wright York County Church Records of the 18th Century._____

financial trouble. He (George) as well as his son, Jacob, also loaned Peter money, which he was continuing to repay 0after he moved to Ohio around 1836. George Beltzhoover owned the property for 48 years and added two more limestone structures between 1812 and 1820; the Mansion House, Stone Lodge and Carriage Room. In honor of George Beltzhoover they have named a new portion 'The Allenberry-Beltzhoover Terrace.' The names of the previous owners are written underneath the windows on one side of the building. [1] [2] [3]

George Beltshoover, of Monroe Twp., Cumberland Co., PA. made a will dated 21 June 1845, filed 29 April 1846. In his will be mentions his wife, Mary, his son, Daniel, providing for Daniel during his minority and then dividing all that is left between his five sons, Michael G., George, Jacob, John and Daniel and his four daughters, Catherine Brandt, Betsy Herman, Rachel Lerue and Sally Vanasdale, share and share alike. He also mentions his granddaughter, Susannah Weaver, the daughter of his daughter, Sally.

All children of the first marriage were born before 1827. Issue: (BELZHUBER/BELTZHOOVER)

> 77-Christina Catharina/Catherine Beltzhoover/Belzhofer[4], b. 15 Apr. 1790; bpt. 9 May 1790, sponsor was Christiana Belzhofer and refers to Regina as the consort of George. York Co., PA. [4] [5] [6] [7]
>
> She m. 16 Oct. 1810, in Carlisle, Martin Brandt, Jr. She later m. Mr. Morrett?
>
> 78-Michael G. Belzhuber/Beltzhoover (1792-1873), b. 14 Jan. 1792; bpt. 19 Feb. 1792, sp. Michael Belzhuber, his uncle; d. 12 Jan. 1873; m. Anna

----

1. Heinze, Kathleen A.   The Allenberry Story   p. 16

2. Courtesy Deanna Oklepek 5/99

3. Frick, Ruth Hudson

4. York County Historical Society Nov. 1992 Courtesy Deanna Oklepek

5. Ibid., Bates, M.   First Reformed & Trinity First Reformed Church   , York Co., PA., p. 96

6. York Co., PA.,   Church Records of the 18th Century   Vol. III, p. 243 Jacob Lischy's private pastoral record.

7. York County PA. Church Records of the 18th Century   Vol. III, Jacob Lischy's Private Pastoral Record. Quickel's (Zion) Lutheran and Reformed Church

Maria Herman. [1]

79-Georg(e) Belshuber/Beltzhoover, (1793-1867) (Georg
    of Georg & Regina), b. 24 Oct. 1793; bpt. 24
    Nov. 1793; sp. were Mich. Leydig and Sara
    LEYDIG/LEIDIG; d. 21 July 1867, g. Longsdorf
    Cem.; m. Mary --?-- (1786-1857). [2]

80-Elizabeth "Betsy" Beltzhoover, b. ca. 1794, m./1
    --?--- Herman; m./2 --?-- Morrett?. She is
    named as Betsy Herman in her father's will.

81-Jacob Belshover/Beltzhoover (1795-1876), b. 26
    Oct. 1795; bpt. 25 Dec. 1795; d. 1876, Wil-
    liamsport; m./1 Rebecca Leidig, d/o Peter
    Leidig and wf. Susanna Stauch. [3]

82-John (John A. ?) Beltzhoover, b. 3 Jan. 1798, York
    Co., PA.: d. 29 Apr. 1881, g. Mt. Zion Cem.,
    Monroe Twp.; m. 1822, Margaret SMITH (1802-
    1881)

83-Rachel Beltzhoover, (1802-1881); m. before 1831,
    Henry Lerew (1791-1871).

84-Sarah "Sally" Belzhoover, b. 16 Mar. 1805; d. 26
    May 1856, g. Old Churchtown Cem.; m. 28 Feb.
    1828, Carlisle, PA., Isaac VANasdlen.

Child of the second marriage:

85-Daniel Beltzhoover, b. 11 Feb. 1830, bpt. 7 Mar.
    1830; d. 23 Apr. 1847, son of George and
    Mary/Polly, g. Old graveyard, Churchtown,
    Monroe Twp., Cumberland Co., PA. (17-2-12)
    [4]   [5]   [6]

21-**JOHN MICHAEL BELTZHUBER**[3] (3), b. 18 June 1772, chr. 9
Aug. 1772, Christ Ev. Luth. Church, York, PA.; d. 3 Oct. 1843
(70-4-13). John Michael was called "Michael" in his mother's
will. Michael Sprenkel and wife sponsored his baptism.   [7]

    John Michael's wife, was Eva Gross. the daughter of
Samuel Gross and wf. Elizabeth Shaeffer (1753-1811).

----

1. Bates, M. F. & F. Edw. White, York County PA Church Records of the 18th Century   1991 Vol. I,
Vol. II Quickel's Zion Lutheran & Reformed Church, York Co., PA., p. 180

2. Ibid., Bates, M.   Quickle's (Zion) Lutheran & Reformed Church   , York Co., PA., p.182

3. Ibid., Quickel's Zion Lutheran & Reformed Church   . York Co., PA., p. 186

4. Ibid., History of Penna.   Part I

5. Ibid., Evangelical Lutheran Church Records

6. Carlisle Herald Newspaper   , Carlisle, PA., Wed. Apr. 28, 1847

7. Cumberland Co. Church Records   p. 275

Samuel Gross settled in York Co., PA and had seven children: (Gross) George, Samuel, John, Daniel, Eva who married Michael Beltzhuber of Cumberland Co., PA., a daughter, Catherina who married Rev. Johm Schmucker, and a daughter, Elizabeth, who married John Strayer of Dover.   [1]

THE GROSS FAMILY

From <u>The Family of Samuel Gross (1749-1831) of Manchester in York Co., PA.</u> by George Paul Gross, BS., PhD.

"Simon and Theobalt Gross (emigrants) referred to also as, Teobalt, Dewalt, Duwalt, Dewald, etc.
Theobald died intestate.
His widow, Anna Margaret, m./2 Peter Moyer/Myer in 1760.
Guardianship was arranged in 1761 for the minor children of Theobald and Anna Margaret. Children: (Gross) Margaret, Samuel, Dewalt Jr. and Anna Barbara. Older children and assumed out of the household, married etc., were (Gross) Maria C., Peter and Elizabeth.

Samuel Gross was born 7 Dec. 1749 which was a preferred date over 25 Apr. 1750, was then an orphan son. He was later in the York Co., Militia of the American Revolution. Samuel died 13 Feb. 1831. He married c. 1771, Elizabeth Scheaffer/Shaffer, d/o Serenius Sheaffer/Shaffer and wf. Margaretha.
Samuel's children (not in order) were: (Gross)
    Catharina, m. the distinguished Lutheran Church pastor, Rev. John George Schmucker, pastor of Christ Lutheran Church, York. After 1836, Rev. Schmucker was at Quickel's until 1852. Catharina and John George Schmucker had five children: (Schmucker) Susan, Catharina, Anna Maria, Henrietta, Sarah who m., Wm. Ebert. Catharina died soon after Sarah's birth and Rev. Schmucker m./2 Anna Marie Hoffman and they had children, Caroline, Isabella, Margaret Anna, Lutherus Melanchthon, Frederick Augustus, Charles Ferdinand and Amanda.
    Eva, b. c. 1776, m. Michael Beltzhoover who died c. 1849. Michael Beltzhoover was an important land and miller owner in Dover. Michael is referred to as being the brother-in-law of Rev. Schmucker. Eva, in her final years lived with one of her brothers. See Beltzhoover file.
    George (Johann George) b. 9 Apr. 1779, m. Barbara Felker
    Samuel (1781-1863)
    John
    Daniel (later Daniel and his son, Samuel owned the

----

1. <u>York Co., PA., Biographies</u> under Michael Gross of Manchester, Twp., York Co., PA., Ancestry.com

mill.
Elizabeth, m. John Strayer"

* * * * * * * * * * * * * * * * * * *

<u>A Pioneer Mill</u>. The mill on the road from York to Dover
is a very old structure. To the right of the road, on the
Little Conewago, and 400 yards northeast from the present old
building. Martin Weigle, about 1738, erected one of the
earliest mills in York Co. He tried first to build a mill on
the Codorus, near York, but found the stream too large for his
pioneer venture. His Indian neighbors came to view his en-
croachment upon their territory with astonishment, but tradition says they helped him construct the mill.

The stone mill which rendered such important service was
built before the Revolution. The owner of this mill during
that period, was not very patriotic toward the new government.
The mill was later owned by Michael Beltzhoover, and in 1802,
bought by Dr. J. G. Schmucker, pastor of Christ Lutheran
Church at York. Daniel Gross and his son, Samuel, were subse-
quent owners and in 1847, George Neiman purchased it. John
Neiman purchased it in 1856. [1] [2] [3] [4]

Issue: (BELTZHOOVER)
> 86-Sarah "Sally" Beltzhoover[4], b. 2 Nov. 1800, bpt.
>   25 Dec. 1800. Sponsors were Samuel and Eliza-
>   beth Gross. Sarah married Oct. 1819, Christ
>   Evangelical Lutheran Church, York, George
>   Eisenhart.
> 87-Samuel Beltzhoover, b. 3 April 1803, bpt. 18 May
>   1803, sponsors were Samuel and Elizabeth Gross.
> 88-Jesse Beltzhoover, b 3 Oct. 1806, bpt. 17 Nov.
>   1806; sponsors were the parents; m. 7 Mar.
>   1839, Catherine Kleinpeter/Klinefelter.
> 89-Michael Beltzhoover, b. 10 Sept. 1809, a twin,
>   bpt. 13 Sept. 1809, sponsors were Catherine
>   Schmucker and the father; m. 9 Jan., 1831,
>   Cassandra (Cassy) Schreiber/Shriver
> 90-Eva Beltzhoover, b. 10 Sept. 1809, a twin, spon-
>   sors were Catherine Schmucker and the father;
>   d. before 1815?
> 91-George Beltzhoover, b. 14 Oct. 1814, bpt. 8 Feb.
>   1815, m. Elizabeth Kuntz

----

1. Ibid., <u>History of York Co., PA.,</u>   Vol. I, p. 1095 Courtesy Deanna Oklepek.

2. Ibid., <u>York Co. Church Records of the 18th Century</u>   p. 199

3. Christ Evangelical Lutheran Church, York, PA., pages 127, 169, 177.

4. Powell, George R. <u>History of York Co., PA.,</u>   J. H. Beers 1907 p. 1095

24-**EVA BELTZHOOVER**[3] (3), b. 12 Feb. 1775, Cumberland Co., PA., d. 9 June 1850, g. Dosh Cemetery, age (75-3-27). Dosh Cemetery is in Windsor Township and must be in York Co., PA. Eva married in 1799, Jacob WITMAN, III, b. c. 1777, s/o Jacob WITMAN, II, b. c. 1735. They moved to Chanceford Township, York Co., PA. Jacob Witman II was the son of Jacob Witman I, who came to America and settled in the vicinity of Ephrata, Chancford Township, then in Lancaster, Co.? He eventually settled across the Susquehanna River. In the information it says that Jacob and Eva WITMAN had seven children. But, the will mentions more, a Polly and Eve, who may have been granddaughters. After Jacob WITMAN's death, Eva married second John KNISLEY/KNISELEY, b. 24 Nov. 1781; d. 12 Feb. 1842 (60-2-18), g. Dosh Cemetery. [1] [2] [3]

Issue: (WITMAN)

92-Jacob Witman, IV[4]

93-Lydia Witman, b. 4 Mar. 1800, bpt. 28 Apr. 1800, Chanceford Township, York, Co., St. Luke's or Stanley's Lutheran and Reformed Church, sp. by Christina Peltzhuber, the grandmother; d. 29 Feb. 1873. [4] [5]

94-Catherine or Rebecca Catherine Witman, bpt. 11 Oct. 1807, York Co., Chanceford Township, St. Lukes's or Stanley's Lutheran & Reformed Church, wife of Conrad Hake, d. 30-35 years of age.

95-Christena Jane Witman, m./1 Jacob Klinefelter. Christena Jane m./2 John Miller.

96-Mary Witman (Anna May or Mary Ann); d/ age 60; m. Rev. Frederick William VANDERSLOOT.

97-Rachel Witman, d. ca. 1908 (90) m., David BAHN

98-Elizabeth Witman, m. Joseph STRICKLER

Children of the second marriage of Eva Witman Kniseley:

99-Sarah Ellen Kniseley, b. 14 Nov. 1819; d. 31 Oct. 1906, wife of John EMIG, Jr.

Fourth Generation

34-**MARGARET BELTZHOOVER**[4] (12), b. 11 Sept. 1798, Pittsburgh, PA; chr. 2 Oct. 1798, German Church, Pittsburgh; d. 2 June 1832, Stewart Co. TN.; g. Montgomery Co., TN; m. 29 Jan.

----

1. Kamp, Gayle O.   The Kamp Papers   Vol. II, 1986 pp. 765-767

2. Heinicke, Milton   History of Ephrata   pp. 9, 28-33

3. York Co., PA. Courthouse Will Book O p. 505

4. Ibid., Gayle O. Kamp   The Kamp Papers   Vol II 1986 p. 765

5. Bates, Marlene S.,   Church Records of the 18th Century   . York Co., PA. vol. 1 Stehli's/Stehley's/Staley's/St. Luke's Unio0n Church p. 240. Courtesy Jerri Burket, Longswamp, PA.

1819, Samuel STACKER, in the Trinity Church on Sixth Street, Pittsburgh, PA. He was born 1788, Radnor Township, Delaware Co.; d. 26 Dec. 1859, Stewart Co., TN. Margaret is buried with Samuel on the former grounds of the Lafayette Furnace, near Southside, TN, now the Yarborough Farm. [1]

After they were married, Samuel and Margaret, moved to TN. Samuel Stacker and his brother, John, built iron furnaces in TN., and had a number of riverboats there too. They were prominent in the area and also quite wealthy. [2]

Mrs. French Deane (Mrs. Francis L. Deane) d. 1985, a desc. of Margaret Beltzhoover and Samuel Stacker. She is buried in Bellefontaine Cemetery, St. Louis, MO.
Issue: (STACKER)
100-Elizabeth C. Stacker[5] (1821-1835),g. Stacker Cem. Cunningham, Montgomery Co., TN.
101-Catherine Beltzhoover Stacker, b. 29 Feb. 1824, Nashville, Davidson Co., TN., d. 26 April 1881, St. Louis, MO; g. Bellefontain Cem. St. Louis, MO; m. 19 May 1841, French Rayburn, s/o James Rayburn (d. Dec. 1814) & wf., Nancy Watterson Shanklin (d. July 1835).
102-George Stacker, b. ca. 1826, Nashville, Davidson Co., TN; d. 9 June 1883, Cumberland City, Stewart, TN.; m./1 Martha J. West (1830-1854), five children. m./2 13 Feb. 1868, Blanche L. Bishop, b. 1847, d. 22 Nov. 1931, Cumberland City, S., TN.
103-Mary Clementine Stacker (1828-1887); d. 29 April 1887, TN.; g. Bellefontaine Cem.; m./1 18 May 1843, Stewart, TN, Isaac Way Taylor (1822-1858),; m./2 --?-- Richards. Issac Way Taylor was a lawyer and represented St. Louis in the Missouri State Legislature. He died in a railroad accident in Pana, IL.
104-John Stacker, (1831-1831), b. 5 Feb. 1831; d. 6 Feb. 1831; g. Lafayette Furn. Montgomery Co., TN.

35-**SARAH BELTZHOOVER**[4] (12), b. 1801; d. 1851; g. Allegheny Cemetery; m.\1, 13 Mar. 1817, Dr. Frederick Bausman. Frederick Bausman was the son of Nicholas Bausman (d. 1804) and wf. Dorothy; Sarah m.\2, Rev. Jermemiah Knox. [3]

"The community of Knoxville takes its name from Rev.
----

1. Family Bible published 1814. Courtesy Deanna Oklepek

2. Ibid., Oklepek, Deanna

3. Family Bible published 1814. Courtesy Deanna Oklepek

Jeremiah Knox, the son, of Rev. Wm. Knox, a Scottish minister, born in Ireland in 1767. Jeremiah Knox came to Coal Hill, above Birmingham, in the year 1840."

Rev. Knox Jr. (1814-1872), either lived with or was a frequent visitor to the Beltzhoover home, eventually married Jacob's daughter, Sarah, who had been previously married to Dr. Frederick Bausman. Although Sarah had received a portion of her father's land as part of her dowry at her first marriage, she returned to her father's home with her only child, Frederick, at the death of her husband." Your compiler feels that this "one child" was in error as there were several children.

"After his marriage to Sarah Bausman, Mr. Knox took over the management of the 100 acre farm, about 40 acres of which were vineyards producing word-famous grapes. When Rev. Knox died in 1872, the farm was taken over by his heirs, but in 1873, the Knox heirs formed Knox Land Improvement Co. and laid out lots." [1]

Issue: (BAUSMAN)
105-Frederick Bausman[5], b. 1825, d. 1908
106-Sarah Bausman
107-Virginia Bausman, m. Thomas H. Shepard
108-Henry Oatis Bausman, b. 1827: wf. Susan
109-Pressley Neville Bausman
110-Jacob Beltzhoover Bausman (1821-1840)
111-Margaret Bausman m. Thomas S. Neel
Children of the second marriage:
112-Amanda Knox, m. ----Mathews
113-William Wilbur Knox

There are many names in Beltzhoover and Pittsburgh that came from this family: Bausman St. was named after Frederick, son of Sarah: Amanda St. named after Amanda Knox; Arabella, a famous grape grown in the Knox vineyard; Juncunta, a famous Knox strawberry; Rochelle for the famous Knox blackberry; Zara, for the famous Knox grape. Arabella and Zara were named after Beltzhoover women.

36-**MARY ANN BELTZHOOVER**[4] (12), b. 1 May 1803, Pittsburgh, PA; d. 25 July 1880; g. Allegheny Cemetery; m. 7 Dec. 1820, Francis Bailey, b. 1783, d. 8 Jan. 1849. His father, Francis Bailey, a member of a family which held a 100-year lease on an estate on the Riber Baum, near Coleraine, Ireland, his mother was a member of the Livingston family. Francis Bailey came to Philadelphia in 1814 and to Pittsburgh about six years later.

----

1. _Knoxville Borough, a History_   Women's Library Club of Knoxville, 1938

Children probably not in order.

Issue: (BAILEY)

114-Sarah Bailey[5] (1822-1869), m. --?-- Moore

115-Elizabeth Beltzhoover Bailey (1824-1866), m. c. 1846, Wm. Kennedy NIMICK (1822-1875)

116-Francis 'Frank' Bailey Jr. (1827-1872), m. Ellen Howe

117-John H. Bailey, Judge (1830-1897), m. Katherine C. Washington (1832-1914).

118-James Madison Bailey, (1833-1903), m. Martha E. Dalzell (1841-1883).

119-Mary Jane Bailey (1839-1842), d. y.

37-HARRIET (HARRI ETTA) BELTZHOOVER[4] (12), b. 25 Mar. 1806; d. 25 July 1877, g. Allegheny Cemetery; m. 12 April 1831, John Murray/Murry. Her name at baptism shown as Herri Etta Belshuber. Harriett inherited the stone house, barn and the home farm that originally belonged to her grandfather, Melchior Beltzhoover. The home was still standing in 1966, near the corner of Climax and Curtin, although substantially remodeled. [3]

Issue: (MURRAY/MURRY)

120-John S. Murray[5] (1833-1901)

121-Jacob B. Murray

122-Melchior Murray (1843-1843)

38-ELIZA "Elelsa" BELTZHOOVER[4] (12), b. 1809; d. 1832; m. 8 Nov. 1830, Rody Patterson. Rody Patterson m./2 -----. In her father's will filed in 1835, Jacob Beltzhoover removed Rody Patterson as one of his executors, and her portion of the estate go to her son, George Patterson, provided Rody Patterson was not his guardian. [4]

Issue: (PATTERSON)

123-George Patterson[5]

39-MELCHIOR BELTZHOOVER[4] (15), b. 1810; d. 17 Sept. 1850, Allegheny Co., PA.; m., Mary/Margaret Hughey. Mary Hughey was the daughter of Joseph Hughey (1790-1844) and wf., Jane Kennedy (1793-1842). Jane Kennedy was the d/o William Kennedy, d. 1821 and wf., Ann Strawbridge. Jane Kennedy was a sister to Samuel Kennedy. [5]

----

1. History of Allegheny County, PA. Vol. II, Western Penn. Gen. Soc. p. 554

2. Ibid., Family Bible

3. Ibid., Family Bible pub. 1814

4. Ibid., Family Bible pub. 1814

5. Will of Joseph Hughey, recorded 18 July 1844, All. Will Book 5, p. 497 Deanna Oklepek

Anne Strawbridge was the d/o David Strawbridge who owned a good deal of present day Castle Sharon.

The Beltzhoover family settled on the hilltop in the early part of the Nineteenth century and owned considerable property. Melchor Beltzhoover conducted a hotel there. This Melchor Beltzhoover was murdered in West Liberty ca. 1847, being mistaken for an enemy by an enraged circus man. [1]

There is a discrepancy in the dates as two Pittsburgh papers on the scene report he was murdered 17 Sept. 1850. Those papers report that Melchior Beltzhoover was murdered at his Tavern on Washington Road by a man named Dan Mackey. There is no mention in the articles of "an enraged circus man". The account states further. Mackey asked for a room, as he was ill, and was given a room. Mr. Beltzhoover's brother, William, went to the room later to prepare for bed and Mackey rushed him and stabbed him in several places. Melchior heard the call for help and went to his brothee's aid and Melchior was also stabbed in several places. Melchior ran downstairs and expired. A third man went to the room and struggled and overcame Mackey. That man was also stabbed. He tied him up with ropes, dragged him down the stairs and continued to beat him. Officers and the Coroner were called.

William Beltzhoover did not die right away, but was considered serious. He had only been married a few days previous. On the 20th Sept. 1850, The Pittsburgh Daily Gazette had the following information, "William Beltzhoover is in a fair way of recovery. His wounds, though severe, being by no means so dangerous (as) at first supposed." [2]

Again, on the 24th Sept. 1850 "William Beltzhoover. This gentleman is in a fair way of recovery."

Melchior left a widow with several small children. [3] [4]

Mary HUGHEY, was the daughter of Joseph HUGHEY, Allegheny Co., PA. Jos. Hughey made a will 10 July 1844 and it was recorded the same date, g. Bethel Church Cemetery. Children: (HUGHEY) Joseph HUGHEY, David HUGHEY, Ephraim HUGHEY, William HUGHEY, George W. HUGHEY; Mary Hughey BELTZHOOVER; Dorcas HUGHEY, Ann Jane HUGHEY EDWARDS; grandchildren, Joseph D. and

----

1. Ibid., _Pittsburgh Gazette Times_   4 Mar. 1907

2. _Pittsburgh Daily Gazette_   , 20 Sept. 1850, p. 3 col. 4 Courtesy Mr. Norman Schwotzer, 12/97

3. _The Daily Morning Post_   , Pittsburgh, PA., Wed. Sept. 18, 1850 Courtesy N. C. Schwotzer 11-18-97

4. _The Morning Chronicle_   , Pittsburgh PA., Sept. 18 1850 Courtesy N. C. Schwotzer 11-18-97

George W. BELTZHOOVER.   [1]
       Issue: (BELTZHOOVER) Children not in order.
          124-Melchor Mason Beltzhoover[5], b. 24 Dec. 1837; d. 3
                 Mar. 1907; m. Charlotte Lotte Wenzel.
          125-Jane Beltzhoover (Mrs. Jane Beltzhoover TROTTER),
                 b. ca. 1837. She lived at Hays Station and was
                 living as of Mar. 4, 1907.
          126-George W. Beltzhoover, b. ca. 1835; d. 7 Mar. 1889,
                 Pittsburgh; bur. 10 Mar. 1889, from his resi-
                 dence, William Street, Mt. Washington, PA.
                 Member Mt. Washington Lodge, Grandview Lodge,
                 Col. Ellsworth Lodge, A O U W, etc. The 1880
                 census shows George, and his wife, Elizabeth
                 and two (three?) daughters. [2]
          127-Joseph D. Beltzhoover, named in the will of his
                 grandfather, Joseph Hughey. Nothing further is
                 known.

       41-**WILLIAM BELTZHOOVER**[4] (15), b. c. 1817; d. before 1867.
                 [3]

       The Pittsburgh Daily Disptach on 18 Sept. 1850 had the
following news. "On Monday evening, a man named David Mackey,
an Irish laborer went to hotel of Mr. (Wm.) Beltzhoover, four
miles out the Washington Road and ask for lodging. Sometime
after the man went to bed, Mr. Beltzhoover went into his room
to retire to bed, as was understood, and Mackey as it appears,
without any provocation attacked Mr. B. with a large knife,
inflicting one very severe and two slighter stabs, and also
cutting Mr. B. across the hand, as he attempted to ward off
the knife. Mr. Beltzhoover called for aid and his brother.
Melchior Beltzhoover, rushed in to afford assistance, when
Mackey stabbed him several times and he died in a few minutes.
A man named Konk next rushed upon Mackey, and he was horribly
cut across the upper lip, but finally succeeded in overpower-
ing Mackey, secured and tied him." "Testimony was also taken
from Wm. Beltzhoover at the time as it was thought that he
would surely die. He was still living the following afternoon." On the 20th Sept. 1850, The Pittsburgh Daily Gazette
had an article about William Beltzhoover, "is in a fair way of
recovery. His wounds, though severe, being by no means so
dangerous as first supposed." On 24 Sept. 1850, "This gentleman is in a fair way of recovery."

       William Beltzhoover married Jane McGibbney, d/o James
----

1. Harris, Helen L. and Elizabeth J. Wall   <u>Will Abstracts of Allegheny Co., PA.</u>   Will books, I
through V . Pittsburgh, PA. 1986 Carnegie Library of Pittsburgh, Pennsylvania Dept. Courtesy Deanna Oklepek

2. Harris, Helen and Eliz. J. Wall.   <u>Will Abstracts of Allegheny Co., PA., Books I-V</u>   Abstact of the
will of Joseph Hughey 10 July 1844.

3. Peach, Elizabeth

McGibbney and wf. Margaret McGibbney.

This information from the Pittsburgh papers, at the time, made available to us through the great courtesy of Mr. Norman C. Schwotzer. [1]

Issue: (BELTZHOOVER)

128-James Beltzhoover[5], b. c. 1854 no further info.

129-George H. Beltzhoover, b. July 1859, PA.; m. Kate P. --?--, b. Sept. 1852, PA., both bur. Mt. Lebanon Cem.

42-MARY MARIA BELTZHOOVER[4] (15), d. 1831; m. 23 Mar. 1824, Thomas A. Varner, (1799-1883/1884?). Thomas A. Varner was b. 22 Aug. 1799, Baldwin Twp. (then St. Clair Twp.); d. 22 Aug. 1884, according to one report. His photo is found on the page referred to in the note. Thomas A. Varner was the son of John and Mary Free Varner (1768-1814). [2] [3]

Some references state that Thomas' father was Thomas, but your compiler feels that Thomas' father was John.

John Varner came from Lancaster Co., PA.; he was a soldier in the Rev. War, a gunsmith by trade. When insurgents (Whiskey Rebellion) burned Neville's house, being opposed to them, he loaded all the guns and sent the family away and awaited them. The insurgents knew better than try and attack the Varner home and avoided him. John Varner and Mary Free had the following children: (Varner) Thomas, Sarah, Christina and Phoebe. John died at age 76; Mary Free Varner d. 28 Nov. 1814 (48). The family were strict Quakers and through his influence the township of Baldwin was erected. [4]

There is an interesting story about Tom Herron, the last slave of the 64 slaves in Pennsylvania in 1894. He served the family of Melchior Beltzhoover having been brought as a child along with his parents and brothers and sisters to Pennsylvania from Maryland by the old Beltzhoover family. He was owned by Harry Beltzhoover of Sawmill Run, when Mary Beltzhoover married Squire Varner, Tom was part of the dower. Tom took care of the Varner children, as they came along and became a member of the family. Tom had been declared "free" many times by Squire Varner, but he clung to the family and would not

----

1. Schwotzer, Norman C. Nov. 1997

2. Ibid., Warner & Co. History of Allegheny Co., PA   Carnegie Library, Pittsburgh, PA

3. Western Pennsylvania Genealogical Society Quarterly   Vol. 23 No. 1 Summer 1996 pp. 33, 34 a study of Surgeon's Hall Postoffice, the various postmasters

4. History of Allegheny Co., PA   , 1889 A. Warner & Co., Vol. 2 p.236

leave. [1]

Squire Varner was the oldest Justice of the Peace in the USA. He received his commission from Gov. Scheurk (sic) (Shunk). Varner was the founder of the Infirmaries of Pennsylvania. Thomas Varner was a member of GAR and F&AM (Masonic).

Melchior Varner, b. 1829; m. Matilda McClurg, d/o Joseph McClurg (1789-1851) and wf. Julia Fleming (-1845).
    Issue: (VARNER) not in order.
        130-Eleanor Gilbert? Varner[5], b. 1828
        131-John P. Varner, b. 1846
        132-Thomas Varner, b. 1818

44-HENRY G. BELTZHOOVER[4] (15), b. 13 Jan. 1819; d. 19 April 1892 (74), at the residence of Silas Pryor Beltzhoover in Castle Shannon, PA., g. Concord Cem., Southern Ave., Pittsburgh, PA. He was apprenticed by his father to a millright, but when he attained his majority he went into the "tavern business" conducting for many years the "Old Stone Tavern." He afterwards took over the 'White Hall Tavern" on the Brownsville Road which he sucessfully operated. In later years he retired and then became superintendent of the Robinson-Rea Boiler Works. The gunboat "Manyunk", which did great service during the Civil War, was built under his direction. He was manager of Gray's Iron Line and retired to his farm at Castle Shannon. He died in 1892 (74). He married 12 Aug. 1846, Hettie/Hattie Talcott Pryor, b. 18 Mar. 1821; d. 20 May 1889 (71) (The Pittsburgh Gazette on 22 May 1889, reported the death of Mrs. Hetty T. Beltzhoover, May 20, 1889 (69) at her residence near 2814 Penn. Ave.)., g. Concord Presbyterian Church Cemetery, Carrick, Allegheny Co., PA. Her name is on the Pryor tombstone. There may have been other chilren.
[2] [3]

Hettie Pryor was the daughter of Silas D. Pryor (1792-1851), g. Concord Cem., and wf. Elizabeth (1795-1850), g. Concord Cem. They had the following children: (Pryor) Hetty, Ann, Catherine, James M. and possibly another son. Her father, S. D. Pryor ran the S. D. Pryor Inn in St. Clair Township (later Baldwin Township, Allegheny Co., PA.) from about 1835-1849; the son, James M. Pryor inherited the property and in 1852 sold it to Henry Beltzhoover. Henry Beltzhoover resold the property to James M. Pryor in 1855; Hetty Beltz-

----

1. The Pittsburgh Dispatch____, Monday, June 18, 1894 p. 2 Col. 3 Courtesy N. C. Schwotzer

2. Pittsburgh Gazette____ Death Notices Apr. 20, 1892. Henry G. died 19 April 1892. Courtesy N. Schwotzer

3. Ibid., History of Pittsburgh and Environs_____ 1922

hoover purchased it in 1855 and held it until 1868. [1]
Issue: (BELTZHOOVER)
133-Silas Pryor Beltzhoover[5], b. 1 July 1847; d. at
Castle Shannon, 14 Nov. 1915; m. Mary E. Harris.
133a-Harry B. Beltzhoover, b. 1850, d. 12 Feb. 1895,
Pittsburgh, g. Uniondale Cem. In the 1880
census he was single, a boarder at the St.
Clair Hotel, corner Penn Ave and 16th St.
134-George McLaughlin Beltzhoover, b. 15 Apr. 1855,
res. Cincinnati, OH; m. Ameliah L. Kaemerling
135-John Dixon Beltzhoover, b. Pittsburgh, PA., (1858-
1894); b. 24 Mar. 1858: d. 29 April 1894,
Cincinnati, OH. (36-3-19), g. internment was 1
May 1894, Spring Grove Cemetery, Cincinnati,
OH., s/o Henry and Hattie Beltzhoover; m. Josephine Goebel.

46-**SAMUEL BELTZHOOVER, M.D.**[4] (15), b. 17 Mar. 1823, d. 10
April 1890, g. St. Clair Cemetery, Scott Road, Mt. Lebanon; m.
Eliza Jane Long, b. 12 April 1826, OH; d. 8 Dec. 1920. [2] [3]

Samuel Beltzhoover was referred to by Geo. M. Beltzhoover
as "Doctor Sam." in 1805. There are records that indicate
that Catherine b. 1 June 1853, was born New Cumberland, Hancock Co., WV. Hancock Co., WV is near Pittsburgh.
Issue: (BELTZHOOVER), see p. 152 for additional data.
136-Alexander Long Beltzhoover, b. 2 May 1848, d. 20
Feb. 1909, funeral from his mothers' home in
Castle Shannon
137-Ruben Henry Beltzhoover, b. 13 Sept. 18, 1850, d.
10 Mar. 1871.
138-Catherine Bell Wilson Beltzhoover, 24 June 1853, d.
23 Nov. 1926
139-Maria Ellen Beltzhoover, b. 17 Jan. 1858, d. 1
April 1877
140-Matilda Long Beltzhoover, b. 23 Feb. 1861, d. 28
July 1871
141-Samuel Blackmore Beltzhoover[5], b. 11 Feb. 1864, d.
14 Sept. 1869.

48-**DANIEL BETZHOOVER**[4] (15), son of Henry B. Beltzhoover,
b. 1825; d. 1886; m. Jane Alderson (1832-1882). Daniel
served in the Civil War, Co. A. 18th PVI; g. Uniondale, Pittsburgh, PA.
Issue: (BELTZHOOVER)
----

1. Schwotzer, Norman C. Letter 11-28-97

2. Peach, Elizabeth. <u>St. Clair Cem</u>. records of Samuel Beltzhoover, M.D. and family.

3. <u>Deceased Physicians Book</u>, Samuel Beltzhoover 12/31/29a (Male); (5.) Allopath); (8) PA, 1887

142-Mary Elizabeth Beltzhoover[5], b. 1849

49-**NANCY BELTZHOOVER**[4] (15) (1802-1883), d. 29 Sept. 1883 (81), res. near Castle Shannon; m./1 Samuel Kennedy; m./2 Samuel COOLEY (1807-   ). Samuel Kennedy was the son of William Kennedy d. 1821 and wf. Ann Strawbridge. Ann Strawbridge was the daughter of David and Ann Strawbridge. [1]

David Strawbridge died in 1794. They had children: (Strawbridge) Samuel, William, Jane m. Joseph Huey/hughey, David m. Dorcas Hughey a sister to Joseph Hughey.

Henry Beltzhoover was named guardian of the children of Nancy Beltzhoover and her husband, Samuel Kennedy. The children later requested and had that guardianship removed.

Samuel Cooley was b. 16 July 1807, farmer, P.O. Castle Shanon, Baldwin Twp., Allegheny Co., PA., the son of Francis Cooley (1767-1842); grandson of William Cooley, a native of England who settled in New York state before the Revolutionay War. William Cooley was a soldier in the War as aid-de-camp under Gen. Wayne. There were three sons, William, Rev. Joseph and Francis. Francis Cooley was born in NY state, became a silversmith. He married Eleanor Vandivolt. Their children were: (Cooley) Robert, Jon, William, Francis, Samuel, Harrison, Elizabeth and Mary. Francis Cooley was a prosperous farmer and active church worker; d. 21 May 1842. [2]

Samuel Cooley owned 130 acres and married Mrs. Nancy Kennedy d/o Henry and Eliz. (Bell) Beltzhoover. Nancy's grandfather, John Bell, was the first civilized settler on Chartiers Creek.

Samuel and Nancy Cooley were members of the Seceder Church.
Issue: (KENNEDY) not in order
    143-Samuel Tarleton Kennedy[5] (1830-1853), m. Nancy Jane
        Stewart (1828-1891).
    144-Henry Kennedy (1825-1854)
    145-Elizabeth Kennedy, m. Robert Hamilton
    146-William Kennedy (1823-1877)
Issue: second marriage (COOLEY)
    147-Eleanor Cooley (1837-   )(Mrs. Eleanor Couch)
    148-Samuel B.(Beltzhoover?) Cooley (1843-   ), m. Jane
        Hultz (1843-   )
    149-William Cooley (1840-   )

----

1. <u>Descendants of William Kennedy   </u>. Courtesy Elizabeth Peach.

2. <u>History of Allegheny Co., PA.   </u> 1889 p. 376. Courtesy of N. C. Schwotzer

52-FREDERICK WILLIAM BELTZHOOVER[4] (16), b. 2 July 1811, Pittbsburgh, PA.; chr. 2 Sept. 1811, German Church, Pittsburgh, PA.; d., 4 Aug. 1843, St. Louis, MO., g. Calvary cem., St. Louis; m. 24 July 1834, St. Louis King Fr. St. Louis, St. Louis Co., Mo., Frances Theresa Knapp, b., 11 Oct. 1812, NY; d. 24 Sept. 18567, g. Calvary Cem. St. Louis, MO. [1]

Frederick William Beltzhoover was bapt. in the First German United Evangelical Church. His sponsor was Elizabeth Beltzhoover, his grandmother.

Frederick W. Beltzhoover was in business with William Robb. They were hatters, making caps and hats.
Issue: (BELTZHOOVER) (children not in in order)
150-Edward Jacob Beltzhoover[5], b. 6 Aug. 1836, St. Louis, MO; chr. 9 Sept. 1838, St. Louis; d. 2 Jan. 1837, St. Louis. Buried with his parents.
151-Samuel G. (George?) Beltzhoover, b. 25 Jan. 1838; d. 20 April 1869, St. Louis, MO. Buried with his parents. He served in the CW, Confederate, 2nd Reg't. Missouri Militia; General and Staff Officers, Non-Regimental Enlisted men, CSA; and 4th Reg't., Missouri Infantry State Guard (8th Division). He served as Adjutant. He was captured and escaped, one of 52 escaping enroute to Johnson's Island, 18 April 1864.
152-Frederick W. Beltzhoover, Jr., b. 12 Nov. 1840; d. 29 Oct. 1858, St. Louis; m. Nancy H. Fitch MCSPIRIT, wid., Thomas MCSPIRIT.
153-Mary E. Beltzhoover, b. 30 Aug. 1843, MO; d. 30 Dec. 1900, St. Louis. In the 1880 Census she was living with her Uncle, John Knapp. She is buried with her parents.

53-ELIZABETH MARY BELTZHOOVER[4] (16), (1813-1877) m./1, 12 Aug. 1830, William Mason Cox. Elizabeth was born 4 April 1813. d. 14 July 1877, g. Greenwood Cemetery, Clarksville, TN.; m./2, 16 Mar. 1846, at Stewart Co., TN., Alfred B. Norris. [2]

Elizabeth Beltzhoover Cox NORRIS was a Civil War heroine who nursed wounded soldiers from Fort Donelson and who later gained renown for her travels and valiant efforts to establish a Civil War Veteran's Orphans Home in Clarksville, Montgomery Co., TN. Eric Thomas said that she was a very tall and large woman. He also said that her husband was inclined to go out drinking and she shot him the foot to keep him at home. The truth is that, Eliz. shot her second husband on June 5, 1856

----

1. Ibid., Family Bible, pub. 1814

2. Ibid., Family Bible pub. 1814

and she was charged with intent to commit murder, and she plead not guilty. Alfred Norris died Oct. 1, 1856 and the charge was changed to murder. Her cousin's husband, Samuel Stacker, posted her bond during the lengthy trial. She was found not guilty of the murder of her husband. There was a large portrait of her in the Orphanage she helped to found. [1]

In the 1860's, Elizabeth Beltzhoover Cox Norris went to California to get donations for her orphanage in Clarksville, TN., Deanna concludes that her g-g-grandmother would not have made such an arduous journey had there not been Beltzhoover's out there with some money. She ultimately collected over $7,000. and in today's money (2005) that would be in excess of $178,000. Efforts are being made to locate those Beltzhoovers in Calif., if they are there.

> Issue: (COX)
> > 154-Mary Jane COX[5] b. 17 Aug. 1833; d. 20 Mar. 1839 (5), Beardstown, IL
> > 155-Frances Louisa Cox, b. 25 Jan. 1837, Pittsburgh; d. 22 Mar. 1886, Cumberland City, TN.; m. 17 Dec. 1857, Stewart Co., TN., Isaiah Willson Evans (1829-1888), d. Dover, Stewart, TN. And their daughter Louisa Dickson Evans (1864-1961), Clarksville, TN., m. John Hill Thomas. Their son, Eric Dewitt Thomas, m. Ella Mae Paige (1900-1984). Their daughter Deanna Nedra Thomas (1942-), m. Milan Gustav Oklepek. Deanna is a wonderful genealogist and it is from her years of Beltzhoover research that this compilation is possible.

57-ELIZABETH ANN ARMISTEAD THOMSON MASON[4] (17), b. 7 April 1803, d. 20 Jan. 1857; m. 9 April 1829, John O. WHARTON.
> Issue: (WHARTON)
> > 156-Mary Armistead Wharton[5] (1830-1850)
> > 157-John Wharton
> > 158-Jesse Barnes Wharton, m. Susan Whiting
> > 159-Elizabeth Wharton, m. Heber Crane
> > 160-Sarah Wharton, m. Clagg Fitzhugh
> > 161-William Fitzhugh Wharton

58-ABRAM BARNES MASON, Jr.[4] (17), 21 Oct. 1807; d. 10 April 1863; m. Margaret St. Clair Clarke PATTERSON, 29 Nov. 1831.
> Issue: (MASON)
> > 162-John Thomson Barnes Mason[5] (1833-)

59-MELCHOR BELTZHOOVER MASON[4] (17), b. 3 Oct. 1812; m. Mary DAILY (1827-1880).
----

1. Clarksville Chronicle   21 July 1877. Courtesy Deanna Oklepek

Issue: (MASON)
163-Melchior Beltzhoover Mason, Jr.[5]; m. Maud Reide.
164-Thomas Mason, m. Mary Collins
165-Virginia Wallace Mason, m. R. W. McMasters
166-Sarah Elizabeth Mason, m. Walter Lewis Sanford

60-**JOHN THOMSON JUNIOR MASON**[4] (17), (1815-1873); m. Margaret Cowan, (1821-1899).
Issue: (MASON)
167-Louisa Gilmer Mason[5], (1844-   ), m. Silas W. Terry.
168-William Temple Thomson Mason (1845-1847)
169-Elizabeth Mason, (1848-   )m. Theoderich Porter
170-John Thomson Mason (1850-   )

64-**MELCHIOR WALLACE BELTZHOOVER, Capt.**[4] (18).b. 23 Mar. 1815, Hatfield, PA. As a small boy he went with his father to Zelienople, Butler Co., PA. Melchior W. returned when he was about 15 years of age. See Virginia Lee Koontz, m. Melchior Stewart Beltzhoover, but the Beltzhoover line of descent is through Virginia Koontz. Melchior Wallace Beltzhoover was born 23 Mar. 1815, Hatfield, PA; d. 12 Nov. 1879. Pittsburgh, PA; g. Alleghheny Cem. Melchior Wallace Beltzhoover never married. It has been speculated that Melchior Stewart Beltzhoover may have been actually the son of Melchior Wallace Beltzhoover, but that Malona/Melona J. Stewart was married (1-Gulick, 2-John B. Burton, 3-Ford) or widowed and that he did not want to marry her, so adopted her son. He adopted Melchior Stewart Beltzhoover. This speculation is further supported by provisions for financial support to Melona J. Stewart in Melchior W. Beltzhoovers' will. [1]

Melchior W. Beltzhoover's Will and Testament was written 2 Dec. 1879. He was the first registered guest at the Monongahela House Hotel when it opened and he resided there until his death. Excepts from the will are herein given. "To John Wright, boot black at the Monongahela House my clothing and wearing apprel and trunks." "to my sisters Arabella and Zara, my pictures and other things in my room.....annuities annually of $2,000 to Arabella and Zara each." "to Melona J. Stewart, now Mrs. John Burton of Baltimore, MD., the mother of my adopted son, my house and lot of ground number twenty Clinton Street, Cincinnati, OH.....annual sum for support for her natural life ($1,000.)." " to my brother, George Beltzhoover $2,000. annually, to the daughters of my brother, Daniel Beltzhoover, deceased (Mary, Sallie, Elizabeth and Jane) $500. annualy to each." "the Trustees to provide $3,000. annually for the education of Mechior Stewart Beltzhoover....provision for $5,000. annually from age 21-25....at age 25 $7500. annu-

----

1. Pittsburgh Gazette   Obituary Nov. 13, 1879. He was referred to as Capt . Melchior W. in the
Pittsburgh Gazette Nov. 13, 14, 1879 Courtesy Norman Schwotzer

ally to age 30 at which time he could claim the whole estate."
"in the event of the death of Melchior Stewart the estate to
be settle, share and share alike by his brother, George W.,
sister, Mary Kountz, sister, Catherine Furgison, sister,
Arabella and sister, Zara, and a share divided between the
daughters of Daniel."

Melchior Stewart Beltzhoover was about eleven years old
when his chosen father died. He was raised by Aunt
"Zora/Zara" and Aunt "Arabella." He was raised and attended
school in Europe by Aunt Arabella, according to one source.

Melchior W. Beltzhoover was quite prominent in business
and wealthy. He was born in the building known as the "Beltzhoover Homestead", which stands in Allegheny Cemetery. When he
was young his father moved to Zelienople, Butler Co., PA., and
at age 15 he returned to Pittsburgh and became a salesman in a
dry good store. He became part owner in several dry good
stores and signed on as a clerk on the steamer 'Robert Morris'. He was connected with the Pittsburgh & Cincinnati
Packet Lines, and then purchasing an interest in the steamers,
Isaac Newton, Brilliant, Buckeye State, and Capt. of the
Buckeye State and Capt. of the steamer, Economy. During the
Civil War he secured contracts to carry troops and supplies
south and made a great deal of money. After the war he had
various businesses and associations.

Issue: (BELTZHOOVER)
   171-Melchior Stewart Beltzhoover[5], b. 18 May 1868,
      Monmouth, IL., d. 20 July 1918, Natchez, Adams
      Co. MS.; m. 1 Sept. 1891, Virginia Lee KOONTZ,
      b. 19 April 1862, Natchez, MS., d. 3 April
      1921, Natchez, MS. See Virigina Lee Koontz.

   70-**DANIEL M. (Melchior?) BELTZHOOVER, Col.**[4] (18), "Uncle
Dan" or "Colonel Dan"; b. 11 April 1826, Zelienople, Butler
Co., PA.; d. 31 Oct. 1870, Mobile, AL.; g. Mountain Cemetery,
Mount St. Mary's Seminary, Emmitsburg, MD., both Daniel and
Lizzie Miles are bur. in the Mountain Cemetery right behind
the Seminary); Col. grad. West Point in 1847 (age 21) and was
an Officer in the Union Army and later in the Confederate
Army. It is believe that he took the middle initial M. later
in life.

Daniel M. m., 7 Jan 1850, Frederick Co., MD., Elizabeth
'Lizzie' Miles, b. 25 Dec. 1826; d. 18 Nov. 1858, g. St.
Anthony's. Eliz. Miles, d/o Wm. & Sarah (Mickle) Miles. The
grandmother was Elizabeth Mickle.

Daniel said that after his graduation from West Point
that he was for several years a Lt. in the 1st Reg't. of
Artillery and served on the Rio Grande in California, Mexico,
Texas and in Florida. Daniel and Elizabeth are shown in the
1850 California census in San Diego. He was assigned to the
Federal Garrison there. He resigned while Jeffersn Davis was

Sec. of War to accept a Professorship of Mathematics and Civil Engineering which he was then holding at Mount St. Mary's College.

On Mar. 1, 1861, he wrote a letter from Mount St. Mary's College, to Jefferson Davis, Pres. CSA, offering his services to serve in the Confederate Army. From <u>Emmitsburg Area in the Civil War</u> by Wayde Chrismer Mount St. Mary's College During the Civil War, the mountain continues, "Though the professors and the students took sides and were firm in their opinions there was never any ill-feeling entertained nor violence indulged in." "No sooner had the war broken out than southern born students made haste to leave for Dixie. Some thirty left with Beltzhoover, who later commanded a Louisiana Battery."

Military Records, Washington D. C., inquiring about Daniel's place of birth and other records. The letter was from John D. Kilbourne, Dir. (U. S. Military Academy?) he was made 1st Lt. 22 Feb. 1851, and resigned his commission on Dec. 6, 1855. He enlisted in the 1st Louisiana Heavy Artillery, a Col. in Confederate Army and served for the duration of the conflict; m., 7 Jan 1850, Frederick Co., MD., Elizabeth "Lizzie" Miles: b. 25 Dec. 1826; d. 18 Nov. 1858, g. Mountain Cemetery, Mount St. Mary's Seminary, Emmitsburg, MD. St. Joseph's Provincial House (Emmitsburg) says that Elizabeth Miles attended St. Joseph's Academy from 1836-1841. Daniel and Lizzie's brother, Henry were both at Mount St. Mary's during this period. Newspaper states that he died of yellow fever.

It was said that Daniel attended West Point with General Grant, but later this was discredited as Gen. Grant left the same day Daniel Beltzhoover entered West Point. In the CW. Confederate Army, Daniel Beltzhoover was appointed, Lt. Col., 14 Aug. 1861; he was at Watson's Battery at Columbus, KY; in July of 1862, he was Acting Inspecor-General at Camp Moore; Dec. 1862 he commanded Heavy Artl. at Vicksburg, MS; he was captured and parolled at Vicksburg, 4 July 1863; he was in parole camp at Enterprise, MS., Oct. 1863-Apr. 1864; he was ill and in hospital quarters in Oct. 1864; on the rolls of Prisoners of War parolled Mobile, AL., May 26, 1865. [1]

There is a monument to Daniel Beltzhoover in Vicksburg, MS., and a map of Vicksburg during the CW shows an area called 'Beltzhoover." Beltzhoover researchers believe that this was the area of encampment of a unit or batallion under the com- mane of Daniel Beltzhoover.

In browsing through the Library of Congress Records,

----

1. <u>Records of Lousiana Copnfederate Soldiers</u>   Vol. II Couresty David Madden, Director, Civil War Center, LSU., Baton Rouge, LA.

Deanna Oklepek found the following information. Under Collections, "American 19th Century Sheet Music. Copyright Deposits, 1870-1885" a "song for piano", entitled, "The Rhine Feast" by D. Beltzhoover. published by William Hall and Sons, New York 1871. It is thought that this is Daniel, who was a Colonel and an accomplished musician. [1] [2]

To your compiler's knowledge all of the children died unmarried and without children. Three of his daughters were nuns. Col. Dan was a professor at Mount St. Mary's College in Emmitsburg, MD before the war (CW). He was a professor of Mathematics and Commandant of the Mountain Cadets Drill Team.

Lizzie Miles had a brother, George Henry Miles, who taught English at Mount St. Mary's before the CW and is bur. in Mountain Cemetery, Mount St. Mary's Seminary, Emmitsburg, MD. He was somewhat of a man of letters, a poet, novelist, playwrite, and penned the words to the unofficial Confederate National Anthem, "God Save the South." George Henry Miles had been a student at the Prep School along with Daniel Beltzhoover. Elizabeth "Lizzie" Miles and her brother, George Henry were the children on William Miles and wf. Sarah "Sally" Mickle Miles. Elizabeth Mickle, the grandmother, converted from Judaism to Catholicism at a very old age. It is not known if her husband was Jewish. Along with Daniel and Lizzie, Mary Paulina, Willie, Eliz. Mickle and Sarah and Wm. Miles are all bur. Mountain Cemetery, Mount St. Mary's Seminary, Emmitsburg, MD.. William Miles served in the U.S. Consular service and whose last posting was at Callao, Peru. [3]

Daniel's connection with Mount St. Mary's was considerable. At the age of 11 he was in the Hagerstown Academy, Hagerstown, MD.; at the age of 13, his father died. He was at Mount St. Mary's Prep School, an all boys school, 1840-1841, 1841-1842. where he studied Latin, Greek, French and Science. There is a notation on a student card that he had a brother, Melchior who was perhaps the one remitting the money. At this time it is not known where he attended schooling between the time at Mount St. Mary's and his entrance into West Point in 1847. [4]

Issue: (BELTZHOOVER) Children may not be in order.
172-William "Willie" Beltzhoover[5], (1851-1852), b. 24
    Sept. 1851; d. 8 Mar. 1852, g. Mountain Ce-

----

1. Courtesy Deanna Oklepek

2. Scharf's History of Baltimore City and County Vol. II, p. 795   . Courtesy Deanna Oklepek

3. Ledoux, Rev. Albert, Asst. Prof. of Church History, Mount St. Mary's Seminary, Emmitsburg, MD. 11/03

4. Ibid., Leoux, Rev.

metery, Mount St. Mary's Seminary, Emmitsburg, MD.

173-Mary Paulina Beltzhoover, b. ca. 1858 (census), no dates on her stone in Mountain Cemetery, Mount St. Mary's Seminary, Emmitsburg, MD.

174-Sarah Beltzhoover, a.ka. Sister Agatha, b. 5 Feb. 1854, Balt. City, MD.; which does not agree with the census dates; d. 16 Nov. 1898, Emmitsburg She was mentioned at her death as being one of four sisters. Bur. Community Cemetery of the Daughters of Charity, Emmitsburg, MD. She entered Daughters of Charity 23 Sept. 1886. Agatha was commisioned to schools in WI., MA., MD., and LA. before her death, age 44.

175-Henry (Harry) Beltzhoover, b. 8 May 1855; d. 14 June 1871, g. Natchez City Cem., Natchez, MS. He died from drowning in quicksand in Homochitto Creek.

176-Elizabeth Rose (Rosa) Beltzhoover, b. ca. 1858 age 12, 1870, Mobile, AL. The 1901 England census shows her age 43, a nun, Supt. St. Margaret's Industrial School, Mill Hill, Middlesex Co.

177-Mary Jane "Jennie" Beltzhoover. a.ka. Sister Berchmans, b. 14 Nov. 1857, on her grave stone which does not square with the census; d. 5 Dec. 1946, g. Community Cemetery of the Daughters of Charity, Emmitsburg, MD. She joined Daughters of Charity of St. Vincent de Paul in Emmitsburg 16 July 1887. She was commissioned to schools in VA. and AL., as well as to hospitals in Ga., MD., Wash. D.C., and NC.

71-**MARY ROANE BELTZHOOVER**[4] (18), b. 24 Sept. 1827, Zelienople, Butler Co., PA.; d. 25 June 1895, Natchez, MS.; m. 21 Oct. 1845 (she was 18), Natchez, MS, George Washington KOONTZ. Geo. Wash. KOONTZ was born 6 April 1816, in Washington, Washington Co., PA., d. 4 April 1876, Natchez, Adams Co., MS.[1]

George Washington Koontz was the son of John H. Koontz and wife Jane Mitchell Koontz. John H. Koontz, b. 8 Jan 1778, Lancaster Co., PA., d. 15 May 1857, Washington, Washington Co., PA. Jane Mitchell Koontz, b. Dec. 1779, d. 28 Oc. 1818, Washington, Washington Co., PA. John H. Koontz was the son of Michael Kuntz (1751-1793). [2]

George Koontz was a banker in Natchez, MS.

----

1. _Ladies Home Journal January_ ____ 1947 "Meet The Beltzhoovers of Natchez, MS"

2. Beltzhoover, Ruth Audley

Issue: (KOONTZ)

178-Mary Koontz[5], b. 29 July 1847, d. 14 Apr. 1923, Natchez, MS.; m. 14 May 1879, Francis Surget Shields.

179-Henriette Koontz, b. 1849, educated in Germany, d. 14 Mar. 1914; m., 19 April 1876, William Dunbar JENKINS.

180-George Wallace Koontz, b. 24 Sept. 1851, educated in Tours, France and Washington College, Lexington, VA., d. 5 Aug. 1914, Natchez, MS. unm. n.i.

181-Kate Beltzhoover Koontz, b. 5 Oct. 1853, educated in Germany, d. 27 Sept. 1908, Natchez MS., unm. ni.

182-Margaret Koontz, b. 19 Feb. 1856, d. Aug. 1927 in France; m. 25 Nov. 1874; m. Andrew D. JONES

183-Lizzie B. Koontz, b. 8 Feb. 1858, d. 14 April 1865, Natchez, MS.

184-Alexander Ferguson Koontz, M.D. b. 11 April 1860, d. 5 Mar. 1917, New York, NY. Educated Univ. of the South, Sewanee, TN and Bellevue. unm. ni.

185-Virginia Lee Koontz, b. 19 April 1862, Natchez, MS., d. 3 April 1921, Natchez; m. 1 Sept. 1891, in Natchez, Melchior Stewart Beltzhoover (chosen), b. 14 May 1868, Monmouth, IL.; d. 20 July 1918, Natchez, MS.

78-MICHAEL G. BELTZHOOVER[4] (20) (1792-1873). b. 14 Jan. 1792, chr. 19 Feb. 1792; d. 1 Jan 1873 (80-11-14), g. Ashland Cem., Carlisle, Cumberland Co., PA.; m. 15 Jun. 1819, First Ev. Luth. Church, Carlisle, Cumberland Co., PA., Anna Maria HERMAN. Ashland Cem. records indicate "Anna Mary Herman Beltzhoover, wife of Michael G. Beltzhoover, b. (11?) 12 Nov. 1799; d. 30 May 1871, g. Ashland Cem." [1] [2]

Mary (Anna Maria), d/o Christian Herman (1761-1829) and wf. Elizabeth Bauer/Bowers (c. 1774), on 15 June 1819, married Michael G. Beltzhoover; dau. Anna, m. Dr. Jacob Bosler, Dayton, OH., and Eliza m., Abram Bosler. [3]

Christian Herman was the s/o Martin Herman (1732-c 1804) and wf. Anna Dorothea Boerst. Christian Herman's sons were, John (who married Rachel\Elizabeth Beltzhoover); Jacob; Mar-

----

1. Ibid., <u>Cumberland Co., PA. Church Records</u> p. 444

2. LDS IGI Index page 2 First buried in First Lutheran burying ground, Carlisle, PA. The body was moved in 1891 to the church plot, NE corner of new addition to the new addition in the old graveyard.

3. <u>History of Cumberland and Adams Counties, PA.</u>, 1886, p 380. Courtesy of Jerri Burket, Longswamp, PA.

tin; Christian and David. [1]

At the birth record of Amanda her parents are shown as Michael Beltzhoover and wf. Mary, also at the birth of Mary Bowers, her mother was shown as Mary. Anna Maria Herman the d/o Christian and Elizabeth Bauer/Bowers Herman.

Michael G. was executor of his fathers will.
Issue: (BELTZHOOVER) Children not in order.
   186-Charles Beltzhoover[5] b. 15 May 1825; d. 4 Dec.
      1862 (37) NY., NY., g. Ashland Cem., Carlisle,
      Cumberland Co., PA   [2]
   187-Christian Herman Beltzhoover, b. 27 Aug. 1826; d.
      27 Feb. 1875, g. Ashland Cem.
   188-Amanda Beltzhoover, b. 26 Feb. 1829; chr. 4 Mar.
      1829, d. 3 Mar. 1829; g. Old Churchyard,
      Churchtown, Carlisle, Cumberland Co., PA
   189-Helen Beltzhoover, b. 15 May 1833; bpt. 8 June
      1834; d. 5 Oct. 1890, g. Ashland Cem.; m. James
      W. Bosler. [3] [4]
   190-Mary Bowers Beltzhoover, b. 5 Nov. 1836; bpt. 6
      Nov. 1836, d. 16 Mar. 1857. (22); m. John A.
      Filbert [5]
   191-Eliza Ann/Elizabeth/Elizabeth Ann Beltzhoover, b.
      22 Dec. 1821; d. 21 Mar. 1876; m. 6 May 1841,
      Henry Hake Grove   [6]
   192-Angelina Beltzhoover, b. 18 May 1838; d. 21 June
      1838, infant daughter of Michael G., g. Old
      Churchtown Cem., Monroe Township. [7] [8] [9] [10]
      Church records show she was born 23 Nov. 1837,
      bpt. 16 June 1838, d/o Michael and wf. Mary.
----

1. SAR Warren Serentus Herman refers to Rachel Beltzhoover Herman.

2. First Evangelical Luth. Church, Carlisle, PA

3. Biographical Annals of Cumberland Co., PA.   p. 215

4. LDS Records IGI Index p. 2 633

5. Ibid., Cumberland Co. PA. Church Records.   First Evangelical Lutheran Church, Carlisle, PA.,
p. 149

6.   History of Cumberland County, PA.,   p. 190

7.   Cumberland Register   Vol. I

8.   Ibid., First Evangelical Lutheran Church

9.   Carlisle Republican   19 July 1838

10. LDS IGI Records 2, 633

(Churchtown)

77-CHRISTINA CATHARINA BELTZHOOVER[4] (20), b. 15 April 1790; d. 8 Sept. 1873 (83-4-20); m. Martin Brandt; d. 24 July 1833 (48-10-7), g. Mt. Zion Cem. Sect H.
 Issue: (other children?) (BRANDT)
  193-Samuel Brandt[5], d 26 Feb. 1859 (40-6), g. Mt. Zion

79-GEORGE BELTZHOOVER[4] (20), (Georg of Georg & Regina) (1793-1867), b. 24 Oct. 1793, York Co., PA.; bpt. 24 Nov. 1793; d., 21 July 1867, g. Longsdorf. Sponsors at his birth were Mich. Leydig and Sara LEYDIG/LEIDIGH. [1]

Your compiler believes that this is George (1793-1867), m. 1816, wf. Margaret --?--; b. ca. 1796; d. 12 April 1874 (in her 78th year), both bur. Longsdorf Cemetery. The Longsdorf Graveyard is near New Kingston Railroad Station, north and west of Mechanicsburg and George and Margaret (Mary?) are the only Beltzhoover's buried there. [2]

Margaret's will of June 1872. Any children dec. before 1872 are not mentioned. She does not mention John Clendenin Beltzhoover (he died in 1870). In 1872 were there other children of Jacob (George Jacob) other than Francis E. Beltzhoover, George Moris/Morris Beltzhoover and Mary A. 'Maggie' E. Hocker deceased? Mary A. Hocker is shown as a housekeeper for Frank Eckles Beltzhoover in 1910 census. Mary Hocker, b. 15 Sept. 1867, PA., d. 30 July 1950, Los Angeles, CA, d/o --?-- Hocker and wife --?-- Eckles. In the 1930 CA., Los Angeles, Census she was 63 years old.

The plot in Silver Spring Presbyterian Church Cemetery showing monuments and graves includes, Agnes Eckles Beltzhoover (1852), Jacob Beltzhoover (1853) son of George and Margaret Beltzhoover, John C. 'Mateer'? Beltzhoover (1870) and Margaret Beltzhoover wife of B. W. Hocker (1919).
 Issue: (BELTZHOOVER) (other children?)
  194-Jacob Beltzhoover[5], b. 25 Sept. 1817, Allen Township, d. 1853, (35) (now Monroe), g. Silver Spring Presbyterian Church Cem., wf. Agness Eckles, g. Silver Spring Presbyterian Church Cem. 1852
  195-Michael B. Beltzhoover, m. Mary A. Brickman belong here?

80-ELIZABETH 'BETSY' BELTZHOOVER[4] (20), referred to as Betsy Herman in her father's will.

----

1. Ibid., Bates, M. <u>Quickle's (Zion) Lutheran & Reformed Church</u>, York Co., PA., p.182

2. Zeemer, Joe Record State Library, Harrisburg, PA XVI '15, Longsdorf Graveyard

81-JACOB BELTZHOOVER[4] (20), b. 26 Sept. 1795, York Co., PA.: chr. 25 Dec. 1795 York Co., PA.; d. 25 Mar. 1880, Williamsport, PA.   Obituary information from The Daily News Gazette, Mar. 26, 1880, states that, Jacob Beltzhoover died Mar. 25, after an illness of nearly three weeks, age 84 years and 5 months.   Funeral service held afternoon at half past two, Market St. Lutheran Church.   There was a request that Cumberland Co., PA., papers, please copy. [1]

The Cherokee History, KS., says that his dates are (1805-1876).

Jacob Beltzhoover, m./1 28 Oct. 1824 (one record says married 28 Sept. 1824), by Rev. Keller, at Cumberland Co., PA, Rebecca Leidig(h)/Leidich. Rebecca Leidig(h) Beltzhoover died 24 Feb. 1829 (27-9-32); Jacob, m./2 c. 1830, Rebecca's sister, Anna Maria Leidigh, b. 28 Sept. 1802, at Schaefferstown, PA., d. 14 Aug. 1832 (29-10-17), burial was in the Beltzhoover plot in the Old Churchtown Cemetery; m./3 22 Aug. 1833, at Carlisle, Cumberland Co., PA., Louisa Jacobs (she was of York Co., PA.   Jacob died in 1880, therefore, Jacob and Louisa were married 47 years.   His residence at the time of his marriage to Louisa Jacobs was Monroe Township, Cumberland Co., PA. [2] [3] [4] [5] [6]

Leidigh family information for Rebecca and Ann Maria Leidigh follows this family information.

Family information says that in 1864 they moved to Williamsport, PA. [7]

Boyd's Directory 1875-1876, shows Jacob Beltzhoover, h. 299 Washington St., Williamsport, PA.   In Boyd's Directory of 1881-1883, Louisa Beltzhoover, widow, Jacob, h. 299 Washington St.

----

1. The Daily Gazette and Bulletin_____, Mar. 26, 1880. James V. Brown Library, Williamsport, PA. 17701, Mar. 1996

2. Ibid., Cumberland Co., PA. Church Records_____ p. 216, 226

3. Harrisburg, PA. Library

4. History of Cherokee Co., KS_____ 1904 Courtesy of Joan M. Moore

5. Moore, Joan C.

6. Ibid., Marriages and Deaths of Cumberland Co., PA., 1821-1830._____ Cumberland Hisorical Society p. 100

7. Boyd's Directory Williamsport_____. 1871-1872. James V. Brown Library, Williamsport, PA. Mar. 1996

Back in the text it says that Jacob was b. ca. 1797. Your compiler has an instruction page as to how to determine the age of birth when you know the tombstone inscriptions. From my compilations, which may not be correct, Jacob the 25th October, 1796. His obituary says, "Cumberland Valley Papers please copy. It appears that he originated in Cumberland Co., PA.

From the first marriage, one child:
Issue: (BELTZHOOVER)
 196-John P. Beltzhoover[5], b. 25 Oct. 1825, bpt. 26 April 1827., d. 1 May 1908; m. Hannah Nagle, b. c. 1826; d. 13 Jan. 1875, Sandoval, IL. The sponsors at the baptism were the parents. [1]

Children from the third marriage:
 197-George Jacob Beltzhoover, b. 14 Jan.1838; d. 7 Nov. 1911, a resident of Cumberland Co., PA
 198-Susanna/Susan Beltzhoover, of Silver Spring Twp., Cumberland Co., PA., m. 10 Jan. 1861, Michael Weaver of Mt. Rock, PA.
 199-Mary Ellen Beltzhoover,
The following two children d. y. and are not mentioned in the Cherokee Co., History, KS.
 200-Eliza Jane Beltzhoover, b. 19 Jan. 1840; d. 18 Sept. 1844, g. Newville Cemetery. d/o Jacob & Louisa.
 201-Joseph Beltzhoover,b. 5 July 1841; d. 2 Mar. 1844, g. Newville; s/o Jacob & Louisa

****

LEIDIGH

Leidigh researchers have not been able to determine who was the actual immigrant in this Leidigh family. There is no evidence that Leonard Michael Leidigh/Leidich is the immigrant.

1-JOHANN PETER LEIDIGH, m. 11 May 1800, Berks Co., PA., Susannah STAUCH, b. ca. 1780. Berks Co., PA., d. ca. 1815, Cumberland Co., PA. Susannah STAUCH was the daughter of Nicholaus and Maria Margaretha STAUCH. [2]
 Johann Peter Leidigh m./2 Elizabeth ---
 Issue: (from marrage one)
  2-Rebecca Leidigh, b. 1801. She m. Jacob Beltzhoover. She died 24 Feb. 1829.

----

1. Ibid., Cumberland Co., PA., Church Records. First Evangelical Lutheran Church, Carlisle, PA., p. 93

2. Frick, Ruth Hudson Leidigh Family resides Oak Brook, IL and gives credits to Katherine Kay Leidigh Meredith. Other credits to Ellen Leidigh McCrory, Ellen Reed Leidigh, Robert Irwin Leidigh, Jr., etc. Our thanks to Deanna Oklepek

3-Anna Maria Leidigh, b. 1802, m. her sisters'
widower and d. 14 Aug. 1832, ni. (See Jacob
Beltzhoover)
4-Enoch Leidigh, b. 1809
5-Henry Heinrich Leidigh, b. 1811
Children from the second marriage
6-Levi Leidigh

2-REBECCA LEIDIGH, b. 2 May 1801, PA., d. 24 Feb. 1829,
Cumberland Co., PA.; m. 28 Sept. 1824, Carlisle, PA., Jacob
Beltzhoover, b. 26 Oct. 1795, d. 1880, Williamsport, PA. After
Rebecca's death, Jacob m,./2, her sister, Anna Maria Leidigh.
(See Jacob Beltzhoover)

4-ENOCH LEIDIGH, b. ca. 1809, PA., d. 7 Apr. 1840 Ashland, Co., OH; m. 13 Oct. 1833, Cumberland Co., PA., Sarah
McClure, b. ca. 1816, PA.
Issue:
7-George Leidigh
8-Samuel Leidigh

★★★★★★★★★★★★

82-JOHN BELTZHOOVER[4] (20), b. York Co., PA., 1798, d. 29
Apr. 1881 (83-3-26), g. Mt. Zion, Sect Q. He came to Cumberland Co., PA. when he was a boy and became a farmer. He
married in 1822, Margaret A. SMITH, b. 3 Jan. 1802; d. 17
April 1881 (79-8-4), g. Mt. Zion Cemetery, Carlisle, PA. John
Beltzhoover and his wife were members of the Lutheran Church
and in politics he was a Republican. He was a landowner near
Boiling Springs and lived on this farm over fifty years.
Their home was the scene of a big, brutal robbery. He lived
to be almost 84 years of age, considered to be one of the best
citizens of the county and always contributed largely of his
means to build up the township. [1] [2] [3]

John Beltzhoover was the first known Fire Chief of the
South Middleton Twp. Fire Company. He was also a joint executor of his father's estate. [4]
Issue: (BELTZHOOVER)
202-George Beltzhoover[5], b. 26 Dec. 1823; d. 5 May
894; m., 25 Mar. 1846, Maria C. Niesley. [1]
----

1. Mt. Zion Cemetery and the Old Churchtown Cem. are one and the same. They are located at Jct. of
Rt. 74 and Allen Road, southeast of Carlisle. George Beltzhoover 12/95

2. Ibid., History of Cumberland Co., PA p. 506

3. Bio. sketch p. 504 History of Penna., Western PA. Historical Library, Pittsburgh, PA.

4. Ibid., Boiling Springs

5. Cumberland Church Recordsm PA. , First Evangelical Lutheran Church, Carlisle,PA., p. 305

203-Anna E. Beltzhoover, b. 14 Jan. 1828; d. 25 Mar.
1839, (11-2-11), g. Zion Cem.
204-Mahala/Manhala/Manala Beltzhoover, b. 12 Oct.
1832; bpt. 9 Nov. 1833; d. 30 Dec. 1902, Cumberland Co., PA, g. Mt. Zion Cem.; m. 17 July
1851, George W. Leidig\Leidigh. [1]

83-**RACHEL BELTZHOOVER**[4] (20), b. before 1810, d. 6 April
1863, m., 1831, Henry Lerew, b. 14 Feb., 1791, Bermudian
Creek, York Co., PA., d. 7 Oct. 1871, son of Jacob Lerew and
wf. Anna STAUFFER LEREW. [2]
    Issue: (LEREW)
        204a-Sarah Lerew,; b. 2 Feb. 1824; m. 1841, Jacob Zinn
        205-Andrew Murphy Lerew[5], b. 1829, Latimore Twp.,
            Adams Co., PA., he moved west with his child-
            ren, living in South Dakota.
        206-Daniel Lerew, b. 24 Sept. 1829
        207-Solomon Lerew, b. 27 July 1831, moved to Dauphin
            Co., PA.
        208-Manassa Lerew, b. 28 Jan. 1834
        209-Mahala Lerew, b. 22 Oct. 1838; d. 3 Feb. 1863
        210-George Lerew, b. 5 April 1842; d. 7 Sept. 1858

84-**SARAH "SALLY" BELTZHOOVER**[4] (20), b. 16 Feb.. 1805; d.
28 May 1856 (51-3-12); m. 28 Feb. 1828, Isaac VANasdlen/Venas-
dlen, at Carlisle, PA, Married by Rev. John S. Ebaugh. [3]
    Issue: (VANasdlen) Possible children taken from cemetery
            records. Additional records from Gendext.
        211-Reuben VANasdlen[5] d. 1837 (3-2-13)
        212-Rachel Ann VANasdlen, d. 1833 (1-11-2)
        213-Sarah VANasdlen
        214-Mary Jane VANasdlen
        215-Isaac VANasdlen
        216-George VANasdlen, d. 1833 (4-0-18)
        217-Susannah VANasdlen, m. --?-- WEAVER (mentioned as
            Susannah Weaver in the will of George Beltz-
            hoover)
        218-Catherine E. VANasdlen

87-**SAMUEL BELTZHOOVER**[4] (21), b. 3 April 1803, bpt. 18 May
1803, sponsored by Samuel and Elizabeth Gross., bur. 2 Mar.
1836, sudden death. This must be Samuel Beltzhoover, m. 27
April 1830, by Rev. F. Pringle, Miss Susan Rherer, both of S.
Middleton, Cumberland Co., PA. A brother to George, not a son

----

1. Ibid., Cumberland Co., PA.   , Church Records, First Evangelical Lutheran Church, Carlisle, PA.,
p. 128 (Churchtown)

2. Lerew, Don 5/10/00

3. Ibid., Marriages and Deaths Cumberland Co., PA.   , (1821-1830) American Volunteer p. 23

Mrs. Susan Beltzhoover, who married 24 Sept. 1839, Isaac Ringwald, United Presbyterian Church. Isaac Ringwald was from South Middleton at the time of his marriage; Mrs. Susan Beltzhoover was from Carlisle, PA. Susan Ringwald, d. 4 Mar. 1885 (73).

There was a Samuel Beltzhoover, of Weiglestown, Dover Twp., York Co., PA., transferred 131 acres for $200. to Jacob Heilman in 1829.

Issue: (BELTZHOOVER)
219-Mary Ann Beltzhoover[5], b. 15 Oct. 1830; bpt. 24 Mar. 1833 (1835?), United Presbyterian Church, Big Spring, Cumberland Co., PA. [2]
220-Eliza (Catherine?) E. Todd Beltzhoover, b. 20 Dec. 1833; bpt. 24 Mar. 1835, First Evangelical Lutheran Church, Carlisle; d. 8 Oct. 1856, g. Ashland Cem., Carlisle, PA., unm.? [3]
221-Cassey/Cassy Beltzhoover

88-JESSE BELTZHOOVER[4] (21), b. 3 Oct. 1806, bpt. 17 Nov. 1806, sponsored by the parents; married 7 Mar. 1839, by Rev. John Ulrich, Catherine Kleinfelter/Klinefelter, both of Middleton Twp., Cumberland Co. Jesse Beltzhoover and Catherine appear in the 1860 census they appear in Union Twp., Porter Co., IN., dated 18 Aug. 1860, Jesse told the census takers that he was 53 and Catherine was 50 and that they were both born in PA. William was age 17. In the household was also Nancy Mitchler (sp?>) age 8. [4]

In the 1870 census, Union Twp., Porter Co., IN. they appear under the name of Bellshoover. William is there age 26, at home; Josiah, 15 (works on the farm, b. Indiana), Lizzie, 18 (a housekeeper born in NY); Minerva (sp?), 2, b. Indiana. Nothing further is known of these children other than William. But the census taker shows that Jesse, Catherine and William all born in Ohio?, which we think is in error.

Your compiler can only assume that Josiah and Minerva are children of Jesse and Catherine Beltzhoover.

Issue: (BELTZHOOVER)
222-William Beltzhoover[5], b. 10 May 1844, Cumberland

----

1. Ibid., <u>Marriages and Deaths of Cumberland Co., PA.</u>, 1821-1830, American Volunteer (Cumberland Historical Society) p. 91

2. Ibid., <u>Cumberland Co., PA. Church Records</u> p. 138

3. <u>Cumberland Co., PA. Cemetery Records.</u> Vol. II, p. 234

4. Nault, Barb, Porter Co. IN Library Gen. Dept.

Co., PA.
223-Josiah Beltzhoover, age 15 in 1870, b. Indiana, no further record.
224-Minerva Beltzhoover, age 2, in 1870, b. Indiana, no further record.

89-**MICHAEL BELTZHOOVER**[4] (21), b. 10 Sept. 1809, York Co., PA., (Quickel genealogy states Michael was born, 14 Jan. 1792, York), a twin, son of Johann Michael and Eva Gross Beltzhoover, bpt. 13 Sept. 1809, Christ Lutheran Church, York, York Co., PA.; sponsors were Catherine Schmucker and the father; d. 8 May 1848, York Co., PA., g. Quickels, Conewago Twp., PA.; m. 9 Jan. 1831, Christ Lutheran Church, York Co., PA., Cassandra 'Cassie/Cassy/Cassia' Schreiber (listed as Shriver), b. 27 Sept. 1816, York Co., PA. Cassandra Schreiber was the d/o --?-- & wf. Christina Ensminger Schreiber. Christine Ensminger was the d/o Conrad Ensminger & wf. Anna Marie Quickel Ensminger. [1] [2]

Cassandra 'Cassie' also called Catherine in the (1850 Census) and in The Family of Samuel Gross (1749-1831). She married second after Michael's death, 1848, Philip Quickel.

The children, John and Sarah, were listed on "Poor Children;s Tax Lists for 1841-1842 and again in 1843. Records of the children and parents, sometimes shown as Beltzhuber/Belshower/Belshouer

Issue: (BELTZHOOVER)
225-George Beltzhuber/Beltzhoover[5], b. 18 Jan. 1832; bpt. 6 April 1832, Christ Evangelical Lutheran Church, York, York Co., PA., sponsors were George and Sally Eisenhart. George d., 6 Aug. 1832, g. Quickel's.
226-John Beltzhoover, b. 22 Oct. 1833 (10 years of age in 1843); d. 10 April 1875 (41-5-18); g. Union Church, Shiloh, West Manchester, York Co., PA. Also known as Neiman's Church, W. Manchester Twp.
227-Sarah (Sarahan) A. Beltzhoover, b. 20 Dec. 1835 (8 years old in 1843; d. 8 April 1861; g. Nieman's, W. Manchester Twp., York Co., PA.
228-Elizabeth Beltzhoover, b. ca. 1837
229-Mary Ann Beltzhoover/Belshower, b. 16 July 1840, chr. 4 Nov. 1840; d. 21 Feb. 1888, York Co., g. Nieman's. In the 1880 census she was living in the home of Philip Quickel and her mother, Kate, in Dover, York Co., PA. In the household was Alice Quickel, age 17 and a granddaughter,

----

1. Descendants of Hans Quickel   . Family Tree Maker

2. Christ Evangelical Lutheran Church   , York Co., PA., Baptisms 1826-1856

Sadie A. Boyer, age 7.
230-Susan/Annie? Beltzhoover, b. c. 1843, York, PA
231-Catherine Beltzhoover, b. 1 Aug. 1846, York, PA.,
        chr. 17 Nov. 1846, Christ Lutheran Church,
        York, PA., m. ca. 1865, Reuben Quickel, b. 10
        Feb. 1840. York; d. 12 Feb. 1919. No children
        in the household in 1880 census.

91-**GEORGE BELTZHOOVER**[4] (21), b. 14 Oct. 1814; d. 1856, g.
Mt. Zion Cemetery; m. Elizabeth Kuntz, b. c. 1825. Elizabeth
Kuntz, wf. of Geo. Beltzhoover, dau. of John Kuntz (Philip[1]
John[2]). John Kuntz b. 1800, Franklin Township, d. 1879 (79),
York Co., PA., m. 1822, Susan HARBOLD, d/o Michael HARBOLD. [1]

George Beltzhoover, of Franklintown; b. ????; d. 1856, g.
Mt. Zion; m. Elizabeth Kuntz, b. c. 1825. Deanna shows that
George d. ca. Apr. 1856? Franklintown Boro, Franklin Twp.,
York Co., PA., may have well been his place of residence at
the time of his marriage, later Manchester Township?

George Beltzhoover resided Manchester Township, York Co.,
PA. His will was written 4 Aug. 1855 and it was probated 25
April 1856. Samuel GROSS was named executor. He refers to
his daughter, Sarah, married to Benjamin Nisely/Niesley and to
children of "my Jesse." He refers to his brother, Samuel's
children, Mary and Cassey and to his brother, Michael's children. [2]

George Beltzhoover, in his will bequeaths to Samuel GROSS
$200, and bequeath's $1. to Mary Beltzhoover and $1. to Cassey
Beltzhoover, chidren of Samuel, dec'd.
    Issue: (BELTZHOOVER)
    231a-Mary (Mary S.?) Beltzhoover?[5]. From the Library
        of Congress Records, a song, "Cling To the
        Rock" published in 1862 by Henry S. Revd and
        dedicated to Mary S. Beltzhoover. Is this the
        right Mary? There was a Mary Emelia Beltz-
        hoover, eldest daughter of George and Elizabeth
        Betlzhoover, d. 20 August 1877, (17 years 3
        months), services at her parents residence,
        Grant Ave., Mt. Washington.
    231b-Sarah Beltzhoover, m. Benjamin NIESLEY/NISELEY

* *

----

1. History of York Co., PA   Vol. II pages 676, 678

2. History of York Co., PA.   Vol. II, p. 675

THE KUNTZ FAMILY

The History of York Co., PA., Biographical Sections has considerable information on the Kuntz family of York Co., PA.
    1   2

Philip Kuntz, b. Germany, d. 1815, his wife was Elizabeth SHIMP. There were eight children. Children not in proper order.

(1) Michael Kuntz, d. 1880, lived at Mt. Rock, he has a son, William Kuntz, who married Miss Brannon and they had three childre: William, Ammie who married Fortenbaugh and May.

(2) Philip Kuntz, d. 1862 (79), m. Mrs. Andy Mumpher (maiden name was Seidle), she died 1882, York Springs. Their children were: John Kuntz, who moved to Nebraska; Lizzie Kuntz who married William Fickel of York Springs; Henry Kuntz, who married Miss Shenk; and Samuel Kuntz who was a Professor in Washington, DC.

(3) Jacob Kuntz, d. 21

(4) Elizabeth 'Betsey' Kuntz, m. Peter Hoffman and they had children: George Hoffman and Mrs. Hughes.

(5) Mary Kuntz, who m. Henry Graybill of York and Hanover: children: Henrietta Graybill, m. Mr. Keeny of York Co., PA.,;Eliza Graybill who resided in Minnesota.

(6) Rebecca Margaret Kuntz, m. George Beltzhoover, and they lived near Kingston. Their children were: (a) Michael Beltzhoover, m., Mary Bricker and they had three children, Frank, an Att'y. in Carlisle (Frank Beltzhoover the Att'y in Carlisle is not the son of George and Rebecca Margaret Kuntz); Jacob, and Alice. (b) George Beltzhoover of Franklintown, who married, his cousin, Elizabeth Kuntz, daughter of John Kuntz.

(7) Susanna Kuntz, m. Henry Sidle, res. MN. Their children were: Samuel Sidle who married Miss Camel; Jacob Sidle, m. Margaret DeHoff and they were in MN., Henry Sidle, m. Katie Katz.

(8) John Kuntz, b. 1800; d. 1879 (79). m. 1822, Susan Harbold, d. 1879, dau. of Michael Harbold and they had ten children: Michael Kuntz, dec., Elizabeth Kuntz, dec. m., George Beltzhoover; Sarah Kuntz, m. Wm. Fuller and had children: Susanna (Mrs. Kapp); Sarah; Anglehard, a son, m. Miss Catherine Day; John Kuntz, Philip

---

1. History of York Co., PA   ., Bio. Section Vol. II, p. 675

2. Coates, Patty (some additional and corrected information) 3/14/99

Kuntz, m. Miss Stauffer; Susanna Kuntz, dec., m./1 Frank Wolf, m./2 Wm. Altland; Polly Kuntz, unm.,: Elizabeth Ann Kuntz, m., Henry Klugh.

This ends the Kuntz Family genealogy.

* * * * * * * * * * * * * * * * * * * *

THE SHIMP FAMILY

This Shimp family information will show the connection to the Beltzhoover family. [1]

Five Shimp brothers came to America from Mesztetten/ Mestadten, Wurttenberger, Germany around 1754.

(1) Johannes Schimpf, d. May 1798, children were: Philip Shimp, d. 20 Dec. 1756; George J. Shimp, b. 13 May 1757, d. 16 Jan. 1833; David J. Shimp, d. 20 Dec. 1758; William J. Shimp, b. 9 Dec. 1764, d. 1800; Andrea Shimp, b 18 Feb. 1767, d. 20 Mar. 1830; Henrich J. Shimp, d. 15 July 1771; Sebastian J. Shimp, d. 5 July 1772

(2) Mathias Schimpf, d. 1777, m. 4 Dec. 1758, Christena Dorothea Rossli, d/o Tobias Rossli. Children: Leonard Shimp (1757-1817); Andrew C. Shimp (1758-1838); Elizabeth Shimp, m. Philip Kuntz and they had children: (Kuntz) Michael, Susanna, Phillip, Jacob, Elizabeth (Betsey), Mary, Rebecca Margaret who m. George Beltzhoover, John whose dau. Elizabeth m. George Beltzhoover s/o Geo.; Mary Shimp and Catherine Shimp. These are the five children living at Mathias' death. There may have been other children. [2]

(3) Jacob Johann Schimpf, m. Christina Mayer, ch: John Shimp (1758-1835); Casper Shimp (1759-   ), m. Elizabeth Marie Geiger.

(4) Frederick Schimpf, no futher information.

(5) Melchior Schimpf, no further information.

This ends the Shimp family informaton.

* *

93-LYDIA WITMAN[4] (24), b. 4 Mar. 1800, bpt. 28 Apr. 1800, Chanceford Township, York, Co., St. Luke's or Stanley's Luthean and Reformed Church, d. 29 Feb. 1873. Mentioned in

----

1. Coates, Patty 14 Mar. 1999

2. Records of Pastoral Acts at Trinity Evangelical Lutheran Church   , New Holland, Lancaster Co., PA., 1730-1799. Marriages by John Samuel Schwerdfeger. Salt Lake City, Courtesy of Patty Coates

her Mother's will as the widow of Frederick SCHENBERGER/SCHOENBERGER, dec. Children: Emanuel; Susan, wf. of Jacob GILLEN; Isabell, wife of Henry SCHENBERGER; Catherine, wife of Henry SIGLER; John SCHENBERGER; Adam SCHENBERGER. [1]

Frederick Schenberger, b. 10 Jan. 1796, Windsor Twp., York Co., PA., d. 11 Dc. 1846, g. Schenberger's, York Co., PA., the son of Adam and wf., Catherine (Dosh) Schenberger.

Lydia Witman, m. Frederick Schenberger, b. 10 Jan. 1786, Windsor Twp., York Co., PA.,; d. 13 Dec. 1846, g. Schenberger's Chapel, York Co., PA. He was the son of Adam and Catherine (DOSH) Schenberger. Adam and Catherine Schenberger owned 50 acres at one location and another 700 acres in Windsor Township, York Co., PA. and 122 acres in Baltimore Co., MD. His executor sold the property to John Knisley, and his step-daughter, Lydia Wittman, owned it. The Adam Schenberger farm was under the name of Fauth until early 1900's. The Dosh Cemetery is on the farm.

Issue: (SCHENBERGER)
- 232-Melville Garrison Schenberger[5], b. 21 Feb. 1819, York Co., PA.,
- 233-Jacob Schenberger (1821-1888), b. 21 Jan. 1821; d. 27 Feb. 1888
- 234-George Frederick Schenberger (1823-1823), b. 9 feb. 1823; d. 11 Feb. 1823
- 235-Susan Schenberger, b. ca. 1818, m. Jacob Gillen.
- 236-Lydia Schenberger, m. --?-- Myers
- 237-Catherine Schenberger, m. Henry ZIEGLER /ZIGER/SIGLER
- 238-Henrietta Schenberger, m. Henry Seidel, res. Michigan
- 239-Sarah (Salome) Schenberger
- 240-Isabell Schenberger, b. 28 Nov. 1832; d. Feb. 1905; m. 29 Nov. 1846, Henry SCHENBERGER, killed in the Civil War.
- 241-John K. Schenberger, b. 19 Mar. 1833; d. 18 Aug. 1902
- 242-Adam W. Schenberger, b. 1837
- 243-Emanuel Schenberger

94-**CATHERINE or REBECCA CATHERINE WITMAN**[4] (24), bpt. 11 Oct. 1807. St. Luke's Lutheran, PA.; m. Conrad HAKE. Conrad Hake may be the son of Jacob Hake who was mentioned in the Adm. papers of Conrad Beltzhuber, York Co. PA., 1787.

Issue: (HAKE)
- 244-Jacob Hake[5]
- 245-John Hake
- 246-Eve Hake, m. Joseph SECRIST/SECHRIST

----

1. Ibid., Gayle O. Kamp   The Kamp Papers   Vol. II 1986 p. 765

95-**CHRISTENA JANE WITMAN**[4] (24), b. 25 Sept. 1803; d. 1878; m./1 Jacob Klinefelter and had children, Mary "Polly"; John, Jacob IV.   Christena Jane m./2 John MILLER and had children: David Miller, Sarah Jane Miller; Samuel Elias Miller; William Henry Miller.   Christena Jane m./3, Peter LEBER. [1]

Issue: (KLINEFELTER)
247-Mary "Polly" Klinefelter[5], b. c. 1823, m. Henry BUSSER.
248-John Klinefelter, b. 13 Nov. 1825; d. 23 Jan. 1905; m. Lucinda ALSPACH
249-Jacob Klinefelter IV, b. c 1827, d. 1839
Children from the second marriage: (MILLER)
250-David Miller
251-Sarah Jane Miller
252-Samuel Elias Miller
253-William Henry Miller

Fifth Generation

101-**CATHERINE BELTZHOOVER STACKER**[5] (34), b. 29 Feb. 1824, Nashville, Davidson Co., TN., d. 26 April 1881, St. Louis, MO; m. 19 May 1841, French Rayburn, b. 15 Jan. 1815; d. 25 Mar. 1888, St. Louis, MO., s/o James Rayburn (d. Dec. 1814) & wf., Nancy Watterson SHANKLIN (d. July 1835).

Issue: (RAYBURN)
254-Samuel Stacker Rayburn[6], b. 14 Dec. 1842, d. 7 June 1888, St. Louis, MO.; m. 3 Oct. 1867, Nancy Elvira WALKER, b. 6 July 1849, St. Louis, MO, d. 18 Mar. 1918, Kansas City, MO.
255-Cora Rebecca Rayburn (1844-1859)
256-Mary Elsie Rayburn (1854-1869)
257-Catherine French Rayburn, b. 1860; d. 1880

102-**GEORGE STACKER**[5] (34), b. ca. 1826, Nashville, Davidson Co., TN; d. 9 June 1883, Cumberland Co., S. TN.; m./1, Martha J. West (1830-1857) m./2, 13 Feb. 1868, Blanche L. BISHOP, b. 1847, d. 22 Nov. 1931, Cumberland City, S., TN.

George was a Col. in the Confederate Army-the 50th Reg't. organized in Clarksville, TN., in 1861.

Issue: (STACKER)
258-Mary Stacker[6] (1849-   )
259-George W. Stacker, b. 30 Aug. 1851; d. 24 Oct. 1851.
260-Kate Stacker, m. George Valliant
261-Willie D. Stacker (1855-1855)
262-Samuel Stacker (1856-1857)
Children of the second marriage:
263-George Stacker, Jr. (1870-1926), m. Eunice Farns-

----

1. Ibid., Kamp, Gayle O.   The Kamp Papers Vol. II 1986

worth
264-Charles Stacker (1871-   ), m. Beatrice Clemmie
        Payne
265-Margaret Stacker[6], b. 5 Aug. 1875; d. 1949, Clarks-
        ville, TN

103-**MARY CLEMENTINE STACKER**[5] (34), (1828-1887), m. Isaac
Way Taylor, (1822-1858); m./2, --?-- Richards.
    Issue: (TAYLOR)
        266-George S. Taylor[6] (1846-1926)
        267-James L. Taylor (1846-1847)
        268-Kate A. Taylor (1848-1949)
        269-Isaac Stockton Taylor (1849-1917)

115-**ELIZABETH BELTZHOOVER BAILEY**[5] (36); b. b. 21 Oct.
1924, Pittsburgh, d 10 May 1866; m. c. 1846, Wm. Kennedy
NIMICK, b. 21 May 1822, d. 19 April 1875.
    Issue: (NIMICK)
        270-Mary Kennedy Nimick[6], b. ca. 1847, PA; m. Anthony
                S. Murray, b. ca. 1846, PA.
        271-Frank Bailey Nimick, b. ca. 1849, PA; d. 21 Nov.
                1924, PA; m. 20 Nov. 1888, Eleanor Howard HOWE.
        272-Elizabeth K. Nimick, b. 27 Sept. 1852; m. John
                Milton Bonham.
        273-William Bailey Nimick, b. 1855, Pittsburgh; d.
                1890.
        274-Jennie Lyle Nimick, b. 1857, PA., m. David Glen
                Stewart.
        275-Alexander Kennedy Nimick, b. 1860, Pittsburgh, d.
                1890, m., Florence N. Coleman.
        276-Blanche Nimick

116-**FRANCIS 'FRANK' BAILEY**[5] (36), b. 17 Mar. 1827, d. 4
Dec. 1872; m. Ellen HOWE.
    Issue: (BAILEY)
        277-Francis Bailey, Jr.[6] (1827-1892), m. Mary SPENCER,
                res. Coraopolis, PA
        278-Thomas Bailey
        279-William Kennedy Bailey

117-**JOHN H. BAILEY, Judge**[5] (36), b. 24 Mar. 1830, Pittsburgh; d. 8 Feb. 1897, m. Katherine C. WASHINGTON b. 11 Mar.
1832; d. 27 Dec. 1914, g. Allegheny Cem., Pittsburgh, Sect 14,
Lot 90.
    Issue: (BAILEY)
        280-Reade Washington Bailey[6], b. 30 Mar. 1856; d. 2
                June 1948, g. Allegheny Cem.
        281-Edward Bailey, b. 19 June 1857, d. 19 June 1857,
                g. Allegheny Cem.

118-**JAMES MADISON BAILEY**[5] (36), b. 23 Aug. 1833, Pittsburgh; d. 6 May 1903, g. Allegheny Cem., Pittsburgh; m., 1867,
Pittsburgh, Martha E. DALZELL, b. 28 June 1841, d. 26 April
1883. He was a steel manufacturer, Pittsburgh.

Shortly after he married he became a dealer in coal. Then he joined the California gold rush and returned home successfully. Upon his return home he engaged in the steel business and this is where he acquired his wealth. He was the sole owner of Phillips, Nimick Co., one of the largest steel companies in the Pittsburgh area. He owned the Sligo Works; became President of the Fourth National Bank of Pittsburgh, the Union Bridge Co., and companies operating the Monongahela and Castle Shannon Inclines. He had many civic activities. Bailey Avenue on Mt. Washington was named after him and Ruth Street was named after his daughter, Ruth Bailey McMehen.

Issue: (BAILEY)

282-Ella Bailey[6], b. 9 Feb. 1870, Pittsburgh; d. 17 Feb. 1870, Pittsburgh.

283-Ruth Bailey, d. 26 July 1954, Shadyside Hosp., Pittsburgh; m. Bimie W. McMechen.

284-Mark Bailey

285-Lois Livingston Bailey, m. Edward Duff Balken

286-infant Bailey (1878-1878)

120-JOHN S. MURRAY[5] (37), (1833-1901), m. Mattie A. Murray, g. Allegheny Cem., Sect 16, Lot 135, Pittsburgh.

Issue: (MURRAY)

287-Margaret Grace Murray[6], (1887-1890)

124-MELCHOR M. BELTZHOOVER[5] (39), b. 24 Dec. 1837; Allegheny Co., PA., d. 3 Mar. 1907, (70), whose family owned Beltzhoover Borough. He was the son of Melchor and Mary Hughey Beltzhoover. In early life he was a blacksmith. He served in the entire Civil War in Co. A. Sixty-Second PA. Volunteers under Col. Samuel Black. He was wounded at Gaines Mills. He was a member of GAR. He married 20 Feb. 1866, Miss Charlotte Lotte WENZEL; b. 6 June 1844; died 31 Dec. 1906 (63). She lived on Williams St., Washington, PA. He was survived by four children, Harry W., Melchor B., William N., Mrs. Mary Humphrey. He also left one sister, Mrs. Jane Trotter of Hays Station. [1]

The Beltzhoover family settled on the Hilltop in the early part of the nineteenth century and owned considerable property. Melchor Beltzhoover, the father of the deceased, conducted a hotel there. He was murdered in West Liberty about 1847, being mistaken for an enemy by an enraged circus man. [2]

Nothing further is known of this family than what is shown.

Issue: (BELTZHOOVER)

288-Harry W. Beltzhoover[6] b., ca. 1867-1868, in the

----

1. Pittsbugh Gazette Times   4 Mar. 1907; Jan. 2,1907

2. Hill T op Record   7 Mar. 1907, Friday p. 7 Col. 4 Courtesy Norman C. Schwotzer 1/29/00

1920 census he is shown in Pittsburgh, age 53, no further information.
289-Melchor Bailey Beltzhoover, b. ca. 1869
290-William N. Beltzhoover, b. ca. 1870
291-Mary A. Beltzhoover (Mrs. Charles (Mary A.) Humphrey) res. Mt. Washington, PA. b. ca. 1873

126-GEORGE W. BELTZHOOVER[5] (38), b. ca. 1835; d. 7 Mar. 1889, Pittsburgh; bur. 10 Mar. 1889, from his residence, William Street, Mt. Washington, PA, g. Mt. Lebanon Cem., All., Co. PA. Member Mt. Washington Lodge, Grandview Lodge, Col. Ellsworth Lodge, A O U W, etc. The 1880 census shows George, and his wife, Elizabeth --?--, b. 13 Feb. 1841, Mt. Lebanon, PA; d. 27 Feb. 1918, both of her parents born in England.
[1] [2] [3] [4]

Census reports has his surname as Belzzhoover and occupation 'teamster.' They were married about 1859, Mt. Lebanon.
Issue: (BELTZHOOVER)
292-Mary Emelia Beltzhoover[6], b. 25 May 1860, Mt. Lebanon, PA., d. y. (17-3)
293-Ida Beltzhoover, b. ca. 1864, PA
294-Carrie Beltzhoover, b. ca. 1867, PA

133-SILAS PRYOR BELTZHOOVER[5] (44), b. 1 July 1847, in the Old Stone Tavern (now the site of the Carson St. Station of the Panhandle RR of Penn.); d. 14 Nov. 1915, at Castle Shannon; g. Mt. Lebanon Cem., Lebanon, PA. In 1876 he went to Texas and was employed by the Texas Central Railroad Co. Locating in Georgetown, TX., he erected a courthouse building and had other building operations. In 1881 he returned to Pittsburgh engaging in the grocery business on Penn Ave. He served as postmaster of Castle Shannon for twenty years. His business which he founded was carried on by his wife, son and daughter, after his death.

Mr. Beltzhoover was very active in several fraternal orgnizations, including the Masonic Lodges and Odd Fellows. He and his wife were long time members of the Baptist Church of Library, Allegheny Co., PA. He married on 20 Nov. 1879, in the First Presbyterian Church in Georgetown, Williams Co., TX., Mary E. HARRIS, b. Georgetown, 28 July 1860, d/o George T. HARRIS and wf. Charlotte A. Eubanke. Mary H. Beltzhoover, d. Thursday, 7 June 1928 at 6:30 P. M. in her 69th year.
----

1. Obituary, Pittsburgh Post Gazette, March 9, 1889

2. Ibid., Harris, Helen

3. Peach, Elizabeth

4. Ibid., Schwotzer, Norman C.

CASTLE SHANNON

"Castle Shannon...From Forest-to-Modern Boro- [1]
In the 1700's the area was virgin wilderness...
Prior to 1768, when the Iroquois through treaty relinquished their rights....there was little interest in settling the area south of Fort Pitt....However a child was born at a homestead along the Mansfield-Elizabeth Road...The house of his birth, a log cabin hewn from the forest surrounding it, is known as the Old Provost Place. The child was named Samuel Beltzhoover, who later became a doctor."

"Shortly thereafter the Beltzhoover family was driven out by the Indians and they returned to Fort Pitt. About 1770, the Beltzhoover's came back to the area, along with other families and were the earliest settlers of Castle Shannon."

"The Cooleys (cousins of direct descendants of the first Beltzhoover's owned the farm, bordering the Wakefield."

"The hub of community activity in Castle Shannon around 1906 was S. P. Beltzhoover's General Store, Post Office and Railroad Depot, all in one. He was the grandfather of J. E. Beltzhoover on Poplar Ave."

Before cars the inclines were the only means of going up and down the hills (Pittsburgh), other than the wagons. Some of the inclines were attached to the horse cars at the bottom and top of the inclines. The Castle Shannon Incline was so used. As of 2002 there were still two of the many former inclines operating in Pittsburgh. [2]

George T. HARRIS was born in 1830 in Franklin, Simpson Co., KY., d. Abilene TX., 1894. He was the son of Nathan R. and Elizabeth HALE HARRIS. Geo. HARRIS, m., Charlotte Amanda EUBANKE, b. 1 June 1833, Mitchellville, Robertson Co., TX., d. Castle Shannon, 27 Nov.1927, d/o Elijah and Annee TURNER EUBANKE. [3]
Issue: (BELTZHOOVER)
295-George Henry Beltzhoover[6], b. 19 Feb. 1883, Pittsburgh, m. 11 July 1906, Margaret HICKS, b. ca. 1884, d/o Richard Hicks.

----

1.   Social Studies classes of the Junior High School and James Kerr, and his personal interviews with J. E. Beltzhoover, Mr. J. P. Kerr, Jr., and Ana Bell Wilson

2.   "The Incline Planes of Pittsburgh",   *WPGS Quarterly 29:1 (Summer 2002)* , pp. 13,14. Jean S. Morris, Compiler

3.   Fleming, George Thornton, compiller.   History of Pittsburgh and Environs   New York and Chicago. The American Historical Society Inc., 1922. Biographical pages 155, 156, 157 Full page photo of Silas Pryor Beltzhoover on p. 154

296-Charlotte Beltzhoover. She assisted in the management of the businesses. She was very active in Masonic circles such as Eastern Star, etc., unm.

297-Endorah Virginia Beltzhoover, m 12 Sept. 1917, Jesse H. LUTZ. She d. 7 Jan. 1919, g. Mt. Lebanon Cem.

298-Thomas Husler Beltzhoover, b. 18 May 1892, Castle Shannon, PA; d. 26 April 1975, Sarasota Memorial Hospital, Sarasota, FL; g. Black Rock Cemetery, Baltimore, MD., res. 2640 Bouganville St. Sarasota; g. Baltimore, MD. Mr. Beltzhoover lived for many years in Dundalk, MD. He moved from Baltimore to Sarasota in 1955 according to his obituary. He was a member of the First Presbyterian Church, Jerusalem Council 2 R. & S. M. and the Ashlar Assoc. all of Baltimore and Lodge 45, F. & A. M. He was a retired foreman, ship builder, for Bethlehem Steel Corp. During the World War, Mr. Beltzhoover was stationed at Sparrows Point as a member of the Emergency Fleet Commission. He leaves a niece, Mrs. Anna Bell Brown, Sarasota and a nephew, George H. Beltzhoover of Wilmington, NC. unm. His Soc. Sec. application spells his fathers' name as Prior and gives his midddle name as Hessler, not Husler, though his wartime rgistration 6/1/1917 reads Husler. [1] [2]

299-Annie Harris Beltzhoover (1894-1923), m. 25 Dec. 1917, Crawford Lindsay WILSON.

300-James Eugene Beltzhoover, b. 22 July 1897, d. Mar. 1972, (1897-1972); according to his Soc. Sec. application, May 12, 1938, signed J. Eugene Beltzhoover. He lived at 3500 Poplar St., Castle Shannon, PA., s/o Silar Pryor and Mary Elizabeth Harris; unm., g. Mt. Lebanon Cem. [3]

134-GEORGE McLAUGHLIN BELTZHOOVER[5] (44), son of Henry, born 15 April 1855 and raised on the Brownsville Pike, White Hall Hotel, six miles from Pittsburgh, PA. His wife's name was Amelia S. Kaemerling/Kammering/Kemerling, b. 8 Jan. 1859, Cincinnati, OH.; d. 3 Dec. 1953. the widow of Geo. M. and arrangements were handled by Chas. M. Beltzhoover; g. Rest

----

1. Obituary Thomas H. Beltzhoover, April 1975. Selby Pblic Library, Sarasota Co., FL. 5/17/96

2. Ibid., Vivian Beltzhoover, July 1997

3. James Eugene Beltzhoover SS app. says he was born 22 July 1897, but the SS Death index says he was born 2 July 1896 and died Mar. 1972

Haven Memorial Park Cem.   They married 17 July 1882. Amer-
lia's mother was Katherine Kaemmering, b. 15 Dec. 1826, Ger-
rmany, d. 30 Dec. 1922, Kennedy Heights, OH, cremated 30 June
1950, g. Rest Haven Memorial Park Cem.

He wrote that his ancestors were Hollanders. George died
at age 69 and it was recorded in the Commercial Tribune,
8/22/25, "organizer of Electric Co., stricken a week ago, came
to Cincinnati at age 24."

George M. Beltzhoover, d. 21 Mar. 1925, res. Kennedy
Heights, OH., entombment, 30 June 1950, by Charles M. Beltzhoover; g. Rest Haven Memorial Park Cem.

George M. Beltzhoover lived in Cincinnati, OH (14 Dec.
1903), owned and operated Beltzhoover Electric Co., 640 Vine
St., 'Electrical Contractors.' He wrote in 1903 to Margaret
STACKER, Cumberland City, TN., that his father was Henry
Beltzhoover; his grandfather was Jacob Beltzhoover. He wrote
on Jan. 18, 1904, that he came to Cincinnati in 1879, met a
girl (Amelia) "who has been his guardian angel for 22 years."
That they have sons Chas. M. Beltzhoover (21 in 1904), who
married 21 Nov. 1903, and son, John D. Beltzhoover, 18. Both
were connected with him in the electrical business.

"Actually, Charles Beltzhoover started the electrical
business and his father, George, owned and operated a grocery
store and joined the electrical firm as a stock keeper. After
the 1913 flood in Dayton, OH., where John D. Beltzhoover and
wife Myrtle lived, they moved to Cincinnati and John D. joined
his brother, Charles, in the Beltzhoover Electric. Later, he
became V-P., to Charles who was Pres. After the 'Noronic'
ship fire, and the death of Charles. John D. became President. Later, after John D. had died and in 1955-1956, after
all contracts were completed the firm was dissolved." [1]

One newspaper article said that Amelia died in the house
of her son, John at 7620 Montgomery Road, with whom she lived.
Another article said that she died at the home of her granddaughter, Mrs. Henry (Jane) Ziegenfelder at 3759 Ferdinand
Place, Cincinnati. Amelia died at age 94, and obituaries were
in the Cincinnati Post 23 Dec. 1953, p. 8:3. The funeral was
handled by Tredway Funeral Home and the body was cremated.

In fact, Amelia died in a nursing home. After Chas., her
son, died she would spend three months with Irene in Columbus,
OH., then three months with Jane Ziegenfelder and then three
months with her son, John. This was the way her care was
handled for several years. Then she would spend six months
with John, and six months with Jane until the care became such
----

1. Ziegenfelder, Jane Beltzhoover letter 10/19/01

that they could not handle.
    Issue: (BELTZHOOVER)
        301-Charles McLaughlin Beltzhoover[6], (1882-1949), b.
            28 Sept. 1882, at 2 o'clock p.m.
        302-John Dixon Beltzhoover, (1885-1967), 18 in 1904,
            b. 24 Mar. 1884(5), a Tuesday at 10 o'clock; d.
            21 Oct. 1967, res. Dillonvale, Hamilton Co.,
            OH. Residence at time of death was zip 45236,
            Cincinnati, OH. [1]

    135-**JOHN DIXON BELTZHOOVER/BELSHOWER**[5] (44) (1858-1894),
b. 10 Jan 1858, Pittsburgh, PA.; d. 29 April 1894, Cincinnati,
OH. (36-3-19), g. Spring Grove Cemetery, Cincinnati, OH., s/o
Henry and Hattie Beltzhoover, at the time of his death he
resided at 7620 Montgomery Road, Cincinnati. His funeral was
arranged by George M. Beltzhoover. He died of acute nephritis
and is bur. in Sect. 26 Lot 3248, Spring Grove Cem.(Cincinnati
Zeibeiny 1 May 1894 p. 5:6); m. 20 Mar. 1883, Hamilton Co.
OH., Josephine nee GOEBEL Belzhoover/Belshower/Beltzhooper (a
misspelling) d., 16 June 1901 (42) (Cincinnati Free Press 17
June 1901 p. 8:1). [2] [3]

    Since these children were minors when their father and
mother died, who raised these children? Your compiler could
never locate them.
    Issue: (BELTZHOOVER
        303-Harry Leonard Beltzhoover[6], b. 4 Jan. 1886, OH; d.
            San Francisco, CA., 27 Nov. 1958, (72), moth-
            er's maiden name Gobel/Goebel, g. Golden Gate
            National Cem., San Mateo, CA., plot 2367, PFC
            SVC Park Unit 517 MTC wf/2?. Anna S. Beltz-
            hoover, b. 20 Dec. 1883, Texas; d. 19 Feb.
            1974, residence was 95486 Villa Grande, Sonoma,
            CA. No issue known. In the 1910 census Harry L.
            Beltzhoover, age 25, OH 0038, b. Hamilton Co.,
            Cincinnati, OH., and wf. Mabel age 20, b. KY.
            So, at age 25 he was still in Cincinnati. In
            the 1920 Census he was in CA., age 34.
        304-George M.? Beltzhoover, Was there a George s/o
            John D. and Josephine Goebel? What are the
            right dates for this George? Or might he have
            been prior to Harry Leonard? What happened to
            this George? Might his wife have been Olive,
            b. 21 Nov. 1891, OH., d. Oct. 1979 zip 45244, .
            Mt. Carmel, OH. Olive must have lived some
            place other than Cincinnati. Locate this

----

1. Social Security death index says b. 24 Mar. 1885

2. LDS Library Record

3. LDS Batch M 513455 1883-1884

George?

143-**SAMUEL TARLETON KENNEDY**[5] (49), m. Nancy Jane Stewart, d/o James and Nancy Agnes Stewart. After Samuel Tarleton Kennedy's death Nancy Jane Stewart Kennedy married James Hays Gibbs (related to the Hays, another founding family, Hays, PA., is named after them). Nancy Stewart was the d/o James Stewart.

Issue: (KENNEDY)
305-Elizabeth Beltzhoover Kennedy[6] (1849-1905), m. Robert Peach (1843-1901)
306-Sarah (Sally) Kennedy, (1852-1894), m. Adam L. Knabe (1850-1910)

147-**ELEANOR (Ellen) COOLEY**[5] (49), b. 1837, m. William CROUCH (1828-   ). William Couch was the son of William Couch (1776-   ) and wf., Elizabeth McIlvain. The Crouch family had property next to Cooley's near Castle Shannon.

Issue: (CROUCH)
307-Mary E. Crouch[6], m. --?-- Wakefield
308-Samuel Cooley Crouch
309-George Crouch
310-Nancy Crouch

148-**SAMUEL B. (BELTZHOOVER?) COOLEY**[5] (49) (1843-   ), m. Jane Hultz\Hulse, d/o Preston and wf. Jane (Williams) Hultz. [1]

Issue: (COOLEY)
311-Ettie/Etta M. Cooley[6] (1867-   ), m. --?-- McDo-nough
312-Mary E. Cooley (1867-   )
313-Francis Cooley
314-James J. Cooley
315-William B. Cooley

155-**FRANCES LOUISA COX**[5] (53), b. 25 Jan. 1837, Pitts-burgh, PA., d. 22 Mar. 1886, Cumberland City, TN., m. 17 Dec. 1857, Isaiah Willson EVANS, b. 28 Aug. 1829, Warren Co., KY., d. 5 Feb. 1888, Dover, Stewart Co., TN.

Issue: (EVANS)
316-William Clay Evans[6] (1859-1885), unm.
317-Elizabeth Evans (1862-1951), m. John Petway Bed-well (1857-1943), n.i.
318-Louisa Dickson Evans, b. 30 Nov. 1864, TN., d. 28 July 1961, Clarksville, TN., m. John Hill Thomas.
319-Mary French Evans, (1875-1973), m./1, John Allman; m./2, Ebbert Bedwell, m./3, Jerrit Holly.
320-Guy Barrow Evans (1877-1900), unm.

156-**MARY ARMISTEAD WHARTON**[5] (57) (1830-1860), m. Richard

----

1. Ibid., <u>History of Allegheny Co.   </u>, 1889 p. 376

Henry Alvey.
  Issue: (ALVEY)
    321-Elizabeth Wharton Alvey[6], b. 29 July 1856-)

  162-**JOHN THOMSON BARNES MASON**[5] (58) (1833-) m./1
Annie Nannie Jamison; m./2 Ellen Hill.
  Issue: (MASON)
    322-Nannie Barnes Mason[6]
    323-Elizabeth Barnes Mason, m. Wm. Judson
  Children from the second marriage:
    324-Sarah Hill Barnes Mason (1881-)

  171-**Capt. MELCHIOR STEWART BELTZHOOVER**[5] (64), b. 18 May
1868, Monmouth, Warren Co., IL., d. 20 July 1918, Natchez,
Adams Co. MS.; m. 1 Sept. 1891, Virginia Lee KOONTZ, b. 19
April 1862, Natchez, MS., d. 3 April 1921, Natchez, MS. See
Virgina Lee Koontz.

  178-**MARY KOONTZ**[5] (71), b. 23 July 1847, d. 14 Apr. 1923,
Natchez, MS.,educated in Tours, France; m. 14 May 1879, Fran-
cis SHIELDS, b. 8 Mar. 1846, Natchez, MS., d. 13 June 1922,
Natchez, MS. He was educated in France and served in the
Civil War.
  Issue: (SHILEDS)
    325-Francis Surget Shields, Jr.[6], b. 6 Nov. 1883,
      Natchez, MS, d. 26 Oct. 1894, (NOL), g.
      Natchez, MS.

  179-**HENRIETTE KOONTZ**[5] (71) 1849-1917, b. d. Natchez, MS.,
m., 19 Apr. 1876, William Dunbar Jenkins, b. 18 Sept. 1849,
Natchez, MS., d. 12 Mar. 1914, Chattanooga, TN, educated in
France and Washington College, Lexington, VA. Served as a
Major in the Spanish-American War.
  Issue: (JENKINS)
    326-Mary Beltzhoover Dacy Jenkins[6], b. 1 July 1878,
      Natchez, MS; d. 24 Jan 1953, Natchez. Educ.
      Wellsley College 1899-1901, taught at Wellsley.
      Served in France in WWI. unm. n.i. [1]
    327-Annis Dunbar Jenkins, b. 2 June 1880, Natchez, MS.
    328-Archibald Dunbar Jenkins, b. 25 Jan. 1884,
      Natchez, MS; d. 6 Sept. 1890, Natchez, MS.

  182-**MARGARET KOONTZ**[5] (71) b. 19 Feb. 1856, d. Aug. 1927
in France; m. 25 Nov. 1874; Andrew Dickson JONES, b. 1846,
Baltimore, MD; d. 29 Mar. 1909, New York, NY., a cotton merchant.
  Issue: (JONES)
    329-Andrew Dickson Talbot Jones[6], b. 3 Apr. 1877, m.
      1917, Julia Montgomery Wood.
    330-George Koontz Jones, b. 11 Mar. 1880, Baltimore,

----

1. Jenkins, Mary Beltzhoover. Courtesy Ruth Coy

MD.; d. 14 Sept. 1900, Baltimore, MD.
331-Allen Penniman Jones, b. 9 Sept. 1882, Baltimore,
MD.; d. 8 April 1908, Seattle, WA.
332-Leonard Roane Jones, b. 11 Mar. 1886, Baltimore.

185-VIRGINIA LEE KOONTZ[5] (71), b. 19 April 1862 at Green
Leaves; d. 3 April 1921; m. 1 Sept. 1891, at Green Leaves,
Melchior Stewart BELTZHOOVER, b. 22 May 1868, Monmouth, Warren
Co., IL., d. 20 July 1918, Natchez, MS. He was the adopted
son of Melchior W. BELTZHOOVER 1815-1879. (See Melchior Wal-
lace Beltzhoover)

Melchior Stewart Beltzhoover's mother was Melona/Malona
Stewart. Melchior W. Beltzhoover was the son of Daniel and
Arabella WALLACE Beltzhoover. Melchior W. BELTZHOOVER never
married. [1]

Melchior Stewart Beltzhoover inherited a fortune from his
father, but his name is not mentioned in the obituary.
Melchior Stewart built a castle-like home in New York state
called Rochroane. He commissioned Louis Tiffany to design a
stained glass window for his music room (Deanna Oklepek says,
"It is gorgeous too." "The home no longer exists. The Tiffany window is now in the Corning Museum in Corning, NY."
[2]

Melchior Stewart was educated at Stonyhurst College,
England. He was a banker and farmer and President of Irvington, NY from 1904-1915. [3]

Since the Beltzhoover line comes down through Virginia
Lee Koontz. The Beltzhoover line follows here, not through No.
164
Issue: (BELTZHOOVER)
333-Melchior Roch Beltzhoover. Sr.[6], b. 24 July 1892;
d. 1 June 1945; m. Ruth Audley Britton Wheeler.
334-Virginia Roane Beltzhoover, b. 14 Sept. 1899; d.
11 Sept. 1969; m. Guy ROBINSON

186-CHARLES BELTZHOOVER[5] (78) b. 15 May 1825; d. 4 Dec.
1862, g. Ashland Cem., Carlisle, Cumberland Co., PA. It is
believed that this is the Charles Beltzhoover involved in
large and successful dealings in stock, in connection with the
AHL family. [4]
Issue:
----

1. Conner, Ruth Audley and Mary Beltzhoover Jennkins

2. Ibid., Oklepek, Deanna

3. Conner, Ruth Audley and Mary Beltzhoover Jenkins, courtesy Ruth Coy.

4. Ibid., History of Cumberland and Adams Counties   pp. 447-448

187-**CHRISTIAN HERMAN BELTZHOOVER**[5] (78), b. 27 Aug. 1826; d. 27 Feb. 1875, g. Ashland Cem., Carlisle, Cumberland Co., PA. [1]

C. Herman Beltzhoover, m. the evening of 15 Mar. 1847, by Rev. J. H. Marsden, to Rebecca R. Wolford, daughter of Colonel John Wolford of Adams Co., PA., and wf. Jane Whitman. [2]

The Chestnut Hill Cemetery, Mechanicsburg, Cumberland Co., PA., records show Rebecca R. Beltzhoover d. 2 July 1873 (42-2-0).

Col. John Wolford was b. 13 Feb. 1800, near Gettysburg, son of Peter and Margaret Albert Wolford, his father afterward moving to York Co., PA., locating near Clear Springs, where John Wolford was reared to the life of a farmer. At age 24 he married Miss Jane Whitman, d/o Daniel and Elizabeth Good Whitman, of Adams Co. Col. John d. 10 April 1883, his widow died 9 Dec. 1883 c. 81. The names of their children were: (Wolford) Albert m. Lucy Martin; Margaret C., m. Anthony K. Myers; Elizabeth m. Richard W. Sadler (Eliz. died leaving two daughters); Rebecca R. deceased m. to Herman Beltzhoover and left a son and daughter; Mary Ann, widow of Abraham Mumper; Clarissa J., m. to Josiah Geiger; Peter; Emily W., m. to Albert Sydney Hartman.

Issue: (BELTZHOOVER) (children not in order)
335-Wunderlich Beltzhoover[6], b. 27 Mar. 1875, bur. 27 Jan. 1877 (1 yr. 10 mo.) g. Old Cemetery
336-Shatto/Shotto Beltzhoover, bur. 4 Feb. 1875, Old Cemetery
337-Harry L. Beltzhoover, b. 1857
338-Mary Ann Beltzhoover, widow of Abraham Mumper. There was a Mary Mumper, b. 18 Feb. 1883, PA., d. Jan. 1972?

189-**HELEN BELTZHOOVER**[5] (78), b. 15 May 1833, chr. 8 June 1834; d. 5 Oct. 1890, g. Ashland Cem. At the brink of the war, she married in 1860, at Rose Balcony, near Boiling Springs, James Williamson BOSLER. Helen Beltzhoover, d/o Michael G. & Mary HERMAN Beltzhoover, and they lived out the war period at Sioux City, IA., returning to Carlisle where they lived out the rest of their lives. [3]

Helen Beltzhoover and James W. Bosler were first cousins. Mary Herman was a sister to Ann and Elizabeth Herman, both Ann

----

1. Ibid., First Evangelical Lutheran Church Records, Carlisle, PA. p. 128

2. Stover, Robert, Abstracts from the Republican Compiler, Adams Co., PA. 1831-1851., Vol. II, p. 361. Gateway Press, Inc., Baltimore, MD., 1976. Courtesy of Jerri Burket, Longswamp, PA. 2/2000

3. Ibid., Bio. and Port. Cyclopedia of Cumberland, York and Adams Co.'s PA., p. 170

and Elizabeth married Bosler's. Ann married Jacob Bosler and Elizabeth married his brother Abraham. Abraham was James WW. Bosler's father, hence the first cousin relationship. [1]

Their home, built in the suburbs of Carlisle in 1886, was called "Cottage Hill" and they were members of the Presbyterian Church.

James Williamson BOSLER (1833-1882), b. 4 Apr. 1832, Silver Springs Twp., Cumberland Co., PA; d. 17 Dec. 1883 (50-7-13); son of Abraham Bosler (1806-1883) and wf. Elizabeth Herman (1810-1885). Abraham Bosler was the son of John Bosler and wf. Catherine Gish. Children of Abraham & Elizabeth Herman Bosler were: James Williamson Bosler 1833-1883); Joseph Bosler (1838-1912; m. 4 Nov. 1868, Sarah Lemen (1845-1868); Elizabeth Bosler, (1840-1903), m. --?-- Bowers. [2] [3] [4] [5] [6]

Joseph Bosler and wf. Sarah had the following children: Margaret, m. M. J. Murry and had son, Samuel Wilson Murry; Joseph, Jr.; Eliza E.; Bessie L.; Mary; Katherine; Susan and Newton L.

James W. BOSLER assisted on the farm until he entered Cumberland Academy, at New Kingston. Two years later he entered Dickinson College and remained there through his junior year. During vacation he conceived the idea of going West, which he did with the approval of his parents. He taught school at Moultrie, Columbiana Co., OH., during the terms of 1853-1854. He then went to Wheeling, WV., where he read law and was admitted to the bar. He then moved to Sioux City, IA., where he formed a partnership with Charles E. Hedges, to engage in the real estate business. Then they established the Sioux City Bank, under the firm of Bosler & Hedges, later they engaged in furnishing goods, cattle and general supplies for the Interior and War Departments of the Government, on the north Missouri River. The partnership was dissolved in 1866, and Mr. Bosler continued the business until his death. During his residence in Sioux City, he was an

----

1. Bosler, Larry, Sugar Creek, OH 5/14/2004

2. Records of First Evangelical Lutheran Church , Carlisle

3. Bio. Annals of Cumberland Co. , p. 215-218

4. LDS Records IGI Index as of Mar. 1992 p. 2 633

5. Young, Henry James Cumberland County Cemetery Records Ashland Cem. 1976

6. Descendants of John Bosler. Personal Ancestry File. Deanna Oklepek

active politician and in 1860 was sent as a delegate to the Charleston Convention. Having, by dint of energy and business capacity, acquired a considerable fortune, he returned in 1866, to his native county in Pennsylvania and built a beautiful home, called 'Cottage Hill', in the suburbs of Carlisle. He was at the time of his death 17 Dec. 1883, President of the Palo Blanco Cattle Co., of NM, and the Carlisle Mfg. Co., and director of the Carlisle Gas & Water Co.

James W. Bosler was the son of Abraham (1806-1883) and wf. Elizabeth HERMAN BOSLER. They had eight children and among them were: Joseph who m. Sarah LEMEN, J. Herman, James W., and Elizabeth (1840-1903, who m. Mr. Bowers.

The contruction of Bosler Hall on the John Dickinson Campus began in 1884 and was completed on June 23, 1886. The building was made possible through a gift by Helen Beltzhoover Bosler and was named the James Williamson Bosler Memorial Library in memory of her husband, a member of the class of 1854. The construction cost was $68,000. [1]

Issue: (BOSLER)
339-Charles "Charlie" Bosler, b. 27 Aug. 1864; d. 29 Dec. 1870, g. Ashland Cem.
340-Frank C. Bosler, b. 1 May 1869; d. 25 Nov. 1918. Frank C. graduated from Harvard in 1894; m. Elizabeth Swank (1882-1944). [2]
341-Mary Eliza Bosler, b., 1872, PA; m. Lewis S. SADLER, s/o Wilbur F. SADLER. Sadler was a member of the law firm of Sadler and Sadler, Carlisle, PA.
342-DeWitt Clinton Bosler, (1873-1903)., b. 25 Apr. 1873; d. 22 Dec. 1903. DeWitt graduated from Harvard in 1897. DeWitt Bosler owned the Fairfield and Allenberry properties from 1898 until his death in 1903. [3]
343-Helen Louisa Bosler, b. 1877. Helen and Frank C., lived in 'Cottage Hill' the home built by their father. Helen was a member of the Presbyterian Church of Carlisle, along with the rest of her family. She married Horace T. Sadler, s/o Wilber F. Sadler.

190-**MARY BOWERS BELTZHOOVER**[5] (78), m. 30 April 1836, Carlisle, PA., John A. (H.?) Filbert, b. c. 1827. PA. They were married at Rose Balcony, near Carlisle, by Rev. A. R.

----

1. <u>Chronicles of Dickinson Education</u>, Bosler/Hall.

2. Ibid., <u>Bio. Annals of Cumberland Co.</u>, 1905

3. Ibid., <u>Bio. Annals of Cumberland Co.</u>, 1905 pp. 215-218

Lilly. They were members of the Zion Lutheran Church and as of the 1880 census they were living in North Manheim, Schuykill Co., PA. (Late arriving information)
Issue: (FILBERT)
344-Benjamin A. Filbert[6], b. ca. 1857, PA
345-Mary E. Filbert, b. ca. 1859, PA
346-J. Harry Filbert, b. ca. 1866, PA
347-Hellen B. Filbert, b. ca. 1873, PA
348-Charles B. Filbert, b. ca. 1875, PA

191-ELIZA ANN or ELIZABETH/ELIZABETH ANN BELTZHOOVER[5] (78), d. 21 Mar. 1876 (56); m. 6 May 1841, Henry Hake GROVE (1817-1870, b. 21 April 1817, of Allen Township, Cumberland Co. He died in Carlisle, 17 Sept. 1870; m. 6 May 1841, First Evan. Luth. Church, Carlisle, PA.

Henry Grove was a member of the Lutheran Church. Eliza Ann was the eldest daughter of Michael G. and Mary HERMAN Beltzhoover. [1]

Henry Hake Grove's gggrandfather settled in Lancaster Co., PA. (Hans Graf), a Menonite from Switzerland c. 1676 to PA., in 1696. Henry Hake Grove was the son of Henry and Catharine Hake Grove. [2] [3]
Issue: (GROVE)
349-Henry Beltzhoover Grove[6], (1842-1865), b. 9 Feb. 1842, bpt. 7 Mar. 1842; d. 29 Oct. 1865. s/o Henry & Eliz. Grove, sponsor Michael and Mary Beltzhoover. Henry Grove was assassinated by a "friend" who then robbed him of $1.25, his gold watch and chain. He had a photograph gallery in Baltimore, which is where he was murdered.
350-Eugene A. Grove, M.D. (1847-1912), g., Ashland Cem., Carlisle, PA; m. Zullieme A. Grove, (1853-1935)

194-JACOB BELTZHOOVER[5] (79) (1817-1853), b. 25 Sept. 1817; d. 1853, the son of George and Margaret BELTZHOOVER. "Jacob Beltzhoover d. age 35, father and mother, George and Margaret Beltzhoover, Allen Township (now Monroe), Cumberland Co., PA., farmer, wife, Agness Eckels/Eckles/Eccles, b. 15

----

1. Ibid., Bio. & Port. Cyclopedia of Cumberland, York and Adams Co.'s p. 399 In bio of Eugene A. Grove. Courtesy Jerri Burket, Longswamp, PA. 2/2000

2. Wing, Rev. Conway   History of Cumberland Co., PA   1879 p. 180

3. Cumberland Co., PA., Church Records

Feb. 1821; d. 11 April 1852, Silver Springs Cemetery." [1] [2]

Jacob (could he have been a George Jacob?) Beltzhoover, b. 25 Sept. 1817, d. 12 Apr. 1853 (35). [3] [4]

Jacob's will was probated in Carlisle, 31 May 1853, executor, George Beltzhoover. Jacob Beltzhoover, m., 24 Dec. 1840, Agness Eckles/Eccles, b. 15 Feb. 1821; d. 11 April 1852, g. Silver Spring, Silver Spring Township, Cumberland Co., PA. [5] [6]

His wife was Agness Eckles/Eccles, d/o Francis ECKLES, Esq., (1787-1861) and wf. Isabella CLENDENIN. d. 1846 Francis Eckles m./2, Jane Reed. Francis ECKLES, b. 1 Apr. 1791, d. 1888, s/o Nathaniel ECKLES (Pvt. Rev. War) and wf. Isabella HUSTON. Isabella CLENDENIN, b. 2 Feb.1790, d/o Lt. John CLENDENIN, PA., (1755-d. July 1, 1802) and wf. Elizabeth CALDWELL. [7]

Lt. John Clendenin, s/o John Clendenin, b. 1704, d. 1802, g., Silver Springs, Cumberland Co., PA., was a 1st Lt. in 1777 in the 6th Co., 3rd Batt. Cumberland Co., Militia; m., Janet 'Jean' Houston, d/o John Houston and wf. Martha Stewart., g. Pine Hill graveyard. Another Revolutionary ancestor, to this line, is probably James Mateer, g. Silver Spring Cem. Lucy A. Beltzhoover Dille became DAR #108899 as a descendant of Lieut. Samuel Huston, Lieut. John Clendenin, and Pvt. Philip Entler. [8]

The York Co., History says that Jacob "left" two sons, whereas the family bible states that he had four children. The children were: Francis E., b. 1841; George M.; John Clendenen and a previous son or daughter who died before he did? There WAS a daughter. List below is correct.

----

1. Schaumann, M. L.   Physicals Return of Deaths 1852, 1853, 1854, 1855, Cumberland Co., PA.   1972 p. 2

2. Cumberland Co., PA., Cemetery Records. Silver Spring Presbyterian Church/. p.147

3. Schaumann, Merri L. S.   Physicians Return of Deaths 1852-55 Cumberland Co., PA.

4. Eckles, William A. and Dr. Charles Eckles Courtesy Joe Cannon, OH

5. Old Beltzhoover Bible information

6. Records of Beltzhoover at State of PA., Library Harrisburg, PA. G. O. Kamp

7. Eckles family information courtesy Joe Cannon 8/10/97

8. DAR Vol. 109, p. 281

Francis would have been 11 years old when his father died in 1853; Geo. and John even younger. in 1841, The mother died in 1852. Was there a court order concerning the custody of the children such as guardian appointed, as was customary at that time? It is thought that the grandparents raised these children.

Issue: (BELTZHOOVER)

351-Frances "Frank" Eckles Beltzhoover[6], b. 6 Nov. 1841, Silver Springs Township, Cumberland Co., PA. He attended Big Spring Academy, Newville, was graduated from Pennsylvania College at Gettysburg in 1862; studied law, admitted to the bar in 1864 and began to practice in Carlisle, PA. He was very active in Democratic politics and served in Congress from 1879-1883 and from 1891-1895. He served in the 46th, 47th. 52nd, and 53rd Congress. In 1910 retired and moved to Los Angeles, CA., d. 2 June 1923, in Los Angles, g. Ashland Cemetery, Carlisle, PA., n. i.
1   2   3   4   5   6

Francis Eckles m., 16 Dec. 1868, Harrisburg, PA., Alwinda Supplee.

There is a fine ink or charcoal drawing of Cong. Beltzhoover's home in Carlisle, PA., in Rev. Conway P. Wing's History of Cumberland Co., PA., 1879. [7]

It was a family rumor (Evertson's) that "the ex-congressman from Carlisle, PA., (Francis Eckles Beltzhoover) was a descendant of one of Eva's brothers."

352-George Morris Beltzhoover Sr., (1844-1935) b. 8 Feb. 1844, Newton twp., Springs, Cumberland

----

1. History of York Co., PA   Bio. p, 606

2. Ibid., Joe Cannon

3. Wiley, Samuel T. Biographical and Portrait Cyclopedia of Cumberland, York and Adams Counties, PA. , Esq. C. A. Ruoff Co., 1897 p. 108, 147, 149, 154, 170, 174, 270, 381, 399. Courtesy Jerri Burket, Longswamp, PA. 2/2000

4. Bio. Dir. of Amer. Congress. 1774-1927

5. Conway, P . Wing History of Cumberland Co., PA., 1731-1879

6. Huston, E. Rankin History of the Huston Families 138-140, 246

7. The Political Graveyard   . Index to Politicians p. 3

Co., PA.; m., 24 Sept., 1873, Lucie Adele
Entler.
353-Margaret E. 'Maggie' Beltzhoover, b. 2 Mar. 1847,
d. 1919; g., Silver Spring Cem., Silver Spring
Twp., m. 17 Jan. 1867, Benjamin F./W. Hocker,
of Middlesex Twp., by Rev. H. R. Fleck. DAR
#115520 (see DAR also under Lucie Dille). They
resided Middlesex, Cumberland Co., PA. [1]
354-John Clendenin Mateer Beltzhoover, b. 9 May 1849:
d. 5 Feb. 1870, (21), un. m., g. Silver Spring
Presbyterian Church Cem. The American Volunteer
gave him the title of Dr.. 10 Feb. 1870. n. i.

195-MICHAEL B. BELTZHOOVER[5] (79), b. 10 Sept. 1824, d. 8
June 1883. g. Mt. Zion, Cumberland Co., PA., m. Mary A. Bricker (1828-1910), Boiling Springs, g. Mt. Zion Cem. Sect. R. [2]
Issue: (BELTZHOOVER)
355-Jacob Beltzhoover?[6], b. 17 Nov. 1855; d. 8 Sept.
1877 (21-9-21).
356-Michael C?/G?. Beltzhoover? Zion Cem. records
show "son of M. G. Beltzhoover (1860-1914)"
357-Alice Beltzhoover, ca. 1861

196-JOHN P. BELTZHOOVER[5] (81), b. 20 Oct. 1825, bpt. 26
April 1827 (First Ev. Luth. Church, Carlisle, PA.), son of
Jacob Beltzhuber and wf. Rebecca; d. 1 May 1908, Baxter
Springs, Cherokee, KS. He was educated at Mt. Rock, PA.;
graduated at age 15; worked 10 years with his father as a
teamster; then worked 12 years (to about age 37) spent on a
farm in Cumberland Co., PA. In 1866 he moved to Clinton Co.,
IL. In 1884 he purchased a farm in Cherokee Co., KS. John
P. Beltzhoover died in 1908, Cherokee, KS. [3]

John P. Beltzhoover married 11 June 1850 "both of West
Pennsboro Twp." Cumberland Co., PA., Hannah NAGLE/NAGEL, b.
1823, d. 13 Jan. 1875, g. Sandoval, IL., Cemetery (North Section). He m./2, 24 June 1876, Mrs. Rachel Watts Thompson, b.
25 Dec. 1844, Allen Co., OH, d/o James and Mary Gilmer Watts.
Mrs. Moore says that she copied Hannah's name off records at
the cemetery and "does not know her maiden name." Her maiden
name is shown as Nagel in the History of Cherokee Co., KS.
The Cherokee Co., KS. History says John P. m. 1857. [4]
----

1. Ibid., E Rankin Huston. History of Huston Families and Their Descedants 1450-1912,
pp. 138-140, 253-254

2. History of York   p. 676, 678

3. Ibid., Hist. of Cherokee Co., KS. and Represenative Citizens   , 1904, pp. 362, 363
Courtesy Joan M. Moore

4. Ibid., Cumberland Church Records   p. 310

There were three children from the first marriage. He married second Rachel Watts, d/o James and Mary Gilmer Watts, born in Allen Co., OH. Rachel Watts was first married to a man named --?-- THOMPSON.

Issue: (BELTZHOOVER)

358-Jacob N.(Nagle?) Beltzhoover,[6] (1850-1935), b. 8 Aug. 1850, Carlisle, PA., m. Josephine Geiger.

359-Ida Mae Beltzhoover, b. 8 Nov. 1859, PA., m. William Leith.

360-Jennie Beltzhoover, b. 1860. m. Edward A. Ennis.

361-Annie Beltzhoover, m. William Stewart.

Children from the second marriage: (mother Rachel Watts Thompson)

362-Rachel Elizabeth Beltzhoover, b. 15 Nov. 1878, d. 24 May 1952,Los Angeles, CA.; m. Orrin Callis

363-Nola Beltzhoover, b. 1881, still at home 1904

364-Mayme Beltzhoover, b. 1883, still at home 1904

197-GEORGE JACOB BELTZHOOVER,[5] (81) (1838-1911). From the tombstone in Newville he was born 14 Jan. 1838 and d., 7 Nov. 1911. (Editor's note: The records of the Stoughtstown Evan. Luth. Church taken from Rev. R. S. Stair's records 1907-1915 are in error). George Jacob Beltzhoover and Jane Mary McKeehan were married 5 Dec. 1861. Jane Mary McKeehan, b. 5 June 1841; d. 24 Aug. 1910. [1] [2] [3]

George Jacob died in Newton Township, Cumberland Co., PA. His will was dated 27 Nov. 1908, Newton Twp.. His will names seven children. Geo. McKeehan Beltshoover, d. i. 1875. Witnesses to George Jacob's will were Harry Leidigh and F. E. Beltzhoover. Both could be his cousins. F. E. being Frank Eckles Beltzhoover, Att'y. Harry Leidig was also an att'y.

The Stoughtstown Evan. Luth. Church was never large enough to be self-supporting. Membership never exceeded 50. The congregation at Stoughstown had an on again off again relationship with Centerville Lutheran as part of the Dickinson Charge. Apparently, when they could afford it they were an independent congregation known as Zion Evangelical Lutheran Church at Stoughstown. The congregation existed until about 1925. The records were still in Centerville Lutheran Church (1999) but they advised they would be forwarding to Lutheran

----

1. Records of Rev. R. S. Starr (1907-1935)   , Stoughstown Evangelical Lutheran Church. Ed.'s note: These records of George Jacob and his wife are in error.

2. Index of Church/Cemetery Records, Cumberland Co., PA.   , Historical Society, 2/9/99

3. Beltzhoover, George Indianapolis, IN Jan. 1996

Historical Institute. [1]
     Issue: (BELTZHOOVER)
          365-Thomas Skiles Beltzhoover[6], b. 5 May 1863; d. 29
               July 1916
          366-Robert Edward Beltzhoover, b. 5 June 1865, n.i.
          367-Clara Belle Beltzhoover, b. 12 July 1867 (Mrs.
               Wesley Cook Thrush in 1895)
          368-Jacob Franklin Beltzhoover, b. 24 Aug. 1869; d. 10
               or 12 Dec. 1959. He joined a threshing crew
               that traveled west and eventually into Canada.
               He lived in Canada for years but returned to
               Carlisle, PA., and is bur. there. unm. [2]
          369-Susan Mae Beltzhoover, b. 1 Feb. 1872; d. 15 Aug.
               1966, m. Mr. Evelhoch
          370-George McKeehan Beltzhoover, b. 31 Mar. 1874; d.
               14 Mar. 1875. d. i. (11 mo. 14 days) [3]
          371-John Graham Beltzhoover, b. 24 June 1877, m. Dessa
               ---?---
          372-William Smith Beltzhoover, b. 15 June 1879; d. 17
               Nov. 1959.

     202-**GEORGE BELTZHOOVER**[5] (82), b. 26 Dec. 1823, Monroe
Township, Cumberland Co., PA.; d. 5 May 1894, (70-4-9), g. Mt.
Zion.   He married, 25 Aug. 1846, at the First Ev. Luth.
Church,   Carlisle,   PA.,   Miss   Maria   C.   (Mary)
Niesley/Nissley/Hiesley, b. 24 Aug. 1829; d. 15 Feb. 1907 (77-
5-21), of this county, g. Mt. Zion Cemetery, Sect. Q., daughter of Jacob Niesley. Mr. and Mrs. George Beltzhoover were
members of the Lutheran Church and in politics were Republican. [4] [5] [6]

     These dates for George and Maria are on their tombstones,
g. Zion.
     Issue: (BELTZHOOVER)
          373-Mary Elizabeth Beltzhoover[6], b. 1847, Cumberland
               Co., PA., m. John Stauffer Hoover.
          374-John A. Beltzhoover, b. ca. 1848-49, in the 1920
----

1. Frantz, Fredrick S., Stoughstown Zion Evangelical Church   information thanks to the
courtesy of Mr. Frantz

2. Beltzhoover, Edw. 3/5/00

3. Lutheran Brick Church graveyard, Upper Frankford Twp., Cumberland Co., PA. Records of
Jeremiah Zeamer

4. Ibid., History of Cumberland Co., PA   p. 506

5. Mt. Zion Cemetery, just outside Carlisle, Cumberland Co., PA., The old portion of the cemetery is
the same as Old Cemetery, Churchtown.

6. Lancaster Mennonite Historical Society. Courtesy Jerri Burket, Longswamp, PA 2/14/2000

PA Census he is shown as age 71, res. South Middleton Twp., Cumberland Co., PA.; m. Mary Emily Brandt.

375-Margaret A. Beltzhoover, b. 20 Feb. 1850, twin; d. 20 Jan. 1851 (11 mos.), g. Mt. Zion Cem.

376-Maria C. Beltzhoover, b. 20 Feb. 1850; d. 22 Mar. 1852, (2-2-1), g. Mt. Zion Cem.

377-Clara E. Beltzhoover, b. ca. 1852

378-Monroe C./G. Beltzhoover, b. ca. 1855, d. 27 Sept. 1879 (24), bur. in same plot of Mt. Zion Cem. as John A. Sect L.

204-MAHALA/MANHALA C. BELTZHOOVER[5] (82), b. 12 Oct. 1833; bpt. 9 Nov. 1833; m. 17 July 1851, George W. Leidig/Leidigh/Leydig, b. 1851; d. 16 April 1901 (72-9-3), g. Churchtown. When they were married they moved to Leidigh Station and lived there ever since. He was 5 years old when his father died and John Brindle became his guardian. George W. Leidigh was the son of Jacob Leidigh and wf. Sarah. The Leidigh family information follows just below this family. At 20 yrs of age he learned the miller's trade from Jacob Goodyear, his brother-in-law. In 1881 he bought the Junction Flouring Mill, one of the oldest on Yellow Breeches Creek. The mill was built in the 1700's, rebuilt in 1828, and again rebuilt by Mr. Leidigh. He was a miller on the same creek for 33 years. The oldest miller on Yellow Breeches Creek. He and his wife were members of the Zion Lutheran Church and he was Republican in politics. [1] [2] [3]

George W. Leidigh had one brother, Samuel Leidigh of Carlisle that survived him.

Issue: (LEIDIGH)

379-John Beltzhoover Leidigh[6], b. 19 Apr. 1852, Cumberland Co.; m. Mattie A. Bowers [4]

380-George Monroe Leidigh, d. 1889, m. Gertie R. Moore

381-Harry M. Leidigh, an attorney, of Carlisle. [5]

* * * * * * * * * *

LEIDIGH

JOHANN MICHAEL LEIDIGH and wf., Appolonia --?--

---

1. Ibid., <u>History of Penna.</u>   Part I p. 511

2. Ibid., <u>Cumberland Church Records</u>   , p. 312

3. Carlisle Sentinel obituary of George W. Leidigh, Tues. 16 April 1901.

4. Ibid., <u>History of Penna.</u>   Part I, by Samuel Bates

5. Ibid., <u>History of Penna.</u>   by Bates p. 511

Issue:
Johann Adam and Magdalena Leidig

JOHANN ADAM LEIDIG, wf. Magdelena --?--
Issue:
(1) David Leidigh
(2) Jacob Leidigh and wf., Sarah
(3) George Leidigh
(4) John Leidigh

JACOB LEIDIGH, wf. Sarah --?--
Issue:
(1) Mary Ann Leidigh, m. Jacob Goodyear
(2) Catharine Leidigh
(3) George W. Leidigh, m. Mahala Beltzhoover
(4) Samuel Leidigh of Carlisle, m. Elizabeth --?--

* * * * * * * * *

222-**WILLIAM BELTZHOOVER**[5] (88), b. 10 May 1844, Cumberland Co., PA.; d. age 92, 14 Feb. 1935, g. Mosier Cem., Porter Co., IN.; m. Elizabeth Bickel/Piskel, b. 15 Mar. 1852, NY., d. 6 April 1921, g. Mosier Cem., Union Twp., Porter Co., IN. [1][2]

William Beltzhoover came to Indiana in 1856. He was a Civil War Veteran. The GAR post assisted at his funeral. There is a record of a William Bellshoover in the 99th Inf. Co. A. from Indiana. Mustered in Aug. 10, 1862; mustered out 5 June 1865, three years. [3][4]

He had, surviving in 1935, a daughter Lenora/Lula?/Lulu? (Mrs. John W. Zea). His obituary states that he was survived by one daughter, one son, six grandchildren, nine gr-grandchildren, and one gr-gr-grandchild. [5]

According to the 1880 census, Union Twp., Porter Co., IN., Wm. (36) b. PA., Elizabeth (28) b. NY., and children Lenora 11, Franklin 8, Calvin 5, Harrison 2. Some of these children as listed in the census might later be known by a different name, therefore may be duplicated in the list of
----

1. Valparaiso Vidette Messenger   , Valparaiso, IN., 14 Feb. 1935, 23 May 1933, 10 Aug. 1943
Courtesy Barb Nault, Genealogy, Porter Co., Library 2003

2. Union Township Cemetery Index, Porter Co., IN.   Courtesy Barb Nault

3. Ibid., Nault, Barb

4. Hewett, Janet B. ed.   The Roster of Union Soldiers 1861-1865

5. Index to Deaths in Valparaiso Vidette Messenger 1927-1967. Courtesy Barb Nault

issue. For want of further information your compiler will assume that Franklin is 'Frank'; Harrison is 'Harry'; Lenora might be 'Lulu'. [1] [2]

Issue: (BELTZHOOVER) may not be in order

382-Lenora Beltzhoover[6]11 in 1880, b. IN., could be Lula/Lulu Beltzhoover, b. 12 Sept. 1868, Union Twp., Porter Co., IN; d. 15 Oct. 1946 (78), wife of John M/W? Zea (1863-1945) (82), g. Graceland Cem., Valparaiso, IN.

383-Franklin 'Frank' Beltzhoover, b. ca. 1872/1874, d. 10 Aug. 1943, Lake Co., IN., g. Crown Hill Cem., Hobart Twp., Lake Co., IN.; m. 23 Nov. 1892, Porter Co., IN., Florence Sawyer (married by Rev. J. H. D. Smith). Other records refer to her as Mrs. Frank, (Mary) b. 1878, d. 26 May 1927, g. Crown Hill Cem., Lake Co., IN., and they had a daughter Gladys Weidman of Valparaiso, IN.; m.\2 Ann Williams, d. 6 Jan. 1950, St. Joseph Co., IN. [3]

384-Calvin Beltzhoover age 5 in 1880, b. c. 1875; m. 17 Nov. 1897, Lake Co., IN., Pearl Kent.

385-Harrison/Harry Beltzhoover, age 2 in 1880, b. c. 1878, Center Twp., Porter Co., IN.; d. 23 May 1933 (55), g. Mosier Cem.; wf. Eva L. Beltzhoover, b. ca. 1876; d. 18 Dec. 1930 (54). The 1930 census shows Harry as head of household, wife Eva L., age 54 and father William age 87 living in Valparaiso, Porter Co., IN.

226-**JOHN BELTZHOOVER**[5] (89), b. 22 Oct. 1833 (10 years of age in 1843); d. 10 (9?) April 1875 (41-5-18); g. Union Church, Shiloh, West Manchester, York Co., PA. Also known as Neiman's Church.

232-**MELVILLE GARRISON SCHENBERGER**[5] (93), b. 21 Feb. 1819, York Co., PA.,d. 23 Feb. 1884, Tompkins Twp., Warren Co., IL., g. Center Grove, Kirkwood, IL.; m. Susan (Susannah) Staley, b. 25 Oct. 1821; d. 13 Oct. 1890, Tompkins Twp., Warren Co., IL. [4]

Issue: (SCHENBERGER)
386-Elias Schenberger[6], b. 13 Jan. 1846, Chanceford Twp., York Co., PA.; d. ca. 7 Jan 1891; m. 17 Feb. 1870, Mary E. Colgrove and they had a

----

1. Illus. Historical Atlas of Porter Co., IN., 1876, A. G. Hardesty, Valparaiso, IN. Courtesy Barb Nault

2. Ibid., Oklepek, Deanna

3. Crown Hill Cemetery, Hobart Twp., Lake Co., IN. Courtesy Barb Nault

4. Kamp, Gayle O. The Kamp Papers Vol. II 1986 pp. 767, 768

daughter, Olgo.
387-Milton R. Schenberger, m. Mary Jane Hall; ch.
     Everett, George
388-Daniel Schenberger, b. 1852; m. 1904, second wife,
     Laura Miller
389-Henry Shenbarger
390-Peter S. Shenbarger, moved to Morris Co., KS, then
     TX in 1885
391-Sarah M. Shenbarger, d. 1912, Tompkins Twp.,
     Warren Co., IL
392-Emerson 'Gus' Shenbarger, b. 5 Apr. 1859; d. 3
     Jan. 1933, Warren Co., IL., m. 9 Mar. 1912,
     Galesburg, IL and had children, Avis (Fleener),
     Melvin, Evelyn, Vernon, Glenn.
393-Alice R. Shenbarger, b. 1 Feb. 1863; d. 10 Dec.
     1864, g. Center Grove, Kirkwood, IL.

233-**JACOB SCHENBERGER**[5] (93), b. 21 Jan. 1821; d. 27 Feb.
1888, g. Craykey, PA., m. Elizabeth Smeltzer.
    Issue: (SCHENBERGER)
     394-Henry Schenberger[6]
     395-Mary Schenberger, m. ---?--- Lehenght

235-**SUSAN SCHENBERGER**[5] (93) also sometimes spelled,
Schenberger/Schoenberger, b. ca. 1821, Chanceford Twp., York
Co., PA., m. 11 Nov. 1845, PA, Jacob GILLEN b. Ireland, res.
of Chanceford Twp., York Co., PA.
    Issue: (GILLEN) Late arriving information
     396-August Gillen[6], b. 1858; m. Ella --?--, b. PA
     397-Noah Gillen, b. ca. 1861

239-**SARAH (SALOME) SCHENBERGER**[5] (93), m. Peter Blair, at
Conrad's Crossing, Chanceford Twp., York Co., PA. [1]
    Issue: (BLAIR)
     398-Rev. Isaac Blair[6]
     399-Elmer Blair
     400-Benjamin Blair
     401-Charles Blair
     402-Horace Blair
     403-Lattimer Blair
     404-Amanda Blair
     405-Susan Blair

241-**JOHN K. SCHENBERGER**[5] (93), b. 19 Mar. 1833, Conrad's
Crossing, York Co., PA., d. 18 Aug. 1902, Newbridgeville,
Chanceford Twp., York Co., PA; m. 12 April 1857, Elizabeth
Louks.
    Issue: (SCHENBERGER)
     406-Ida Schenberger[6]
     407-Charles Schenberger
----

1. Ibid., Kamp, Gayle O.   The Kamp Papers Vol. II 1986)

408-Alice Schenberger
409-Minera Schenberger
410-John W. Schenberger
411-Fred H. Schenberger
412-Dr. William Schenberger
413-Jacob Schenberger

242-**ADAM W. SCHENBERGER**[5] (93), b. 1837; m./1 Susan F. Moody; m./2 Elnora Swartz.
    Issue: (SCHENBERGER)
       414-Adam W. Schenberger, Jr.[6]

248-**JOHN KLINEFELTER IV**[5] (95), b. 13 Nov. 1825, York Co., PA., d. 23 Jan. 1903 (77), Jones Co., IA., (falling from a horse), g. Forest Hill Cemetery; m. 20 Nov. 1845, Morrow Co., OH., Lucinda ALSPACH, d/o Henry ALSPACH and wf., Mary Ann WILDERMUTH. Lucinda d. 17 Oct. 1916, g. Forest Hill Cem. They resided in Anamosa, IA., for many years. There were 15 children, 4 dying in infancy. This line can be continued for several generations in The Kamp Papers Vol. II [1]
    Issue: (KLINEFELTER)
       415-infant[6], b. 20 Aug. 1846, near Calendonia, OH., d. at birth.
       416-Sarah Ellen Klinefelter, b. 1848
       417-William Henry Klinefelter, b. 1850, Morrow Co., OH
       418-Mary Ann Klinefelter (1851-1874)
       419-Rozilla Klinefelter, b. July 1853; d. Nov. 1853
       420-Martha Alice Klinefelter, b. 14 Sept. 1854, Jones Co., IA
       421-Charlotte Amanda Klinefelter, b. 30 May 1856, Jones Co., IA
       422-Amy Louisa Klinefelter, b. 15 May 1857, Jones Co., IA
       423-Olive Lucinda Klinefelter, b. 11 April 1860, Jones Co., IA
       424-John Isaac Klinefelter, b. 14 Feb. 1862
       425-Infant son, died at birth, 23 Oct. 1865
       426-Jennie Elizabeth Klinefelter, b. 13 May 1867, Jones Co., IA
       427-Nettie Isabella Klinefelter, b. 28 Feb. 1870; d. 28 Aug. 1887 (17-6-0), TB, engaged to Bill Meeks
       428-Lillian May Klinefelter, b. 15 Mar. 1873

Sixth Generation

254-**SAMUEL STACKER RAYBURN**[6], (101), b. 14 Dec. 1842, d. 7 June 1888, St. Louis, MO.; m. 3 Oct. 1867, Nancy Elvira WALKER, b. 6 July 1849, St. Louis, MO, d. 18 Mar. 1918, Kansas City, MO.

----

1. Kamp, Gayle O. The Kamp Papers Vol. II 1986

Issue: (RAYBURN)
 429-Catherine French Rayburn[7], b. 1869; m. Charles
   Clarke BRECKENRIDGE, b. 1869
 430-Julia Walker Rayburn, b. 1 Oct. 1870; m. Samuel
   Cortland YEAMAN, b., 1871
 431-French Rayburn, b. 14 July 1873, St. Louis, MO.,
   d. 14 Dec. 1923; m.\1 Mary Withers RATHEL;./2
   on 2 Sept. 1902, Rose Celeste STEBER (1873-
   1963).
 432-Mary Morgan Rayburn, b. 1875; m. William Agadie
   BEALL
 433-James Walker Rayburn, b. 1876
 434-Virginia Elsie Rayburn, B. 1878; m., Frederick
   SURRIDGE, B. 1878
 435-Taylor Rayburn, b. 1880, d. 1921; m./1 Lola SAUN-
   DERS, b. 1880; m./2 Rosalie OSBORN, b. 1880

260-**KATE STACKER**[6] (102), b. 1854, TN; m. George VALLIANT,
b. 1854, MD. George was a druggist in Pine Bluff, Jefferson
Co., AR.
 Issue: (VALLIANT)
  436-George Stacker Valliant[7], b. 1877, TN
  437-Martha Valliant, b. 1875, TN
  438-Rigby Valliant, b. 1880, AR.

264-**CHARLES STACKER**[6] (102), b. 18 Nov. 1871; m. Beatrice
Clemmie PAYNE.
 Issue: (STACKER)
  439-Mary Beatrice Stacker[7]
  440-Charles Stacker, Jr., b. 28 July 1909, d. 26 Oct.
   1920.

270-**MARY KENNEDY NIMICK**[6] (115), b. ca. 1847, PA; m.
Anthony S. Murray, b. ca. 1846, PA.
 Issue: (MURRAY)
  441-Alexander Murray[7]
  442-William Nimick Murray, b. ca. 1869, PA., m. Elizabeth Charliere.

271-**FRANK BAILEY NIMICK**[6] (115), b. ca. 1849, d. 21 Nov.
1924, Pittsburgh; m. 20 Nov. 1888, Ellen Howard HOWE, d/o
Thomas Marshall Howe & wf. Mary Anne Palmer Howe. The name
was sometimes spelled Nimitz.
 Issue: (NIMICK)
  443-Francis Bailey Nimick[7], m. Mary Wilson SPENCER.
  444-Thomas Marshall Howe Nimick, m. Genevieve Dorton
   MURTLAND
  445-Wm. Kennedy Nimick, b. 16 Nov. 1896; d. 26 Oct.
   1920.

272-**ELIZABETH K. NIMICK**[6] (115), m. John N. BONHAM.
 Issue: (BONHAM)
  446-Elizabeth N. Nimick Bonham[7]

274-**JENNIE LYLE NIMICK**[6] (115), m. David Glen STEWART
Issue: (STEWART)
    447-David Glen Stewart, Jr.[7], m./1, Gretta HOSTETTER;
        m./2, Jacquelin Archer.

275-**ALEXANDER KENNEDY NIMICK**[6] (115)
Issue: (NIMICK)
    448-William Coleman Nimick[7]
    449-Alexander Kennedy Nimick, Jr., m. Nell PIERCETON

285-**LOIS LIVINGSTON BAILEY**[6] (118), m. Edward Druff BAL-
KEN.
    Issue: (BALKEN)
    450-Bailey Balken[7] (1904-1993)
    451-Wilkelmina Balken

295-**GEORGE HENRY BELTZHOOVER**[6] (133), b. 19 Feb. 1883; d.
14 Dec. 1953 (70-9-25) in Pittsburgh and was prominent in
business and civic circles in Castle Shannon. He was in the
insurance and real estate business there for many years. He
married on 11 July 1906, Margaret HICKS, b. c. 1884, Austin-
town, Mahoning Co., OH., d. 1956? (d. 1 Jan. 1955), Castle
Shannon, d/o Richard and Bridget DONNELLY HICKS of Castle
Shannon. Bridget Donnelly Hicks was b. 16 Mar. 1865, Colland,
Lanarkshire, Ireland, the daughter of Hugh Donnelly and wf.
Margaret McCartney. [1]

A well known member of the Masonic community. He served
many years as Justice of the Peace. Four sons.

Castle Shannon was the scene of a daring bank robbery and
murder, 14 May 1917. Geo. H. Beltzhoover age 34 was involved
in the attempt to capture the robbers. Two cashiers were
killed. Eventually the robbers were caught and brought to
justice. [2]

Mr. Beltzhoover, at his death, was a retired accountant,
a descendant of Melchor Beltzhoover, a farmer, who in 1806
willed some land in what is now known as the Beltzhoover
District, to his wife, five sons and a daughter. He is survived by wife, Margaret Hicks Beltzhoover, two sons, S. Pryor
Beltzhoover of Houston, Tex., George H. Beltzhoover, Jr. of
Toledo, Ohio and two brothers, Thomas H. Beltzhoover of Baltimore, MD., and J. Eugene Beltzhoover of Castle Shannon. [3]

----

1. St. Ann's Rectory, Castle Shannon, PA., St. Charles Branch. 1146 Ladies Catholic Benevolent Assoc.

2. Pittsburgh Post-Gazette   18 May 1997, Sunday Magazine Section. Castle Shannon Bank Robbery by
Roger Stuart and Edward Hale. Ibid., Vivian Beltzhoover.

3. Remembrance card of George H. Beltzhoover Dec. 1953, courtesy Vivian Beltzhoover 7/97

Bridget Hicks died intestate as per Allegheny Co records, Baldwin Township, 27 Jan. 1919.

Issue: (BELTZHOOVER)
452-Silas Pryor Beltzhoover II[7] (1883-ca.1932) (1905-1957?)
453-Robert Henry Beltzhoover, d. 21 Mar. 1924, died of respiratory failure. He had been wounded by his brother, Thomas, 21 Jan. 1921 in the home of their grandmother, Mrs. Mary Anna Beltzhoover, Castle Shannon. [1]
454-Thomas Hessler Beltzhoover, d. 5 Aug. 1920/1921 d.y. He was killed by a drunken hit-and-run driver, while in his own front yard.
455-George Henry Beltzhoover, Sr., b. 28 Feb. 1920; d. 20 Dec. 1983 (63), resided in Wilmington, NC., wf. Vivian Louise Krecker.

299-ANNIE HARRIS BELTZHOOVER[6] (133), b., 1894; d. 1923, g. Mt. Lebanon Cem., Lebabon, PA.; m. 25 Dec. 1917, Crawford Lindsay WILSON. She died 7 Jan. 1919? We also have the death year as 1923. Annie Harris was educated at local schools and Union High School. Active in the Masonic order of Eastern Star, 353, Castle Shannon. Also active in Carlisle Shannon Temple #99, Pythian Sisters. [2]

Issue: (WILSON)
455a-Mary Virginia Wilson[7] d.i., b. June 1919, d. Sept. 1919, g. Mt. Lebanon.
455b-Annabelle Wilson, b. 1922; m./1 --?-- Brown; m.\2 Bill Carey. She lived in Castle Shannon with her aunt and uncles, Charlotte, James Eugene and Thomas most of her life.

301-CHARLES McLAUGHLIN BELTZHOOVER[8] (134), (1882-1949), b. 28 Sept. 1882, OH; d., 17 Sept. 1949 in the fire of the Cruise ship SS Noronic, when docked at Toronto, Canada. He would have been 67 on Sept.28, 1949. He m./1 18 Nov. 1903, his wife was named Myra T. Anna Dale Beltzhoover. [3]

Myra T. Anna Dale, b. 25 Aug. 1888, Louisville, KY., died 25 Sept. 1925 at West Baden, IN, g. Rest Haven Memorial Park Cem.; d/o Jeptha Dale b. 6 Jan 1851, d. 9 Mar. 1917, Evanston, Cincinnati, OH., g., Braesville Cem., IN; and wf., Mary Katherine 'Kate' Frilingsdorf Dale (1855-1893), both of Louisville, KY.

There were two Beltzhoover daughters. In 1927, he m./2

----

1. <u>Pittsburgh Gazette</u>, 23 Mar. 1924. Courtesy Vivian Beltzoover 7/97

2. <u>History of Pittsburgh and Environs</u> American Historical Society 1922, courtesy Deanna Oklepek

3. 1910 Census

Anna Kotz, a secretary in the firm. Anna Kotz Beltzhoover died in the cruise ship fire also, 17 Sept. 1949, res. Indian Hill, OH., g. Rest Haven Memorial Park Cem. She left two brothers, Harry and Al Kotz and three sisters, Mrs. Marie Wilson, Mrs. Anette Taylor and Helen Eshelman, all of Cincinnati. Her funeral was at St. Patrick's. Both Charles and Anna Kotz Beltzhoover were buried in Rest Haven Cemetery.

With Mr. and Mrs. Beltzhoover on the fatal cruise ship SS Noronic were their friends from Cincinnati, Mr. & Mrs. John G. Kidd, book store owners. Mrs. Kidd was formerly Olive Statler and they resided at 3222 Observatory Drive. Mr. Kidd was bur. in Spring Grove. Mrs. Kidd's body may never have been located or identified at the time of the obituaries in Cincinnati.

Charles M. Beltzhoover resided on Algonquin Dr. Indian Hill. He graduated from Woodward High School. He was a member of the Masons, Rotary, Cincinnati Executives Assoc.

The identification of Charles M. Beltzhoover and his wife Anna, were made by his nephew, George, son of John D., in Toronto.

In 1903-1904, Chas. M. Beltzhoover is shown on the Beltzhoover Electric Co. letterhead along with his father. Actually, Charles founded the Beltzhoover Electric Co., and brought in the other family members.

At a Fiftieth Year anniversary of the firm a list of the major contracts (too long to present here) included such electrical constructions as Cincinnnati Gardens, Seagrams, Fifth Third Bank, the New Public Library, Sears, Gwynne Building, Johnson & Harding Co., Engineering Depot at Sharonville and on and on.

His grandson, Don Hall recalls, "that there was an "electric strike" or "door buzzer" installed on the door to Gramp B's office and was actuated by one of the office workers to admit people to his inner sanctum. The door knob spun uselessly in my hand until it was "buzzed", took hold and would open the door."
Issue: (BELTZHOOVER)
456-Irene Myra Beltzhoover[7], b. 7 Sept. 1904, Cincinnati.
457-Jane Elizabeth Beltzhoover, b. 10 Dec. 1912, Cincinnati

302-**JOHN DIXON BELTZHOOVER**[6] (134) (1885-1967), b. 24 Mar. 1884/5, Pittsburgh; d. 21 Oct. 1967 (82) widowed, Jewish Hospital, Cincinnati, g. Rest Haven Memorial Park Cem. He owned a bakery in Dayton, OH., until he sold and came to Cincinnati to be in the electrical business in 1909 with his brother, Charles. John Dixon Beltzhoover's wife was Myrtle May Tomlinson Beltzhoover, b. 22 Feb. 1882, Williamsville,

OH., d. 19 Oct. 1955, of cancer, Bethesda Hospital, d/o Joseph Tomlinson and wf. Lide Prickett Tomlinson. (Rhea Jeanne Beltzhoover said her grandmother was Myrtle Pickett but your compiler believes that her grandmother's maiden name was Prickett). Mr. Beltzhoover was a member of the Masons, a past patron of the Eastern Star and the Kiwanis club. He was also Pres. and Treas. of Belver Realty Co. He and his wife resided at 4820 Montgomery Road. Mr. Beltzhoover was VP of Beltzhoover Electric when his brother, Charles, who was Pres. died in the tragic fire of the SS Noronic. John D. Beltzhoover at that time assumed the Presidency of the firm. He later resided at 7620 Montgomery Road, Kenwood.

John Dixon Beltzhoover, on his Soc. Sec. application dated, 1 Dec. 1936, stated that he was born 24 Mar. 1884, in Pittsburgh, PA; that he lived at 6463 Ridge Road, Pleasant Ridge, OH; that his father was George M. Beltzhoover and his mother was Amelia L. Kaemerling and that he was employed at Beltzhoover Electric Co.

Myrtle May Tomlinson Beltzhoover d. ca. 10/20/1955 (73), Bethesda Hospital. Funeral arrangments were by Tredway funeral home, Norwood. A native of Withamsville, OH., she was a past Pres. of City Gospel Mission and served as fund raising chairman for many years. She was a member of Norwood Story Tellers Club, Kenwood Garden Club, Eastern Star, Norwood Christian Church. She left a dau. Rhea Weller, a son, George (C.?) Beltzhoover of Morrow, OH, a V-P of Beltzhoover Electric, a sister Mrs. Maude McGuire, St. Petersburg and a brother, Fred Tomlinson of Chicago, and two grandchildren. Burial was in Rest Haven Memorial Park. (Cincinnati Times Star 1/20/1955 p. 40:1)
    Issue: (BELTZHOOVER)
       458-Rhea Grace Beltzhoover[7], b. ca. 1906, m./1, Frank Joseph Weller, b. 6 June 1899, d. 17 Nov. 1956 (57), Ft. Worth, TX; g. Rest Haven Memorial Park Cem. (in John Beltzhoover's lots); m./2 Frederick Dempsey, Ft. Worth, TX. n. i.? She was age 87 IN 1992. The 1930 census, Hamilton Co., OH., states that Frank J. Weller was an attorney and Rhea was a teacher.
       459-George McCook Beltzhoover, b. 22 Sept. 1911; d. 11 Jan. 1965 (53), Morrow, OH.

305-ELIZABETH BELTZHOOVER KENNEDY[6] (143) (1849-1905), m. Robert Peach (1843-1910).
    Issue: (PEACH)
       460-James Stewart Peach[7] (1871-1929), m. Hannah Massing (1871-1942).)
       461-Byron Peach (1873-   ), m. Margaret M. Swisher (1879-   ).
       462-Hugh Wood Peach (1876-), m. Cora Belle Schaub (1878-)
       463-Robert Foster Peach (1879-1913), m./1 Teresa Wei-

gand (1880-   ), m./2, Lillian Gertrude Best
(1879-   )
464-Viola Peach (1893-1894)
465-Viola Peach (1891-   ), chosen. (Married Adah H.
Knabe (1873-   ) Ch: (Knabe) Myrtle D., Ottos
S., Andrew S., Idela D., Byron S., Lleola D.,
Harvey S.)

318-**LOUISA DICKSON EVANS**[6] (155), b. 30 Nov. 1864, TN., d.
28 Jul. 1961, Clarksville, TN.; m. John Hill THOMAS, b. 5 Nov.
1859, Guices Creek, TN; d. 1 Jan. 1911. Cumberland City, TN.
John Hill THOMAS (1859-1911), s/o John Hill THOMAS (1809-
1859), Stewart Co., TN., and wf. Nancy Louise ALLEN (1820-
1868). John Hill THOMAS (1809-1859), s/o Nathan THOMAS and
wf. Sarah HILL. Nathan THOMAS, s/o William THOMAS and wf.
Hannah PRATT.
    Issue: (THOMAS)
        466-Ethel Gertrude Thomas[7] (1884-1960), m. Walter
            Gabriel Rowland
        467-John Hill Thomas (1886-1976), m. Mary Johnson
            Parchman.
        468-Louis Orville Thomas (1889-1976), m. Lottie Ione
            Clifford.
        469-Fannie E. Thomas, (1890-1977) m. L. M. Jackson.
        470-William Thornton Thomas, (1894-1955), m. Myrtle
            Mae Vaughn.
        471-Leonard P. Thomas (1896-1909)
        472-Knox Bryan Thomas (1898-1983), m. Offie Ethel
            Clark.
        473-Nannie Magdalene Thomas (1900-1983), m. Herbert
            Rodney Averitt.
        474-Alice Ruth Thomas (1903-1904)
        475-Eric Dewitt Thomas (1906-1973), m. Ella Mae Paige.
        476-Buford Evans Thomas (1908-1971), m. Mabel Idel
            Stavley.
        477-Charles French Thomas (1911-2000), m. Sarah Louise
            Ash.

319-**MARY FRENCH EVANS**[6] (155), (1875-1973), m./1, John
Allman: m./2, Ebbert Bedwell; m./2, Jerrit Holly.
    Issue: (ALLMAN)
        478-Edwina A. Allman[7], (1899-1974), m. James Dewey
            Smith.

327-**ANNIS DUNBAR JENKINS**[6] (179), b. 2 June 1880, Natchez,
MS.; d. 31 May 1960, Morris Plains, NJ.; m. 8 Nov. 1906, at
Rockroane, Irvington, NY., Leonard Nicholson Snedeker, b. 15
June 1881, Brooklyn, NY; d. 14 Oct. 1943, Brooklyn, NY.
Educated Princeton, New York Law School.
    Issue: (SNEDEKER)
        479-Leonard Dunbar Snedeker[7], b. 23 Dec. 1907, Broo-
            lyn, NY.; d. Jan. 1988, Brooklyn, NY.; m. 1936,
            Beatrice Bishell, b. 12 Jan. 1907, Ipswick,
            England.

95

480-Virginia M. Snedeker, b. 25 Nov. 1909, Brooklyn, NY.; m. 1942, William L. Taylor.

481-George Snedeker, b. 14 June 1911, Brooklyn, NY.; m. 1941 Gladys M. Knapp.

482-Richard Stockton Snedeker, b. 14 April 1927, Brooklin, NY, m. 27 Sept. 1952, at Sea Girt, NJ., Mary Ellen Burroughs, b. 20 June 1929, Spring Lake, NJ. [1]

329-**ANDREW DICKSON TALBOT JONES**[6] (182), b. 3 Apr. 1877, Brooklyn, NY. m. 1917, Julia Montgomery Wood.
 Issue: (JONES)
  483-Geoffrey Montgomery Talbot Jones[7], b. 12 Oct. 1919, Newport, R. I., m. Mary --?--, div. They had one son Kiley Christopher Talbot Jones, b. 6 June 1967, in New York, NY. Geoffrey Jones served with the OSS in WWII.

333-**MELCHIOR ROCH BELTZHOOVER, Sr.**[6] (185), b. 24 July 1892, Natchez, MS.; d. 1 June 1945, Natchez, MS., m. ca. 1916, Ruth Audley Britton WHEELER, b. 8 Oct. 1897; d. 2 Mar. 1991, Natchez. Melchior Roch was a banker; Ruth Audley was a Department Store Owner and one of the founders of the Natchez Pilgrimage in 1932. [2]
 Issue: (BELTZHOOVER)
  484-Melchior Roch Beltzhoover, Jr.[7], b. 5 Jan. 1918;
  485-Ruth Audley Britton Beltzhoover, b. 22 Aug. 1921
  486-Virginia Lee Beltzhoover, b. 19 Nov. 1926

334-**VIRGINIA ROANE BELTZHOOVER**[6] (185), b. 14 Sept. 1899, Ardsley, Westtchester, NY; d. 11 Sept. 1969, Irvington, NY; m. 1920, Guy Robinson, b. 27 Mar. 1891, Yonkers, NY.
 Issue: (ROBINSON)
  487-Virginia Lee Robinson[7], b. 5 June 1921, Irvington, NY.; d. 14 Feb. 1991.
  488-Anne Roane Robinson, b. 25 Jan. 1925, Irvington, NY.; 18 July 1989, Princeton, NJ.

340-**FRANK C. BOSLER**[6] (189), b. 1 May 1869; d. 25 Nov. 1918. Frank C. graduated from Harvard in 1894. He was a Director of Carlisle Deposit Bank and Farmer's Trust of Carlisle. Also, the principal owner of Iron Mountain Ranch of Wyoming. [3]

Frank C. Bosler, m. Elizabeth SWANK, b. 5 May 1882; d. 19 May 1944, g. Ashland Cem.

----

1. Snedeker, Richard, West Windsor, NJ

2. Beltzhoover, Ruth Audley

3. Ibid., Bio. Annals of Cumberland Co. , 1905

Issue: (BOSLER) (other children?)
489–James Dudley Bosler[7], b. 12 Sept. 1918; d. 20 July
1926

352–GEORGE MORRIS BELTZHOOVER Sr[6] (194), b. 8 Feb. 1844,
Boiling Springs, PA., the son of Jacob and Agness Eckles
Beltzhoover; d. 23 Jan. 1935, Shepherdstown, WV. He married
24 Sept. 1873, Lucy/Lucie Adele McElroy Entler, born 15 Feb.
1854, daughter of Jacob Philip Adam Entler and wf. Ellen
McElroy. Jacob Philip Adam Entler s/o Philip Entler & wf.
Catherine Welsh. Your compiler is not sure of the relation-
ship betweem Joseph Entler, and Lucy's father, Jacob. Joseph
Entler was a hotel owner and prominent in Shepherdstown. Lucy
died 2 Mar. 1934 [1]

Philip Entler, b. 1740, York Co. PA; d. 1793, Berkeley
Co., VA., m. Catherine Welsh. Children: son, Daniel Entler
(1785–1866), m. 1809, Margaret H. Weltsheimer (1791–1866).
Children of Daniel and Margaret H. Entler were: Jacob Philip
Adam Entler (1818–1900) who m. Ellen McElroy (1823–1856).

Lucie A. Beltzhoover obtained membership in the DAR on
the Rev. War. record of Philip Entler. [2]

Lucie/Lucy Entler's sister, Anne Entler (30), single, was
in the household in the 1880 census.

He attended Cumberland Valley Institute at Mechanicsburg,
PA and was graduated from Pennsylvania College (Gettysburg) in
1864. He enlisted as a volunteer in Company A 26th Pennsylvania Regiment, serving as a Courier. He was present when
Lincoln delivered the Gettysburg address. In Feb. 1866, he
came to Shepherdstown and opened a law office. He had been
admitted to the bar in Carlisle, PA. He was a member of the
West Virginia House in 1870; county prosecuting attorney 1871–
1875; a pillar in the Lutheran Church; Supt. of Sunday School
for 35 years; a founder and trustee for Shepherd College.

George M. Beltzhoover, Sr., spent his last 69 years in
Shepherdstown as a lawyer, banker, churchman and college
patron.

George Beltzhoover had joined a Pennsylvania regiment
during the Civil War before returning to Shepherdstown and
marrying the daughter of Jacob Philip Adam Entler. Beltzhoover transferred numerous properties to blacks after the
----

1. Kenamond, A. D.   Prominent Men of Shepherdstown (WV) During
It's First 200 Years   pp. 37, 38 Jefferson County
Historical Society, Charleton, WV., 1963

2. Kamp, Gayle O. research

Civil War, and his sale to a black man, John Wesley Seibert in Feb. 1878 (Deed Book F. p. 239, Jefferson Co.) was consistent with a rising black ownership in Shepherdstown. John Wesley Seibert was a waiter and barber in the Entler Hotel for many years, and had close ties with the Entler family, into which, George Beltzhoover had married. During the Civil War, Seibert was recruited to the southern cause and served in the illustrious Stonewall Brigade of the Confederate Army.

Excavations on High St., in the historic neighborhood in Shepherdstown; the easternmost parcel was owned by Joseph Entler (Entler Hotel and cellar); by 1876 Mary Bowers sold (66) 'a certain ground lot and house to trustee, George Beltzhoover Sr.' The construction of the home must have been between 1854 and 1860. [1]

George Beltzhoover, Jr., like his father was an attorney with an active practice in the county. His acquisition of this property was probably for rental income, since his law practice was in Charles Town. Beltzhoover sold the property in 1933 and it eventually became the property of Shepherd College. [2] [3]

Issue: (BELTZHOOVER) (children not in order)

490-Frank Entler Beltzhoover[7], b. 11 Jan. 1877; d. 3 Mar. 1894. He died at Gettysburg College as the result of a fall.

491-Helen Carson Beltzhoover, b. 21 Sept. 1881; d. 18 Aug. 1882

492-George Morris Beltzhoover Jr., b. 22 Mar. 1880; d. 1958 (1880-1958)

493-Lucie/Lucy Adele Beltzhoover, b. 30 Mar. 1885; m. 8 Jan. 1915, Clarence Brown (C. B.) Dille, of Morgantown, Monongalia Co. WV., b. 28 May 1857, Kingwood, WV., d. 22 Aug. 1932; s/o James Adam Dille & wf. Linnie Suter Brown Dille. Mrs. Lucie A. Beltzhoover Dille, DAR ID #108899, descendant of Lt. Samuel Huston, Lt. John Clendenin and Pvt. Philip Entler (1740-1793)

494-Kathryn Eckels Beltzhoover, b. 21 June 1893, WV; m. --?-- Hess, of Fairmont, Marion Co. WV. DAR membership #115621.

495-Agnes McElroy Beltzhoover, b. ca. 1875, WV; m. 6 Feb. 1902, at Leesville, Carroll Co., OH., Don Meredith Carr, res. Toppenish, Yakima Co. WA. She must have been deceased by 1958.

----

1. Deed Book D. p. 257, Jefferson Co   . Courtesy Vic Dunn 10/5/97

2. Shepherdstown Register   , Shepherdstown, Jefferson Co., WV., Thurs. Jan. 24, 1935

3. Huston, E. Rankin   History of the Huston Families and Their Descendants.   pp. 138-140, 246, 254

353-**MARGARET 'MAGGIE' H. BELTZHOOVER**[6] (194), b. ca. 1846/1847; m. Benjamin W. Hocker, probable son of Adam Hocker. In the 1880 census, Hocker's were in Middlesex, Cumberland, Co., PA.
    Issue: (HOCKER)
        496-Minnie A. Hocker[7], 11 in 1880
        497-Adam S. Hocker, 9 in 1880
        498-Nora L. Hocker, 7 in 1880
        499-Helen A. Hocker, 3 in 1880
        500-Frank Hocker, 6 months in 1880

358-**JACOB N. (Nagle?) BELTZHOOVER**[6] (196) (1850-1935), b. 8 Aug. 1850, Carlisle; d. 10 Mar. 1935, g. St. Lawrence Cemetery (part of the Sandoval IL Cemtery, the Catholic section); m. Josephine GEIGER, b. 24 Feb.1859, Huey, Clinton Co., IL., d. 14 Feb. 1936. They resided, Meridian Twp., Clinton Co., IL. [1] [2]

Josephine Geiger the d/o George Geiger and wf. Augusta Kuhn Krogholdze, a widow. Josephine b., 24 Feb. 1859, Huey, Clinton Co., IL; d. 14 Feb. 1936
    Issue: (BELTZHOOVER)
        501-Clara E. Beltzhoover[7], b. 17 Feb. 1878; d. 3 Oct.
            1961; m. 1905, August Voss, b. 8 Oct. 1884,
            Clinton Co., IL; d. 23 Aug. 1952. [3]
        502-Dorothea Beltzhoover
        503-George G. Beltzhoover, b. 14 July 1886; d. Mar.
            1978, Sandoval, Marion Co., IL.
        504-Anna Beltzhoover, b. 16 Nov. 1887; d. Dec. 1978,
            unm.? Her SS was issued in MO. before 1951,
            494-09-8056
        505-Mazie Beltzhoover
        506-John Beltzhoover
        507-Edith Beltzhoover; m. _____ MATTHEWS

359-**IDA MAE BELTZHOOVER**[6] (196), b. 8 Nov. 1859, PA.; d. 7 Nov. 1951, g. Sandoval, IL. cemetery; m. 10 Oct. 1878, William LEITH, (Wilhelm Johann von der Lieth); b. 12 Aug. 1856, Basbeck, Germany; d. 12 Oct. 1932, g. Sandoval (IL) Cemetery. [4]
    Issue: (LEITH)
        508-Charles Leith[7], b. 24 July 1880; m. Henrietta
            ANDERSON
        509-Jennie Mae Leith, b. 1 Dec. 1882, m. James Henry

----

1. <u>Portrait and Biographical Record of Clinton, Washington, Marion, and Jefferson Counties, IL.</u>
Chicago 1894 Chapman Publ. Co.

2. Voss, Lisa Renee 15 May 2003

3. Voss, Lisa Renee 5/15/03

4. Moore, Joan Miller, 21 Feb. 1996

MERIDITH
510-Clarence Leith, b. 12/10/1884, m. Lillian Heister
511-Jessie Leith, b. 26 Jul 1886, m. Emitt WOOD
512-John Leith, b. 19 June 1888, m. Lizzie ANDERSON
513-Cora Leith, b. 15 Feb. 1890, William SINK/SINN
514-Annie Leith, b. 31 May 1892, Walter MARSHALL
515-Dollie Leith, b. 9 Jan. 1896, m. Relza TROUT
516-Katie Leith, b. 23 Mar. 1898, m. R. L. KLEYSTUBER
517-Nellie Leith, b.31 Mar. 1901, m. George BRUMFIELD
518-William Leith, Jr. b. 7 May 1907

360-**JENNIE BELTZHOOVER**[6] (196), b. 1860; m. Edward A. EMMIS/ENNIS, a dealer in musical instruments and they lived in Centralia, IL.
> Issue: (ENNIS)
> 519-Harry Ennis[7]
> 520-Della Ennis
> 521-Thomas Ennis
> 522-Edgar Ennis

361-**ANNIE BELTZHOOVER**[6] (196), m./1, William STEWART; m./2 Frederick BARTOLE.
> Issue: (STEWART)
> 523-Lola Stewart[7]
> From the second marriage: (BARTOLE)
> 524-Mona Bartole

362-**RACHEL ELIZABETH BELTZHOOVER**[6] (196), b. 17 Nov. 1878, IL; d. 24 May 1952. Los Angeles, CA; m. Orrin Callis, b. 1875, KS., a farmer of Spring Valley Twp., Cherokee Co., KS., s/o William Callis (b. England) and wf. M. Catherine (b. Mich.).
> Issue: (CALLIS)
> 525-Jessie Callis[7]
> 526-John William Callis

365-**THOMAS SKILES BELTZHOOVER**[6] (197), b. 5 May 1863; d. 29 July 1916; m. Jennie K. Allison, b. 1867, PA; d. 1954. In the 1920 PA census she is shown age 52 in Newville Twp., Cumberland Co., PA.
> Issue: (BELTZHOOVER)
> 527-Mary Beltzhoover[7], b. 28 Apr. 1897, d. 1 Dec. 1948; m. 20 Dec. 1922, Samuel Armstrong Johnston, b. 3 May 1898; d. 28 Jan. 1954. Children (Johnston), (1) Edyth Kathryn Johnston[8], b. 1 July 1924, m. 9 Apr. 1944, Paul E. Beard, Jr. and they had children (Beard), Susan Beard[8] and Betsy Beard[8]. [1]
> 528-Edith Beltzhoover, m. Clarence Cohick

367-**CLARA BELLE BELTZHOOVER**[6] (197), b. 12 July 1867; bpt.

----

1. Kleppenger, Stanley J. Kleppender-Clippinger-Klepinger Family History 1956, p. 111

3 Oct. 1891, d. 28 Jan. 1934, g. Newville; m. Wesley Cook Thrush. Buried next to her is W. Cook Thrush, b. 15 Nov. 1872; d. 9 Aug. 1909, Newville. She communed at the Stoughstown Evangelical Lutheran Church, Stoughstown, PA., rather regularily (although communion was celebrated only a few times per year) from 1891 through 1905. In 1895, her name appears as Clara Thrush. There is no mention of her husband's name, he must not have been a member. No marriage is listed for her. Nor are there baptism records for her children. She probably survived the congregation but did not transfer to Centerville. [1]

From somewhere there was information that this family removed to Thurmont, MD. Your compiler was unable locate any such family members in census reports. Your compilers therefore believe that this family never went to Maryland.
        Issue: (THRUSH) (children not in order)
            529-George B. Thrush[7], b. ca. 1904
            530-Edward B. Thrush, b. ca 1896
            531-Raymond B. Thrush, b. ca. 1905

369-SUSAN MAE BELTZHOOVER[6] (197), b. 1 Feb. 1872; d. 15 Aug. 1966, PA; m. Alexander C. Evelhoch, b. 24 Dec. 1866, d. 1923. Evilhoch/Evelhoch/Evilhock/Evilhawk/Uebelhack are spelling variations. Alexander Evelhoch s/o Thomas C. Evelhoch and grandson of George Evelhoch. [2]

Deanna Oklepek found Susan M. Evelhoch in the 1930 census, Carlisle, PA., widowed, age 58. The Wagner's William J. and wf. Sarah J. were renting from Susan M.
        Issue: (EVELOCH)
            532-John Evelhoch[7], b. 1891, d. 1918
            533-Susan Jane Evelhoch, b. 1893; d. 1957, m. J. William Wagner,b. 1887, d. 1949 and they had a daughter, Loretta Wagner

371-JOHN GRAHAM BELTZHOOVER[6] (197), b. 24 June 1877, m. Dessa --?--. [3]
        Issue: (BELTZHOOVER)
            534-George Beltzhoover[7]
            535-Florence Beltzhoover

372-WILLIAM SMITH BELTZHOOVER[6] (197), b. 15 June 1879; d. 17 Nov. 1959, m. Charlotte Grace 'Lottie' GOODHART, (1875-1945), dau. of Calvin GOODHART & wf., Anna Bell ALLEN. Anna Bell ALLEN was born 4 Nov. 1859, Shippensburg, PA. The Al-

----

1. Frantz, Fred Centerville Lutheran Church, Centerville, PA 1999

2. Lippert, Earl H. 2/23/03

3. Beltzhoover, Edward 2/19/99

len's came to Salisbury, MA., from England in 1639. An ancestor of this line was a Minuteman and fought at Lexington and Concord. [1]

Issue: (BELTZHOOVER) (not in order.)
536-Charlotte Grace Beltzhoover[7], m. Harold Wise
537-Reba Pauline Beltzhoover, m. Leroy T. Stammel
538-George Calvin Beltzhoover[7], b. 17 May 1911, Quarryville, PA., d. Dec. 1964, PA. Married Hazel O. Walker
539-Creedon Beltzhoover, b. 8 Oct. 1921; d. 13 Jan. 2004; m. Dorothy Shaw, n.i.

373-MARY ELIZABETH BELTZHOOVER[6] (202), b. 31 July 1847 in Cumberland Co., PA.; d. 9 Oct. 1906, Cumberland Co., PA. Mary married 15 May 1873 in Cumberland Co., PA., John Stauffer Hoover, b. 24 May 1820; d. 29 Oct. 1911. John S. Hoover m./1, Fannie R. Steman; m./2, 15 May 1873, Mary Elizabeth Beltzhoover. John Stauffer Hoover was the son of John Hoover (1798-1878) and wf. Catherine Stauffer (1800-1879). The 1880 census shows, Clayton Hoover age 27 in the household of John S. Hoover. [2]

Issue: (HOOVER)
540-Henry 'Harry' Monroe Hoover[7], b. 01 Mar. 1874; d. 06. Aug. 1939
541-George Bender Hoover, b. 23 June 1875, Cumberland Co., PA., d. 07 Dec.1952 Cumberland Co., PA., m. Fannie Irene Herr.
542-Anna Emma Laura Hoover, b. 22 Aug. 1878, Cumberland Co., PA., d. 10 Aug. 1955, m. William Knaub.
543-John Addison Hoover, b. 07 Dec. 1881, Cumberland Co., PA., d. 25 June 1947, m. Mae Weaver

374-JOHN A. BELTZHOOVER[6] (202), b. 4 Sept. 1848; d. 8 Feb. 1927, PA.(78-5-4); m. Mary Emily Brandt (1851-1910), b. 16 Sept. 1851; d. 25 Mar. 1910 (58-6-9); g. Mt. Zion Cem. Sect. L. John A. Beltzhoover purchased a lot in Boiling Springs in 1882. He built the house at 200 Walnut St., known as the "Beltzhoover House", and retired there from his farm in Monroe Townshhip. He and his family lived there for about thirty years. The home remained in the Beltzhoover Estate for many years. It was willed to his daughter Nellie Beltzhoover Meixel whose heirs sold it to Esther Shenk and Paul Miller in 1966. Mrs. Shenk made the home into two apartments. She sold it to the current owner, William Grove, in 1976. [3]

----

1. Ibid., George Beltzhoover, Indianapolis, IN

2. Burket, Jerri, Longswamp, PA. 2/13/00

3. Tritt, Richard L. and Randy Watts, Ed's. *At a Place Called Boiling Springs* pp. 95 and 95. Notable Buildings.

John A. Beltzhoover is shown as J. A. Beltzhoover and Co., "Dealers in Agricultural Implements, Hardware, Seeds, Cement, and Farmer's Supplies in general. The stationery is owned by Sarah Schultz. [1]

In the 1910 census, Ida D. Tehman, 41, was a housekeeper in John A.'s household.
> Issue: (BELTZHOOVER)
>> 544-Nellie M. Beltzhoover[7] (1879-1974), m. 1900, Jacob B. Meixel, d. 1934.

379-JOHN BELTZHOOVER LEIDIGH[6] (204), b. 19 Apr. 1852, Cumberland Co., PA., d. 9 Sept. 1921, Cumberland Co., PA., m. 13 Oct. 1870, Mattie A. Bowers, b. 16 May 1850, Cumberland Co., PA., d/o Jeremiah (Jere) Bowers. John and Mattie are buried in Mt. Zion Cemetery, Churchtown, PA. The 1880 census of Mt. Holly Springs shows John's occupation as a butcher.
> Issue: (LEIDIGH)
>> 545-George J. Leidigh[7], b. 11 Oct. 1871, Cumberland Co., PA., d. 7 June 1876 (4-7-25)
>> 546-Harry B. Leidigh, b. 14 Sept. 1873, d. 19 May 1958, Cumberland Co., PA., m. Mae Warden, b. 11 April 1873, d. 20 Jan. 1963, Cumberland Co., PA.
>> 547-Cora L. Leidigh, b. 16 Aug. 1875; m. William H. Boyd, b. 1875
>> 548-Clara B. Leidigh, b. 9 Jan. 1878, Cumberland Co., PA.; m. Curtis F. Walker.
>> 549-Myrtle Leidigh, b. 3 Nov. 1879, d. 24 Apr. 1939, m. John K. B. Brandt, b. 22 Feb. 1878, d. 4 Apr. 1952
>> 550-Mahala Leidigh
>> 551-Bessie Leidigh, d. 3 May 1912
>> 552-Norman Monroe Leidigh. b. 11 Aug. 1889; d 4 May 1969.
>> 553-Flavilla Maude Leidigh, m. Gordon Warner

381-HARRY M. LEIDIGH[6] (204), b. 26 Dec. 1861; d. 16 Oct. 1933, Cumberland Co., PA., m. 27 Dec. 1893, Clara Elizabeth Herman, b. 8 Feb. 1861; d. 23 May 1904. He was an attorney. Both are buried at Churchtown. [2] [3]
> Issue: (LEIDIGH)
>> 554-George Leidigh[7]
>> 555-Marjorie Leidigh
>> 556-Ruth Leidigh, b. 27 Dec. 1898, d. 19 Feb. 1979, Lauderhill, FL., m. John A. White.

----

1. Ibid., *A Place Called Boiling Springs*

2. Carlisle Evening Sentinel , 27 Dec. 1893, wedding of Clara E. Herman

3. Ibid., Dr. Brandt

382-**LENORA BELTZHOOVER**[6] (222), 11 in 1880, b. IN., could be Lula/Lulu Beltzhoover, b. 12 Sept. 1868, Union Twp., Porter Co., IN; d. 15 Oct. 1946 (78), wife of John M/W? Zea (1863-1945) (82), g. Graceland Cem., Valparaiso, IN.
>   Issue: (ZEA))
>   557-Earl Zea (1887-1970) of Detroit and he had a daughter, Loretta Zea Morris.
>   558-Harry Zea (1889-1965), WWI, res. Los Angeles, CA.
>   559-William J. Zea, WWI, d. 24 Dec. 1968 (76), res. Valparaiso, IN.
>   560-Olive Zea, d. 19 Jan. 1912; m. Douglas Maxwell; Ch: Virda Maxwell and Ollie Maxwell. [1] [2]

384-**CALVIN BELTZHOOVER**[6] (218a), b. 18 Dec. 1875, Indiana, m. 7 Nov. 1897, Lake Co., IN., Pearl Kent.
>   Issue: (BELTZHOOVER)
>   561-Fern Beltzhoover[7], b. 2 Sept. 1899, IN., d., 23 Mar. 1891, Los Angeles, CA., m./1, 15 April 1917, Lake Co., IN., Harry Martin Hilton, b. 29 Sept. 1894, IN., d. 2 May 1953, Siskiyoy, CA., son of Wayne Eldon Hilton and wf. --?-- Greenwalt; m,/2, after 1953, --?-- Ott, CA. (First Marriage) They had a son, Wayne E. Hilton, b. c. 1918, whose residence in Sept. 2004 is shown as, 5013 Elmdale Dr., Rolling Hills Estate, CA.

422-**AMY LOUISA KLINEFELTER**[6] (248), b. 15 May 1857, Jones Co., IA., d. 26 Oct. 1939, Kimball, NE., m. 4 Mar. 1876, Jones Co., IA., George E. EVERTSON (1855-1928), s/o Lewis EVERTSON and wf., Mary Ann TAYLOR. In June of 1883 or 1884, George EVERTSON moved with his family, three small children and a 2 mo. old baby, to Nebraska.
>   This line can be continued in The Kamp Papers Vol. II 1986 by Gayle O. Kamp.
>   Issue: (EVERTSON)
>   562-Nellie Grace Evertson[7], (1877-1931)
>   563-Evert Jay Evertson, (1878-1956)
>   564-Lee Wolford Evertson, (1880-1961)
>   565-Bertha Dale Evertson, (1881-1968)
>   566-Myrtle Jennie Evertson, (1883-1935)
>   567-Charles Edgar Evertson, (1884-1951)
>   568-Hattie Blanche Evertson, (1885-1965)
>   569-George Edgar Evertson, (1887-1955)
>   570-Sadie Adaline Evertson, (1888-1964)
>   571-Francis Elmer Evertson, (1890-1958)
>   572-Kathryn Gladys Evertson, (1892-1985)
>   573-Glenn Henry Evertson, (1894-1895) whooping cough

----

1. History of Porter County, Indiana   Vol. II, Lewis Publishing Co. Chicago 1912 pp. 683, 684.
Courtesy of Barb Nault, Porter Co., IN Library 2003

2. Graceland Cemetery, Valparaiso, IN.   Courtesy Barb Nault

574-Lulu Maude Evertson, (1896-1958)
575-Beulah May Evertson, (1898-1961)
576-Velma Zephyr Evertson (1899-1982)

Seventh Generation

431-**FRENCH RAYBURN**[7] (254), b. 14 July 1973, St. Louis, MO., d. 14 Dec. 1923, Chicago, IL.; m./1 Mary Withers RATHEL, b. 1873; m./2 Rose Celestine STEBER, b. 1873-1963).
    Issue: (RAYBURN) from the second marriage.
        577-French Rayburn[8], (1903-1985); m. Frances L. DEANE
            (1903-1995).
        578-Elsie Rayburn

442-**WILLIAM NIMICK MURRAY**[7] (270), b. ca. 1869, PA., m. Elizabeth Charliere.
    Issue: (MURRAY)
        579-Elizabeth Murray[8], m. Sidney Doolittle.

443-**FRANCIS BAILEY NIMICK**[7] (271), m. Mary Wilson SPENCER Res. Coraopolis, PA.
    Issue: (NIMICK)
        580-Francis Bailey Nimick, Jr.[8]; m./1, Eleanor Christine GRIGGS; m./2, Katherin Chew K. Leighton.
        581-Eleanor Howe Nimick
        582-Charles Spencer Nimick, m. Mary Carolyn SCHMERTZ
        583-William Kennedy Nimick
        584-David Acheson Nimick, m. June Hodgon
        585-Reade Bailey Nimick, m. Anne Simmons Cockran
        586-George Guthrie Nimick, m. Deborah Shupert

444-**THOMAS MARSHALL HOWE NIMICK**[7] (271), m. Genevieve Dorion MURTLAND.
    Issue: (NIMICK)
        587-Kathleen Murtland Nimick[8]
        588-Thomas Marshall Howe Nimick, Jr.; m. Florence Dilworth LOCKHART
        589-George Allaire Howe Nimick, m. Elizabeth WHETZEL

449-**ALEXANDER KENNEDY NIMICK, Jr.**[7] (275); m./1 Nell PIERCETON; m./2 Beatrice A. NIMICK.
    Issue: (NIMICK)
        590-Alexander Kennedy Nimick,III[8]
        591-Pierceton Nimick
        592-Coleman Nimick
    Children from the second marriage:
        593-James Nimick
        594-Florence Nimick
        595-Beatrice Nimick, m. James H. POLHEMUS and they had a son, James H. Polhemus, Jr.

452-**SILAS PRYOR BELTZHOOVER II**[7] (295), b. 1905; d. 20 Jan. 1957, (one source says he died at Castle Shannon?). He

married Bernice Badgley. [1]
     Issue: (BELTZHOOVER) (survived)
          596-B. G. (Glenda) Beltzhoover[8], m. William Malone,
               res. Baytown, TX., n.i.
          597-James Pryor Beltzhoover, res. Mexia, Limestone
               Co., TX. This is James P. Beltzhoover, Lufkin,
               Angelina, TX. James P. Beltzhoover, SS 465-92-
               3730 issued TX in 1967, b. 25 Nov. 1939; d. 21
               May 1999, resided zip 75902, Lufkin, Angelina,
               TX.

     455-GEORGE HENRY BELTZHOOVER, III, then Sr.[7] (295), b. 28
Feb. 1920, Castle Shannon, PA., d. 20 Dec. 1983 (New Haven)
Wilmington, NC.; m. 23 Aug. 1945, Harrish Co. MS., Vivian
Louise Krecker, b. 25 Apr. 1920. George and Vivian were both
in the Navy and were married 38 years, "filled with adventure
and our kids". He owned and operated General Business Servic-
es, Inc., Wilmington, NC. for ten years prior to his death.
Mr. Beltzhoover, an accountant, worked for the former Willys
Motors Inc. until 1959, when he joined Chrysler Corp.,
Intern., as Controller, South Africa. [2] [3]

     They resided in Toledo until 1959. They were in South
Africa for two years; two years in Switzerland; and 2 years in
London, England. They were members of Wesley Memorial United
Methodist Church, Wilmington, NC.
     Issue: (BELTZHOOVER)
          598-George Henry Beltzhoover, Jr., then Sr., b. 18
               Dec. 1947, Toledo, OH
          599-Ruth Ann Beltzhoover[8], b. 19 Sept. 1949, Toledo,
               OH.
          600-Barbara Louise Beltzhoover, b. 3 Nov. 1951, Tole-
               do, OH.

     456-IRENE MYRA BELTZHOOVER[7] (301),b. 4 Sept. 1904, Cin-
cinnati, OH., d. 15 Dec. 1993, m., William Kenneth Hall, b. 8
June 1906, Columbus, OH., d. 23 Sept. 1961, s/o Carl Seymour
Hall and wf. Olive Moore Hall. They were married 29 June
--?--in the Evanston Christian Church, Cincinnati, OH. Resided Columbus, OH. Both Irene and William Hall died Ft. Lauder-
dale/Pompano Beach FL., and were cremated. Irene B. Hall
m./2, 4 May 1963, Horace James 'Jack' Oldham who died in Dec.
1979.
     Issue: (HALL)
          601-David Charles Hall[8], b. 2 May 1932, Columbus OH.
               res. Rochester, NY
----

1. Ibid., Vivian Beltzhoover, Wilmington, NC 7/97

2. The Blade , Toledo Ohio, Tues. Jan 3, 1984

3. Ibid., Vivian Beltzhoover 7/97

602-Donald Seymour Hall, b. 3 June 1940, Columbus, OH., res. Rochester, N. Y.

457-**JANE ELIZABETH BELTZHOOVER**[7] (301), b. 10 Dec. 1912, m. 29 June 1940, Henry James Ziegenfelder, Cincinnati, OH. They were married in the Evanston Christian Church, Cincinnati, OH. Heny Ziegenfelder b. 2 Nov. 1908, d. 16 Aug. 2001, Cincinnati, OH., g. Hyde Park Community Methodist Church, Columbus, OH., cremated, s/o Thomas Ziegenfelder and wf., Caroline Heist Ziegenfelder. [1]

Mrs. Jane Beltzhoover Ziegenfelder wrote, "My grandmother, Amelia, my Mother Myra, my sister and I used to travel by Ohio River Boat from Cincinnati to Pittsburgh to meet an 'Aunt Mary' who lived in Beltzhoover Borough. She was old and could have been Amelia's aunt? or my grandfather's aunt."

Your compiler/researcher feels that this was probably the widow of Jane's grandfather's brother, Silas Pryor Beltzhoover, one Mary E. Harris Beltzhoover (b. 1860) who carried on the grocery business after Silas P.'s death in 1915. Mary carried on the business with her son and daughter.
Issue: (ZIEGENFELDER)
603-Dale Thomas Ziegenfelder[8], b. 12 April 1951, Cincinnati

459-**GEORGE McCOOK BELTZHOOVER**[7] (302), b. 22 Sept. 1911; d. 11 Jan. 1965 (53), of cancer in Christ Hospital (burial was authorized by Mrs. Mary Beltzhoover), his wife, g. Rest Haven Memorial Park Cem.; m. 27 June 1934, Mary Margaret Mueller, who was b. 14 May 1914; d. 3 Dec. 1988. Her last residence was zip 45152, Morrow, Warren Co., OH. George attended Withrow High School, Cincinnati and later went to the Ohio Mechanical Institute and became an electrician.

George McCook Beltzhoover, on his Soc. Sec. application, Nov. 24, 1936, gave his employer as Acacia Mutual Life, Washington, D. C. (Cincinnati Branch). He named his father as, John Dixon Beltzhoover and his mother as, Myrtle M. Tomlinson and his birth date as 22 Sept. 1911.

Myrtle M. Tomlinson Beltzhoover's obit 20 Oct. 1955, states that her son, George Betzhoover, Morrow, OH., VP Beltzhoover Electric Co. George worked for Beltzhoover Electric in Cincinnati until about 1960 when he opened Bel-Wood Country Club near Morrow.

Rhea Hughes writes that she did not know exactly who laid out the course at Bel-Wood, but a man named Taylor Boyd helped her father build (and I guess designed it).
----

1. Dale Bible Records. Courtsey Mrs. Jane Beltzhoover Ziegenfelder 2001

The Cincinnati Enquirer 12/5/88 C 4:1, reported that Mary Mueller Beltzhoover owned and operated the Bel-Wood Country Club in Morrow from 1965 to 1979. George and Mary Mueller lived from 1950 until their deaths in Morrow, OH.

Her daughter Rhea B. Hughes reported that she was a marvelous woman. She added that although her mother ran a country club she did not play golf. She was the offical hostess. The obit. continues to report that she left a dau. Rhea B. Hughes and a son, John D. Beltzhoover of Morrow; a sister, Ruth M. Oettinger, of Lakeside and a brother, Donald R. Mueller of Piedmont, CA., and three grandchildren.

Mrs. Mary Beltzhoover R#2 Box 326, Morrow, OH, 45152 authorized the burial of John D. Beltzhoover in Rest Haven Mem. Cem. John D. was her deceased husband's father.

Issue: (BELTZHOOVER)

604-Rhea Jeanne Beltzhoover[8], b. 30 Mar. 1939, m. Charles Evans Hughes, res. Brookville, IN.

605-John Dixon Beltzhoover 'J. D.', b. 19 May 1941.

460-JAMES STEWART PEACH[7] (305) (1871-1929), m. Hannah Massing (1871-1942).

Issue: (PEACH)

606-Robert Peach[8] (1896-1947), m. Betty Gorse (1907-1998)

607-Anna Peach (1899-), m. David Williams

608-Louis Peach (1907-1974), m. Mildred Miller

609-Margaret Peach (1905-1905)

610-Elmer Peach (1907-1909)

611-Elizabeth Beltzhoover Peach (1903-1927), m. David Williams. He married first Elizabeth B. Peach and then Anna Peach.

612-James Peach (1910-), m. Irma Beiler

461-BYRON PEACH[7] (305) (1873-), m. 1900, Margaret Jane Swisher (1879-).

Issue: (PEACH)

613-Lorina (Edna) Peach[8], (1901-), m. Byron Haley

614-Clara Peach (1904-)

615-Lucille Peach (1908-)

616-Margaret Peach (1910-)

462-HUGH WOOD PEACH[7] (305), b.31 May 1876, m. Cora Belle Schaub (1878-)

Issue: (PEACH) (children not in order)

617-Milton Oliver Peach Dr.[8], b. 15 May 1910, d. 12 Sept. 2003, m./1, Nov. 1941, Frances Seese; m./2, Virginia McQuiston.

618-Virginia E. Peach (1911-), m. Elmer Miller

619-Olive Marie Peach, m. Donald Campbell

620-Clifford Allen Peach (1909-1939), m. Dorothea Erbe

621-Gladys Belle Peach (1917-)

463-**ROBERT FOSTER PEACH**[7] (305), m./1,Teresa Weigand (1880-): m./2 Lillian Gertrude Best (1879-). They had a son.
Issue: (PEACH)
622-a boy Peach[8]

466-**ETHEL GERTRUDE THOMAS**[7] (318), b. 18 Dec. 1884, TN; d. 29 Oct. 1960, Cumberland Co., TN., m. 1904, Walter Gabriel Rowland, b. 15 Feb. 1881, d. 29 June 1967, TN.
Issue: (ROWLAND)
623-Stephen Thomas Rowland[8], b. 9 June 1904, TN., m. Bessie Mae Harris.
624-Roger Graden Rowland, b. 3 Sept. 1907; m. Annie Elizabeth Sykes, b. 1912.
625-George Walker Rowland, b. 18 Feb. 1909, Tn., d. 21 May 1909.
626-Leonard Ralph Rowland, b. 10 May 1910, d. June 1964; m. 1930, Eunice Olivia Mickel, b. 1908.
627-Woodrow Allison Rowland, b. 1912, TN; m. 1943, Margaret Rosalie Rawson, b. 1943.
628-Kenneth Vernon Rowland, b. 16 April 1916; m. 1944, div., Agnes Jane Mickel.
629-Austin Wilbur Rowland, b. 10 May 1923, TN., m. Doris Jean Boyd.

467-**JOHN HILL THOMAS**[7] (318), (1886-1976), m. 1910, Mary Johnson Parchman (1893-1971).
Issue: (THOMAS) not in order.
630-Louise Dora Thomas[8], b. 1911, d. 2001, m. 1930, John Thurman Wilson, b. 1905; d. 1991.
631-Leonard Ellis Thomas (1913-1996), m. 1935, Christine Suggs (1915-1973)
632-Bessie May Thomas (1914-1980), m. Garland Edgar Lyle, b. (1912-1988).
633-Alice Elizabeth Thomas (1916-1918)
634-Velma Nannie Thomas (1918-), m. 1938, Rev. James Max Sykes (1912-1998).
635-this number voided.
636-John Alvin Thomas (1919-1975), m. Dorothy Ora Morgan (1920-1999).
637-Margaret Gertrude Thomas (1921-1988), m. 1941, Carlos Dexter Moore.

468-**LOUIS ORVILLE THOMAS**[7] (318) (1889-1976); m. 1922, Lottie Ione Clifford (1894-1987).
Issue: (THOMAS)
638-Louis Orville Thomas, Jr.[8] . b. 1931; m./1, 1961, Lavada Henegar, b. 1925: m./2 1978, Donna June Allen, b. 1951

469-**FANNIE E. THOMAS**[7] (318), (1890-1977); m. 1915, Lawrence M. Jackson (1887-1956).
Issue: (JACKSON)
639-Lawrence M. Jackson, Jr.[8] (1921-1970); m. 1946,

Dorothy Virginia Schichtel (1921-1996)

470-**WILLIAM THORNTON THOMAS**[7] (318), (1894-1955); Myrtle
Mae Vaughn (1896-1971).
Issue: (THOMAS)
    640-Finas Malone Thomas[8] b. 1916; m./1 Minnie Lee
        Powers, div., m./2 Dorothy Rae McGilton, div.,
        m./3, 1951, Helen Louise Lancaster, (1923-
        1990).
    641-Geneva Mae Thomas, b. (1919-1983); m. 1940, Ralph
        Clarence Shofner (1912-1986).

472-**KNOX BRYAN THOMAS**[7] (318) (1898-1983), m. 1022, Offie
Ethel Clark, (1903-1997).
Issue: (THOMAS)
    642-Alice Ruth Thomas[8] , b. 1923, m. 1942, George
        Edward Sanford, Rev., d. 2004.
    643-Gladys Ione Thomas, (1924-2001); m. 1944, Leo
        Dean Echelbarger (1922-).
    644-Baby Thomas (1926-1926)
    645-Knox Thomas, Jr., (1929-1995); m. 1947, Charlene
        Martha Abernathy, b. 1930.

473-**NANNIE MAGDALENE THOMAS**[7] (318) (1900-1983), m. 1923,
Herbert Rodney Averitt (1899-1976).
Issue: (AVERITT)
    646-Thomas Rodney Averitt[8], (1923-1943)
    647-Audrey Gertrude Averitt, (1925-1967); m. Howard
        Patterson
    648-Martha Frances Averitt, b. 1927, m. Wallace Carney
        Harris, b. 1913.
    649-Mary Estalene Averitt, b. 1929; m. William Carlyle
        Patterson, b. 1921
    650-Eloise Eugenia Averitt, b. 1932, m. Earl Thomas
        Allison (1918-1993)

475-**ERIC DEWITT THOMAS, Col.**[7] (318) (1906-1973), m. 1928
Ella Mae Paige, (1900-1984). He retired from USAF in 1964.
Issue: (THOMAS)
    651-Madeline Mussette Thomas[8] (1929-1929)
    652-Louella Saundra Thomas, b. 1937, m/1, 1958, div.,
        John Allen Burnett, b. 1937.
    653-Deanna Nedra Thomas, b. 1942, m. 1965, Milan
        Gustav Oklepek, b. 1929.

476-**BUFORD EVANS THOMAS**[7] (318) (1908-1971), m. Mabel
Idel Stavley, (1908-2001).
Issue: (THOMAS)
    654-Nelda Jo Thomas[8],b. 1937. m./1, 1957, div., Hunter
        Campbell Harrell, b. 1937; m./2, 1977, Melvin
        Eugene Kersey, n.i.

477-**CHARLES FRENCH THOMAS**[7] (318), (1911-2000); m. 1941,
Sarah Louise Ash, b. 1917-1998).

Issue: (THOMAS)

    655-John Charles Thomas[8], b. 1946; m. Audrey Nell An-
        haiser, b, 1947.

    656-Patricia French Thomas, b. 1952, m. Richard Dean
        Hodge.

479-**LEONARD DUNBAR SNEDEKER**[7] (327), b. 23 Dec. 1907,
Brooklyn, NY.; d. Jan. 1988, Brooklyn, NY; m., 1936, Beatrice
Bishell, b. 12 Jan. 1907, Ipswick, England.

    Issue: (SNEDEKER)

    657-Robert Dunbar Snedeker[8], b. 13 Jan. 1943, New
        York, NY.

    658-Jane Grayston Snedeker, b. 30 June 1947, New York,
        NY.

480-**VIRGINIA M. SNEDEKER**[7] (327), b. 25 Nov. 1909, Brooklyn, NY.; m. 1942, William L. Taylor.

    Issue: (TAYLOR)

    659-Jean Dunbar Taylor[8], b. 5 Aug. 1946

    660-Robert Bell Taylor, b. 12 May 1948, New York, NY.

481-**GEORGE SNEDEKER**[7] (327), b. 14 June 1911, Brooklyn,
NY.; m. 1941, Gladys M. Knapp.

    Issue: (SNEDEKER)

    661-George Knapp Snedeker[8], b. 3 Nov. 1942, Ayer, MA.,
        d. 8 Mar. 1981; m. 2 Mar. 1962, Janice Mae
        Colquitt, b. 15 May 1942, Columbus, GA.

    662-James Leonard Snedeker, b. 6 Dec. 1943; d. 31 Dec.
        1943.

    663-Donald Charles Snedeker, b. 16 July 1946

482-**RICHARD STOCKTON SNEDEKER**[7] (327), b. 14 Apr. 1927,
Brooklyn, NY; m. 27 Sept. 1952, Mary Ellen Burroughs, b. 20
June 1929, Spring Lake, NJ.

    Issue: (SNEDEKER)

    664-Mary Jenkins Snedeker[8], b. 10 June 1954, Prince-
        ton, NJ., m. 27 Aug. 1977, William Kevin Dugan,
        b. 1946.

    665-Katherine Annis Snedeker, b. 24 Jan. 1956; d. 26
        Jan. 1956.

    666-James Peter Snedeker, b. 24 Apr. 1959, Princeton,
        NJ.

    667-Amy Elizabeth Snedeker, b. 12 Nov. 1960, Prince-
        ton, NJ.

483-**GEOFFREY MONTGOMERY TALBOT JONES**[7] (329), b. 12 Oct.
1919, Newport, R. I.; m. Mary --?--, div.

    Issue: (JONES)

    668-Kiley Christopher Talbot Jones[8], b. 6 June 1967,
        New York, NY.

484-**MELCHIOR ROCH BELTZHOOVER, Jr.**[7] (333), b. 5 Jan.
1918, d. 14 Mar. 2002, Natchez, g. Natchez City, Cemetery; m.
11 Sept. 1940, Mary Jane BUTLER, b. 23(22?) Sept. 1918, Mc-

Comb, Pike Co., MS., d. 11 Aug. 1995, Natchez, d/o Bertram Eugene Butler & wf. Mamie Gaye "Mom" Komrunpf. [1]

Family information is that they ran off and were married in Bude, MS.

Issue: (BELTZHOOVER)

669-Melchior Roch Beltzhoover III[8], b. 5 Mar. 1954, Natchez, MS.; m. 20 June 2000, Sherry French-Gardner.

485-RUTH AUDLEY BRITTON BELTZHOOVER[7] (333), b. 22 Aug. 1921, Natchez, Adams Co., MS., d. 12 Sept. 1996, Richmond, Madison Co., KY., g. Natchez City Cem.; m. 17 Dec. 1944, Natchez, MS., Richard Ellis CONNER, III, b. 22 Jan. 1917, Vickburg, Warren Co., MS., d. 14 Mar. 1955, Tuscaloosa, AL., s/o Richard Ellis Conner, Jr., and wife, Caroline Routh Williams. [2]

Issue: (CONNER)

670-Ruth Audley Britton Conner[8], b. 21 Sept. 1946, Natchez

671-Aylett Buckner Conner, b. 16 Sept. 1947, Vicksburg, MS.

672-Richard Ellis Conner, IV, b. 6 Nov. 1951, Natchez

673-Dennison Macrery Conner, b. 23 Sept. 1954, Bay Shore, L. I., NY.

674-Anne Gaillard Conner, b. 18 Aug. 1956, Natchez

675-William Beltzhoover Conner, b. 12 May 1961, Mobile, Mobile Co., AL.

486-VIRGINIA LEE BELTZHOOVER[7] (333), b., at 'Green Leaves' 19 Nov. 1926, bpt. First Presbyterian Church, Natchez, MS.; m. 15 Jan. 1950 at Natchez, George MORRISON Jr., b. 25 Mar. 1923, New Orleans, LA., d. 27 Aug. 1993, Natchez, s/o George Morrison & wf. Bertha Elizabeth Evans. [3]

Green Leaves Mansion, Natchez, MS., has been owned and lived in by the family since 1849. Mrs. Virginia Beltzhoover Morrison's grandmother was born here during the Civil War. In the spring and again in the fall some of these mansions are open for touring by tourists. [4]

Issue: (MORRISON) (all children born Natchez, MS)

676-George Beltzhoover Morrison[8], b. 24 Nov. 1950

677-Ann Borodell Morrison, b. 12 April 1953

678-Joie Stanton Morrison, b. 14 Nov.1959, chr. Easter

----

1. Conner, William Beltzhoover May 2002

2. Conner, William Beltzhoover, May 2002

3. Virginia Lee Beltzhoover Morrison information to Mrs. Francis Nimick.

4. USA News Thurs. Aug. 12, 1993 *Step Back into History in Natchez, MS*   .

1960,, Trinity Episcopal Church, Natchez, MS., n.i.
679-Daniel Beltzhoover Morrison, b. 8 Dec. 1964, Natchez, m. 31 Jan. 1997, Uta Schaefer.
680-William Beltzhoover Morrison, b. 5 Nov. 1968

487-VIRGINIA LEE ROBINSON[6] (334), b. 5 June 1921, Irvington, NY.; d. 14 Feb. 1991; m. 1942, Weymouth Stone Kirkland, b. 1919.

Issue: (KIRKLAND)
681-Weymouth Stone Kirkland, Jr.[7], b. 10 Aug. 1942, Tarryton, NY.
682-Guy Robinson Kirkland, b. 16 Apr. 1948, Chicago
683-Virginia Lee Kirkland, b. 21 Apr. 1949, Chicago

488-ANNE ROANE ROBINSON[7] (334), b. 25 Jan. 1925, Irvington, NY.; d. 19 July 1989, Princeton, NJ.; m. 18 Mar. 1950, William Thomas McCleery.

Issue: (McCLEERY)
684-Samuel Adams McCleery[8]

492-GEORGE MORRIS BELTZHOOVER Jr.[7] (352), b. 22 Mar. 1880, Shepherdstown, WV, s/o the late George M. Beltzhoover and wf., Lucy Entler. George M. Beltzhoover, Jr., (78) retired lawyer of Brucetown, d. 13 Apr. 1958 at the Winchester Memorial Hospital. [1] [2]

Mr. Beltzhoover graduated from Shepherd College and then from West Virginia Univ. into law in 1899. He played football for WVU and kicked left footed. He was very left handed. He opened his law office in Charles Town in 1901 at the age of 21. He appeared before the highest courts in VA., MD., NC., FL., and WV. He was a veteran of WWI. He was survived by his wife, Miss Corrie B. Swimley, of Brucetown, whom he m./2, 1948. Funeral services were held in his home, by Rev. George D. Jackson, Pastor of the First Presbyterian Church. Internment Mt. Hebron Cemetery, Winchester, VA. Corrie Swimley Beltzhoover, b. 30 June 1891; d. Nov. 1969, VA. Her residence at her death was 22622 Brucetown, Frederick, VA. [3]

G. M. Beltzhoover, Jr., m./1, 22 June 1910, Bessie Davis Baker Beltzhoover, Charles Town, WV.; b.31 July 1873; d. Friday May 23 1947 (73). she was born in Jefferson Co., WV., d/o Capt. Eugene Baker and wf., Anna Wiltshire Baker of the Leetown community Her father was for several years sheriff of Jefferson County. Her grandfather was Joseph Baker; g. Edge

----

1. <u>Winchester Evening Star</u>, Monday Apr. 14, 1958

2. Butzner, Mrs. William Jr. (Catherine Tod Beltzhoover)

3. Social Security Record ssn 229-60-1730 issued in VA. in 1962

Hill Cemetery, Charles Town, WV. [1]

Bessie Beltzhoover spent some time in a Baltimore Hospital prior to her death. She was active in several organizations, Charles Town Woman's Club, U.D.C., Democratic Executive Committee, and Secy., of the Committee. She was a member of the Baptist Church. She was survived by her daughter, Mrs. William W. Butzner, Jr., and a brother, Dr. Charles L. Baker of Augusta, GA. The funeral was held in her home. [2]

Catherine Tod Beltzhoover Butzner in correspondence with your compiler answered the question, "your great-uncle Frank, was the Congressman from Carlisle?" right. "he never married, right?" Correct. This last that he did not marry is in error your compiler believes.

Issue: (BELTZHOOVER)

685-Catherine Tod Beltzhoover[8], b. 3 Aug. 1911

501-CLARA E. BELTZHOOVER[7] (358), b. 17 Feb. 1878; d. 3 Oct. 1961; m. 1905, August Voss, b. 8 Oct. 1884, Clinton Co., IL; d. 23 Aug. 1952.

Issue: (VOSS)

686-Walter Richard Voss[8], b. 1 Mar. 1912; d. 22 Aug. 1979, Marion Co., IL; m. Mar. 1935, Flossie Carlyle, b. 7 June 1979, Marion Co., IL., d. 17 May 1981, Madison Co., IL. Harry Eugene Voss, son of Walter and Flossie Voss, b. 30 Sept. 1935, Clinton Co., IL; d. 21 July 2002, St. Clair Co., IL.,; m. 4 Feb. 1960, Marion Co., IL., Mary Alice Edwards, b. 10 June 1940, Clinton Co., IL. They had a daughter, Lisa Renee Voss, b. 23 Nov. 1960, Marion Co., IL. [3]

509-JENNIE MAE LEITH[7] (359), b. 1 Dec. 1883; d. 16 July 1966, Centralia, IL., g. Sandoval Cem.; m. 27 Oct. 1904, Salem, Marion Co., IL., James Henry MERIDITH, b. 28 Mar. 1878, Carrigan Twp., Marion Co., IL.; d. 10 Oct. 1965, Odin, IL, g. Sandoval Cem., s/o William MERIDITH and wf. Sarah SPITLER. [4]

Issue: (MERIDITH)

687-Elsie Mae Meridith[8], b. 28 Nov. 1905, Sandoval, Marion Co., IL; m. 10 May 1925, Cecil HICKS

688-Martha Marie Meridith, b. 28 Dec. 1906, Marion Co., IL; m. 10 Oct. 1925, George Newton SMITH.

689-Margaret Fern Meridith, b. 16 Sept. 1908; d. 8

----

1. Ibid., Butzner, Mrs. William Jr.

2. Farmers Advocate   Wed. May 28, 1947. Charles Town, WV.

3. Voss, Lisa Renee 5/15/03

4. Moore, Joan M. Salem, IL 2/96

July 1909, g. Sandoval Cem.
        690-Helen Genevive Meridith, b. 10 April 1910, d. 20
            July 1910
        691-James William Meridith, b. 26 Aug. 1912; d. Mar.
            1978; m. 10 May 1934, Eunice M. SNYDER.   All
            Marion Co., IL.
        692-Dorothy Viola Meridith, b. 11 Oct. 1914; m. 19
            Dec. 1933, Harry Lee LUSCH
        693-Juanita Lucille Meridith, b. 26 Feb. 1918, m. Jan.
            1935, Ray Everett Miller. 10 ch.
        694-Irma Jean Meridith, b. 17 Mar. 1920; m. 15 May
            1937, Fred KLEYSTUBER/KLEYSTEUBER.
        695-Richard Harold Meridith, b. 20 Jan. 1923, a twin,
            Sandoval, IL.; m. 20 Feb. 1947, Univ. Church,
            Champaign, IL. Martha TELLING, m./2 Jean ALF.
        696-Russell Darrell Meridith, b. 20 Jan. 1923, a twin,
            Sandoval, IL., d. 28 Nov. 1996, Marion, IL.; m.
            24 Sept. 1944 at Carbondale, IL., m./1, Kathern
            Marie BUSH. [1]

        510-**CLARENCE NORWOOD LEITH**[7] (359), b. 10 Dec. 1884, IL.,
d. 26 June 1966, Wichita, KS., g. Kingman, KS.; m. 01 July
1917, at Robinson, IL., Lillian Gladys Heister, b. 4 Mar.
1898, Auglaize Co., OH., d. 01 Dec. 1995, Wichita, KS. [2]
        Issue:
        697-Hester Alberta Leith[8], b. 13 Apr. 1918, Robinson,
            IL., d. 13 Apr. 1918, Robinson, IL.
        698-Clarence Edwin Leith, b. 16 June 1919, Midian,
            KS., d, 31 Oct. 1999, Wichita, KS., m. Nellie
            Mae Baker.
        699-Vivian Geraldine Leith, b. 12 Sept. 1923, Midian,
            KS.

        533-**SUSAN JANE EVELHOCH**[7] (369), b. 1893; d. 1951; m. J.
William Wagner (1887-1949).
        Issue: (WAGNER)
        700-Loretta Wagner[8]

        536-**CHARLOTTE GRACE BELTZHOOVER**[7] (372), m. Harold Wise
        Issue: (WISE)
        701-Jerry Wise[8]

        537-**REBA PAULINE BELTZHOOVER**[7] (372), m. 5 Nov. 1925, York
Co., PA., Leroy T. Stammel, b. 22 Dec. 1894; d. July 1976.
Res. Harrisburg, Dauphin Co., PA. In the 1930, PA census he
and Pauline are shown in Souh Middleton Twp., Cumberland Co.,
PA.
        Issue: (STAMMEL)
----

1. Meridith, Roger

2. Devor, Craig Warren

        702-Ron Stammel[8]
        703-Bob Stammel

    538-**GEORGE CALVIN BELTZHOOVER**[7] (372), b. 17 May 1911, Quarryville, PA., d. Dec. 1964, PA, g. Mt. Zion Cemetery Sect. L., m. Hazel Odella WALKER, b. 4 Jan 1909, Centerville, PA., d. 15 Jan. 2002, d/o Hiram WALKER and wf., Annie PENNER. [1][2]

    George Calvin Beltzhoover signed his Soc. Sec. application 26 Dec. 1951, as Geo. C. Beltzhoover, b. 17 May, 1911, at RFD, Bucks, PA., s/o William S. Beltzhoover and Charlotte Grace Goodhart, he resided at 1001 N. West St., Carlisle, PA., self employed.

    George Calvin Beltzhoover was County Commissioner, Cumberland Co., PA., 1956-1984; County Treasurer 1951-1956; President & COB PA. Grocers Assn.,
        Issue: (BELTZHOOVER)
            704-Delores Corinne 'Dotty' Beltzhoover[8], b. 10 June
                1929, m. Dale Morrow.
            705-Phyllis Eileen Beltzhoover, b. 25 Oct. 1930, Hano-
                ver, PA., d. 2 Nov. 1930, Hanover, g. Center-
                ville, PA
            706-George Edward Beltzhoover, b. 22 May 1932, m. Rita
                Ruscin.
            707-Janice Marie Beltzhoover, b. 12 Mar. 1934, m.
                George Waricher.
            708-Kay Lavonne Beltzhoover, b.15 Feb. 1937, m. Elwood
                Kaylor.
            709-Richard Lee Beltzhoover, b. 3 Feb. 1940, Carlisle,
                PA
            710-Carole Ann Beltzhoover, b. 23 Oct. 1941, m. Don
                Schwartz.
            711-Bonita Raye Beltzhoover, b. 24 Oct. 1943, m. Skip
                Kuhns.

    540-**HENRY 'HARRY' MONROE HOOVER**[7] (373). b. 1 Mar. 1874, d. 6 Aug. 1939, m. 1894; m. 24 Dec. 1894, New Kingston, Cumberland Co., PA., Sarah Jane Knaub, b. 16 Oct. 1876, d. 2 June 1945, the daughter of Daniel Knaub and wf. Agness Pentz. Sarah Jane Knaub, christened, buried, Mt. Zion Cem. Churchtown, Cumberland Co., PA.
        Issue: (HOOVER)
            712-Ethel Hoover[8], b. 19 June 1896, d. 17 Dec. 1988,
                m. 20 July 1915, Logan Pechart.
            713-Emily Irene Hoover, b. 2 Feb. 1899, Cumberland,
                PA., d. 13 Feb. 1972, Shepherdstown, Cumberland

----

1. Ibid., George Beltzhoover, Indianapolis, IN

2. Ibid., Beltzhoover, Edward 2/19/99

Co., PA

714-John Henry Hoover, b. 12 June 1901, Cumberland
Co., PA., d. 24 Dec. 1996, S. Middleton Twp.,
Cumberland Co., PA.
715-Pearl Elizabeth Hoover, b. 25 Dec. 1904, Cumberland Co., PA., d. 22 Feb. 1978, Cumberland Co.,
PA., m. 24 Sept. 1921, Gordon Cullings.
716-William Ray Hoover, b. 10 Oct. 1906, Cumberland
Co., PA., d. 30 Dec. 1921, Cumberland Co., PA.
William Ray Hoover, Christened, bur. Mt. Zion
Cem., Cumberland Co., PA.
717-Clair Monroe Hoover, b. 02 May 1909, d., 11 Feb.
1977, m. Sept. 1931, Carrie Myers.
718-June Isobel Hoover, b. 09 June 1912, m. 20 Sept.
1943, Clarence Weigle.
719-Lila Iona Hoover, b. 18 June 1916, Cumberland Co.,
PA., m. 05 Dec. 1933, Charles E. Moore.
720-a voided number, not used

544-NELLIE M. BELTZHOOVER[7] (374), m. Jacob B. MEIXEL. In 1900 Jacob and Nellie Beltzhoover Meixel were deeded the "Asbury Derland House" in Boiling Springs, when they took up residence there as newlyweds. The house was sold at auction for $3805. to satisfy Derland debts. The home was known as "Oak Hall". Mr. Meixel died in 1934, but his widow remained in the house and maintained it until 1974, when she died at the age of 95. [1] [2]

Jacob B. Meixel was the son of Jacob H. Meixel, b. 22 Jan. 1846 and wf. Clara Bricker, d/o Peter Bricker.
Issue: (MEIXEL)
721-Rhae B. Meixel (Mrs. Elias H. Otto), b. 1902.
Elias H. Otto, b. ca. 1893. PA.
722-Emily Beltzhoover Meixel, deceased by 1976, b.
1904
723-Nellie M. Meixel (Mrs. James Brymesser, b., 1912
724-Sarah Beltzhoover Meixel, b. 1914, m. Lawrence
Schultz, and they resided in the house. The
oak tree was more than 11 feet in circumfer-
ence.

546-HARRY B. LEIDIGH[7] (379), b. 14 Sept. 1873, Cumberland Co., PA., d. 19 May 1958, Cumberland Co., PA., m. Mae Warden, b. 11 April 1873, d. 20 Jan. 1963, Cumberland Co., PA. For many years Harry worked as a butcher in Mt. Holly Springs and later in the meat department of Swigert's Grocery in Carlisle. They were members of the Lutheran Church.

----

1. Ibid., *In a Place Called Boiling Springs* p. 98

2. Historic South Middleton Township   Bicentennial Celebration of Boiling Springs and Surrounding
South Middleton Area. 1976 p.75

Mae Warden d/o George and Sarah GENSLER WARDEN.

Harry and Mae are buried in Mt. Holly Springs Cem., Mt. Holly Springs, PA.

Issue: (LEIDIGH)

725-Luther Linwood Leidigh[8], b. 24 Oct. 1895, Cumberland Co. PA., d. 4 Aug. 1977, Cumberland Co., PA., m. Grace Reed, b. 9 Mar. 1903, d. 29 Aug. 1979, Cumberland Co., PA. He served in WWI. Both bur. Mt. Holly Springs Cem. n. i.

726-Vaughn Warden Leidigh, b. 27 Sept. 1897, Mt. Holly Springs, d. 14 Jan. 1987, Camp Hill, PA., m. 21 Jan. 1920, Florence Edna Horning, b. 28 May 1899, Harrisburg, PA., d. 4 April 1977.

727-Brenda Mae Leidigh, b. 21 Dec. 1899, Cumberland Co., d. 20 June 1993, Cumberland Co., PA; m. June 1920, William Brillhart, b.26 April 1898.

728-William Irwin Leidigh, b. 14 May 1903, Cumberland Co., PA., d. 10 Nov. 1911, g. Mt. Holly Springs Cem.

729-George Leidigh, b. 30 Dec. 1901; d. 14 May 1902, d. y.

730-Harry Frederick Leidigh, b. 27 June 1905, Cumberland Co., PA., d. 19 Sept. 1905, g. Mt. Holly Springs Cem.

731-Richard Owen Leidigh, b. 27 Dec. 1906, Mt. Holly Springs, PA, d. 16 April 1988, Baltimore, MD; m. 2 Jan. 1930, Mary Jane Davis, b. 11 Sept. 1905, Carlisle, Cumberland Co., PA.

732-Thomas B. Leidigh, b. 27 June 1909, Cumberland Co., PA., d. ca. 1978, Cumberland Co., PA.; m./1 --?--, m./2 Betty Gesser.

733-Robert Irwin Leidigh, b. 30 Oct. 1911, Carlisle, PA., d. 22 Dec. 1979; m. Mae Elizabeth Kerrigan, b. 15 Oct. 1908, Baltimore, MD., d. 6 June 1988.

734-Edwin R. Leidigh, b. 27 Dec. 1915, Cumberland Co., PA., d. after 13 June 1916, Cumberland Co., PA.

547-**CORA L. LEIDIGH**[7] (379), b. 16 Aug. 1875, m. William H. Boyd, b. 16 Aug. 1875.

Issue: (BOYD)

735-Pauline BOYD[8]

548-**CLARA B. LEIDIGH**[7] (379), b. 9 Jan. 1878 Cumberland Co., PA., d. 1968; m. Curtis F. Walter, b. 1865, d. 1945.

Issue: (WALTER)

736-Lila Walter[8]
737-Albertus Walter

552-**NORMAN MONROE LEIDIGH**[7] (379), n. 11 Aug. 1889. Monroe Twp., Cumberland Co., PA., d. 4 May. 1969, g. Mt. Holly Springs Cem. Mt. Holly Springs, PA: m. 1909. Lillie Irene March, b. 6 Apr. 1889, d. 20 Feb. 1985, Cumberland Co., PA.,

g. Mt. Holly Springs Cem.   Norman Leidigh was a motorman on the historic 'Trolly to Holly'. He was born in Monroe Twp., and a member of the Lutheran Church. He was a painter and restored antique furniture. As a young man he worked in his father's restaurant in Mt. Holly Springs. Patrons of the restaurant remember him for his turtle soup, escalloped oysters and pan-fried chicken. He excelled as a drummer in the Mt. Holly Springs Liberty Band.

Lillie was born in Cumberland Co., PA., the daughter of Sterrett and Mary Ann FINKENBINDER MARCH. At the time of her death, she was the oldest member of the Mt. Holly Springs Evangelical Lutheran Church. Lillie was a quiet lady, remembered for her homemade cooking. People commented to her children that they recalled her dressing up in big hats with flowers, white gloves, etc. They are both buried in Mt. Holly Springs Cemetery.   [1]

Issue: (LEIDIGH)
738-Paul Monroe Leidigh, Jr.[8], b. 13 Aug. 1909, Mt. Holly Springs, PA.; m. Louise Margaret Thomas.
739-Mary Amanda Leidigh, b. 23 Oct. 1912, m. 28 Aug. 1938, Charles Andrew Kennedy, b. 5 May 1908, York Springs, PA., d. 9 Nov. 1988. n.i.
740-Bernice March Leidigh, b. 17 Jan. 1922, m. 28 Aug. 1943, Conrad Clifford Janashak, b. 2 May 1917, Virginia, MN., d. 28 Apr. 1989, Carlisle, PA., n.i.

553-**FLAVILLA MAUDE LEIDIGH**[7] (379), m. Gordon Warner
Issue: (WARNER)
741-Helen Warner[8]
742-Ethel Warner
743-Boyd Warner

556-**RUTH LEIDIGH**[7] (381), b. 27 Dec. 1898, d. 19 Feb. !979, Lauderhill, FL., g. Westlawn Memorial Garden Mausoleum, Ft. Lauderdale, FL., m. John A. White.

Ruth was a graduate of Carlisle High School and Dickinson College.
Issue: (WHITE)
744-John A. White, Jr.[8], res. Columbia, MS
745-Samuel B. White, res. Livingston, TX
746-Ruth W. White, m. --?-- Grosz, Mechanicsburg, PA

Eighth Generation

572-**KATHRYN GLADYS EVERTSON**[8] (422) (1892-1985), m.   13 May 1916, Cheyenne, WY., Earl B. CASS, b. 19 Sept 1889, d. 8 Dec. 1975, Ft. Wayne, IN., g. Garden of Memory, Huntington

----

1. Ibid., Frick, Ruth

Co., IN.
    Issue: (CASS)
        747-Earl L. Cass[9] b. 30 Mar. 1917, Kimball Co., NE; d.
            29 Jan. 1990, Decatur, IN; m. Virginia BUNCE
        748-Thelma Louisa Cass, b. 6 Nov. 1919, Kimball Co.,
            NE
        749-Doyleen Kathryn Cass, b. 24 Nov. 1932, Huntington,
            IN; d. 17 Feb. 1987, Fort Wayne, IN, res.
            Huntington, IN.

580-**FRANCIS BAILEY NIMICK, JR.**[8] (443), m./1, Eleanor
Christine Griggs; m./2, Katherine Chew Knight Leighton.
    Issue:
        750-Marion Griggs Nimick[9]
        751-Francis Bailey Nimick
        752-Thomas Griggs Nimick, m. Ann --?--.
        753-Eleanor Howe Nimick
        754-Malcolm Guthrie Nimick, m. Sally Spencer De Lazzra

582-**CHARLES SPENCER NIMICK**[8] (443), m. Mary Carolyn
Schmertz.
    Issue:
        755-William Kennedy Nimick[9], m. Linda Trujillo
        756-Daniel Spencer Nimick, m. Nancy Reed
        757-Ellen Hamilton Nimick
        758-Jeffery Alexander Nimick

584-**DAVID ACHESON NIMICK**[8] (443), m. June Hodgon.
    Issue:
        759-Susan Spencer Nimick[9]
        760-David Acheson Nimick Jr., m. Angie Ieprohon
        761-Carol Hodgon Nimick

585-**READE BAILEY NIMICK**[8] (443), m. Anne Simmons Corkran.
    Issue:
        762-Reade Bailey Nimick, Jr.[9], m. Laura Lee Nimick
        763-Anne Simmons Nimick, m. Carl L. Neilson
        764-John Gribbel Nimick

586-**GEORGE GUTHRIE NIMICK**[8] (443), m. Deborah Shupert.
    Issue:
        765-George Guthrie Nimick, Jr.[9], m. Alba Yolanda
            Salvado Penman.
        766-Andrew Supplee Nimick, m. Daleen Renee Bixler
        767-Margaret Campbell Nimick

588-**THOMAS MARSHALL HOWE NIMICK**[8] (444), m. Florence Dil-
worth LOCKHART.
    Issue:
        768-Charles Lockhart Howe Nimick[9]
        769-Cathleen Harwood Mutland Nimick, m. Peter Single-
            ton Austin.
        770-Vistoria Marshall Howe Nimick

589-**GEORGE ALLAIRE HOWE NIMICK**[8] (444), m. Elizabeth WHET-
ZEL.
Issue:
    771-Theresa Nimick[9], m. John Ahern.
    772-George Allaire Howe Nimick, Jr.
    773-Genevieve Nimick
    774-Earl Nimick
    775-Burr Nimick
    776-Mary Butler Nimick

598-**GEORGE HENRY BELTZHOOVER, Jr., then Sr.,**[8], (455) b.
18 Dec. 1947, Toledo, OH., m., 18 Aug. 1973, Detroit, MI.,
Lynda Carole Rice, b., 23 April 1951, Detroit, MI., d/o
Fredrick V. Rice and wf., Carole Elizabeth TRINKAUS RICE.
    Issue: (BELTZHOOVER)
        777-Jeremy Wolfe Beltzhoover[9], b. 5 Sept., 1974, Cary,
            NC.
        778-Aaron Frances Beltzhoover, b. 20 Aug. 1979, Royal
            Oak, MI.
        779-Faith Alexandra Beltzhoover, b. 11 June 1981,
            Southfield, MI.

599-**RUTH ANN BELTZHOOVER**[8] (455), b. 19 Sept., 1949,
Toledo OH., m. 14 June 1969, m. Harley Eugene Craft, b. 1
Sept. 1946. Cresco, IA., s/o Harley Miles Craft, Cresco, IA.,
and wf., Doris Anna KIPPE Craft, Dubuque, IA).   Ruth Ann and
Harley divorced 13 June 1982.
    Issue: (CRAFT)
        780-Sarah Michelle Craft[9], b. 11 Mar. 1974, Silver
            Spring, MD., grad. University of North Caroli-
            na, Wilmington, Dec. 1998, m. 17 Oct. 1998,
            John Patrick Draffin, b. 29 Oct. 1970, Ohoskie,
            NC., s/o Douglas Frank Draffin and wf., Pamela
            QUICK Draffin.   John Patrick grad., Univ. of
            North Carolina May 1994.
        781-Stacey Margaret Craft, b. 14 Feb., 1977, Toledo,
            OH, grad. Meredith College, Raleigh, NC., May
            1999

600-**BARBARA LOUISE BELTZHOOVER**[8] (455), b., 3 Nov. 1951,
Toledo, OH., m., 18 Sept. 1976, Wilmington, NC., James C.
Orrell, s/o James Clarke Orrell, Wilmington, NC., and wf.,
Mary Charlotte LEWIS, Wilmington, NC.

    Barbara and James divorced 31 May 1979, Wilmington, NC.
Barbara, m./2 17 Jan. 1998, Myrtle Beach, SC., Charles Dana
Hinkle, Jr. b, 22 June 1952, Adrian, MI., s/o Charles Dana
Hinkle and wf., Marilyn Lynn REED.

    Barbara's step children ("happily acquired by marriage to
Chuck") are: Kyle Matthew Hinkle, b. 22 May 1983, Addison,
MI.; Dana Lynn Hinkle, b. 1 Aug., 1986, Addison, MI; Kelsey
Lynn Hinkle, b. 17 June 1990, Addison, MI.
    Issue: (ORRELL) Children of the first marriage:

782-Mary Margaret Orrell[9], b., 31 May 1979, Wilmington, NC.
783-Christopher Clarke Orrell, b. 23 Aug. 1981, Wilmington, NC.

601-DAVID CHARLES HALL[8] (456), b. 2 May 1932, Columbus,
OH., m. 16 Jan 1958, at Wright Patterson Air Force Base Chap-
el, Fairborn, Dayton, OH., Gloria Napier. b. 24 Mar. 1937,
Dayton, OH., d/o Elwin Harrison Napier and wf. Frances Helen
Blue Napier.
    Issue: (HALL)
        784-Suzanne Irene Hall[9], b. 24 May 1959, Millard Fil-
            more Hospital, Buffalo, NY.
        785-Scott David Hall, b. 30 April 1962, Strong Memori-
            al Hospital, Rochester, NY.

602-DONALD SEYMOUR HALL[8] (456), b. 3 June 1940, Columbus,
OH., m., some twenty fives years and div.
    Issue: (HALL)
        786-Elizabeth Elaine Hall[9], b. 13 Feb. 1971

603-DALE THOMAS ZIEGENFELDER[8] (457), b. 12 April 1951,
Cincinnti, attended Woodward H. S. Cincinnati, class 1969,
grad. BA degree and Masters degree from Purdue Univ. Electrical Engineering, (Roll of Honor 1997-1998). In addition, Dale
has an MBA from Marist College (1985). Resides Glenford, NY.
He plays classical organ, ski race and sailing as hobbies. A
Gold Medal winner in NASTAR ski racing (downhill Alpine skiing
and racing). Employed for fifteen years at IBM and presently
(2001) a landlord.

    Married 4 Aug. 1979, near Woodstock, NY., Diana Dziura,
b. 11 Jan. 1947, New Brunswick, NJ., d/o Stanley Dziura and
wf. Anna Zalesky Dziura. Diana grad. with a BS in Education
in 1970 from Concordia Teachers College, NE., MS Education
SUNY. Diana is an Elmentary School Teacher, New Paltz, NY.
    Issue: (ZIEGENFELDER
        787-Noelle Jeong Ziegenfelder, chosen, b. 11 Aug.
            1987, Korea, Yeo Jeong Kim

604-RHEA JEANNE BELTZHOOVER[8] (459), b. 30 Mar. 1939; m..
Charles Evans Hughes, b. 27 June 1959 (married on her parents
25th wedding anniversary) div., her fiance was 'Bobby' In
1992 Rhea Hughes was operating a Bed and Breakfast called
Country Manor, 6315 Zoar Road, Morrow, OH. She wrote 7 July
1992 that she talked with her aunt, Rhea in Florida, who was
the daughter of John Dixon Beltzhoover and Myrtle Pricket (?)
of Chicago. The record seems to show that her mother was
Myrtle Tomlinson.
    Issue: (HUGHES)
        788-Justin Jeffrey Taylor Hughes[9], b. 4 April 1960.

605-JOHN DIXON BELTZHOOVER 'J.D.'[8] (459) b. 19 May 1941,
m./1, Joyce Sargent; b. 1 Oct. 1942; d. 22 Mar. 2002. In the

Cincinnati Post 6/10/1983 14: 2, a column on 4-J Homes. "Although Beltzhoover lives in Morrow, he has done most of his building in Hamilton Co., OH. He has built extensively in Milford, Indian Hill, Montgomery and Anderson Twp.'s. Beltzhoover is a 41 year old University of Cincinnati graduate who owned and operated Bellwood Country Club in Morrow for 19 years. During that time he did a lot of building on the property. When he sold in 1979 he decided to go into home building full time. At first he worked with a partner and then formed 4-J Homes in the fall of 1981. He and his wife, Joyce have two children--one is an Ohio State junior and the other is a Little Miami High School sophmore."

J. D. m./2 ---?----. He resides Maineville, OH.
Issue: (BELTZHOOVER)
 789-Jody Ann Beltzhoover[9], b. 1 Mar. 1962 m. -?--
  Metz, has two children, and resides near
  Blanchester, OH.
 790-John Kevin Beltzhoover,b. 9 Mar. 1967-- may be the
  J. Beltzhoover residing in Morrow, OH in 2001.

617-MILTON OLIVER PEACH, Dr.[8] (462), b. 15 May 1910, Bellevue, PA; d. 12 Sept. 2003, Houghton, MI. He earned his first degrees from Calif. State Teachers College of PA., where he met Frances Julia Seese of Scottdale. They were married in the Scottdale Methodist Church Thanksgiving 1941. They moved from Pittsburgh to South Bend, IN., and then to Houghton, MI. Frances Peach died in an auto accident, Good Friday 1981.

Dr. Peach was known internationally for his scientific research in the behavior of crystals under pressure. With another scientist he identified what came known as the "Peach-Koehler Force", which is today found in all foundational metallurgy texts used by researchers around the world.

In 1980 he was confirmed as Professor Emeritus by Michigan Tech., but continued to research and guiding students until 1985 at which time he joined his families in Willts, CA. where he met and married 5 Sept. 1999, Virginia McQuiston.

From his obituary the grandchildren were: Terra Peach of Portland, OR,; John Mitchell of Kealekekua, Hawaii; Wendy Schrader of Seward Alaska; Toby and Amber Ferlman of Willits; Matt Peach of Michigan. His wife and a sister, Gladys Peach of Pittsburgh also survived. [1]
Issue: (PEACH)
 791-Hugh Gilbert Peach[9], res. Beaverton, OR
 792-Jamy Peach, m. --?-- Mitchell, res. Willits, CA
 793-Judy Peach, m. --?-- Ferlman, Willits, CA
 794-James 'Jim' Peach, Saute St. Marie
----

1. Dr. Milton Oliver Peach obituary, Daily Mining Gazette, 11/12/2003. Courtesy Deanna Oklepek

624-**ROGER GRADEN ROWLAND**[8] (466), b. 3 Sept. 1907; d. 19 June 1998, TN., m. Annie Elizabeth Sykes, b. 1912.
Issue:
795-G. Hartwell Rowland[9], b. Jan. 1929, TN

627-**WOODROW ALLISON "AL" ROWLAND**[8] (466), b. 1912, TN m./1, Margaret Rosalie Rawson; m./2, Margaret (div.). He was in the Battle of the Bulge WWII.
Issue: (ROWLAND)
796-James Rowland[9], b. 1943
797-Gail Rowland, b. 1947
798-Gary Rowland, b. 1948

628-**KENNETH VERNON ROWLAND**[8] (466), b. 16 Apr. 1916; m. 1/, bef. 1945, (div.) Agnes Jane Mickel; m./2, Nellie Carter Masters, m./3, 24 Nov. 1960, Elizabeth Rebecca Grove, b. 17 Apr. (?).
Issue: (ROWLAND)
799-Kenneth Rayburn Rowland[9], b. 7 Oct. 1944, TN; m. 25 Aug. 1964, div. Karen Sherrard; m./2 Lea --?--.

630-**LOUISA DORA THOMAS**[8] (467) (1911-2001), m. 1930, John Thurman Wilson (1905-1991).
Issue: (WILSON)
800-Thomas Milton Wilson[9], (1933-   ), m. 1957, Ruth Arjean Little, b. 1937.
801-Mary Evelyn Wilson (1935-   ), m. 1952, Harold Wayne Kennedy, b. 1930.
802-Delma Grace Wilson (1937-   ), m. 1954, David Joe Kennedy, b. 1934.

631-**LEONARD ELLIS THOMAS**[8], (467) (1913-1996), m. 1935, Christine Suggs (1915-1973), m./2 Pauline Suggs, div.
Issue: (THOMAS)
803-Walter Hill Thomas[9], (1936-1983), m. Mary Ann Poindexter, div.; m./2, 1970, Rose Clause; m./3 Doyline Miller, b. 1940.
804-James Leonard Thomas, (1941-   ), m. 1965, Martha Keith
805-Linda Christine Thomas (1944-   ), m. 1965, David Tucker.
806-Perry Edward Thomas (1951-   ), m. 1969, Debbie Henderson.

632-**BESSIE MAY THOMAS**[8], (467) (1914-1980), m. Garland Edgar Lyle (1912-1988).
Issue: (LYLE)
807-Raybourne Edwin Lyle[9], (1934-   ), m. 1954, Bernice Parker, b. 1936.
808-Mary Lynn Lyle, b. 1943; m. Charles Bowyer

634-**VELMA NANNIE THOMAS**[8] (467), b. 1918; m. 1938, James Max Sykes, Rev. (1912-1998).

Issue: (SYKES)
   809-Barbara Ann Sykes[9], b. 1940, m. 1959, Glenn Brew-
       er, b. 1939.
   810-Janet Louise Sykes, b. 1943, m. 1963, Billy Hunt,
       b. 1941.
   811-Velma Maxine Sykes, b. 1947, m. 1970, John Robert
       Brown, b. 1947.

636-JOHN ALVIN THOMAS[8] (467), (1919-1975), m. Dorothy Ora
Morgan (1920-1999).
   Issue: (THOMAS)
   812-Anita Ann Thomas[9], b. 1951; m. 1970, Larry Lee
       Wilder.
   813-Betty Jane Thomas, b. 1954.

637-MARGARET GERTRUDE THOMAS[8] (467) (1921-1988); m. 1941,
Carlos Dexter Moore,
   Issue: (MOORE)
   814-Jerry Dexter Moore[9], b. 1943, m. Dorothy Bailey,
       div.
   815-Judy Gertrude Moore, b. 1949, m. James Fields,
       div.

638-LOUIS ORVILLE THOMAS Jr.[8] (468), b. 1931, m./1, 1978,
Lavada Henegar, b. 1925; m./2 1978, Donna June Allen, b. 1951.
   Issue:
   816-Angela Dawn Thomas[9], b. 1980; m. Scott Roberson.

639-LAWRENCE M. JACKSON, Jr.[8] (469), (1921-1970); m.
1946, Dorothy V. Schichtel (1921-1996). Lawrence M. Jackson,
Jr. M.D. served in the US Army as Chief of Surgery for several
different hospitals. He was Col. Jackson as head of Kenner
Hospital and Director of MEDDAC when he died. He is buried in
Arlington National Cemetery.
   Issue: (JACKSON)
   817-Janet V. Jackson[9], b. 1947, m. 1971, Robert Sil-
       verman.
   818-Jo Ann Jackson, b. 1949, m. 1969, William Frank
       Harrell.
   819-Lawrence Monroe Jackson, b. 1951, m. 1974, Patri-
       cia Colleen Fink.
   820-David F. Jackson, b. 1954
   821-Mark Steven Jackson, b. 1960, m. 1985, Sandra Sue
       Keel.

640-FINAS MALONE THOMAS[8] (470), (1916-1989); m./1 Minnie
Lee Powers, n.i., div.; m,.2 Dorothy Rae McGilton, n.i., div.;
m./3 1951, Helen Louise Lancaster (1923-1990).
   Issue: (THOMAS)
   822-Timothy Lancaster Thomas[9], b. 1961

641-GENEVA MAE THOMAS[8], (470) b. (1919-1983); m. 1940,
Ralph Clarence Shofner (1912-1986).
   Issue: (SHOFNER)

823-Donna Lynn Shofner[9], b. 1942, m. 1961, Lonnie N.
Allison, b. 1939.
824-David Stanton Shofner, b. 1947, m. 1968, Elizabeth
Ballard, div.

642-**ALICE RUTH THOMAS**[8] (472), b. 1923, m. 1942, George
Edward Sanford, Rev., d. 2004.
Issue: (SANFORD)
825-Sherry Lynette Sanford[9], b. 1943, m. 1962, Quinn
F. Earl, Jr.
826-Merry Annette Sanford, b. 1943, m./1, Truett
George; m./2 1963, James Douglas Maddox.
827-Charles Stephen Sanford, b. 1946, m. Alice Rebecca
McCown.
828-Susan Elizabeth Sanford, b. 1966

643-**GLADYS IONE THOMAS**[8] (472), (1924-2001); m. 1944, Leo
Dean Echelbarger, b. 1922.
Issue: (ECHELBARGER)
829-Michael Dean Echelbarger[9], b. 1945, m. 1966, Kathleen Ann Jenkins, b. 1947.
830-Patrick Thomas Echelbarger, b. 1948, m. 1969,
Marilyn Lodell Miller, b. 1948.
831-Lindsey Leo Robinson Echelbarger, b. 1952, m.
1980, Carolyn Elizabeth Updike, b. 1949.

645-**KNOX THOMAS, Jr.**[8] (472), (1929-1995); m./1 Charlene
Abernathy, b. 1929.

Knox B. Thomas, Jr., d. 17 Mar. 1995, at Centennial Medical Center, Nashville, TN. He was b. 10 July 1929, Montgomery
Co. He was an innovative farmer, using an underground irriga-
tion system and operated a cattle feeder system.
Issue: (THOMAS)
832-Deboray Kay Thomas[9], b. 1948, m. 1967, James Ireland, div., m/2 1988, James Masters, b. 1947.
Res. Haslett, MI., in 1995.
833-Knox Thomas III, b. 1951, m. 1973, Debbie Lynn
Shelton, b. 1956.
834-Charles Larry Thomas, b. 1953, m. 1983, Amy Banton
div., b. 1964.
835-Scott Alan Thomas, (1962-1984), m. 1979, Cynthis
Rene Shearon, b. 1962.

648-**MARTHA FRANCES AVERITT**[8] (473), b. 1927, m. 1947,
Wallace Carney Harris, b. 1913, d. 2000.
Issue: (HARRIS)
836-Wallace Carney Harris II[9], b. 1953, m. 1977, Dawn
Renee Sloan, div.
837-Jerold Rodney Harris, b. 1958
838-Thomas Averitt Harris, b. 1966.

649-**MARY ESTALENE AVERITT**[8] (473), b. 1929; m. 1947, William Carlyle Patterson, b. 1921;

Issue: (PATTERSON)
>   839-David William Patterson[9], b. 1952, m. 1989, Neena
>   White.
>   840-Susan Patricia Patterson, b. 1955, m. George
>   Randall Hinson.

650-ELOISE EUGENIA AVERITT[8] (473), b. 1932, m. 1957,
Joseph Boone; m./2 1966, Earl T. Allison (1918-1993); m./3,
1999, Billy Weaver. Issue: (ALLISON)
>   841-Lou Ann Allison[9], 1962

652-LOUELLA SAUNDRA THOMAS, PhD.[8] (475), b. 1937; m.
1958, div. John Allen Burnett. b. 1937. (PhD from FL State
Univ.)
>   Issue: (BURNETT)
>   842-Steven Eric Burnett[9], b. 1960; m./1, 1978, div.,
>   Joni Carr, b. 1960; m./2, 1986, div., Sheila
>   Wilson, b. 1961; m,/3, 1988, Jennifer Knight,
>   b. 1971
>   843-Saundra Suzanne Burnett, b. 1963; m. 1993, Paul
>   Michael Kretschmer, b. 1963.

654-NELDA JO THOMAS[8] (476),b. 1937. m./1, 1957, div.,
Hunter Campbell Harrell, b. 1937; m./2, 1977, Melvin Eugene
Kersey, n.i.
>   Issue: (HARRELL)
>   844-Sherri Jan Harrell[9], b. 1958; m. 1984, div.,
>   Bruce Page Arnell, b. 1957; m./2 Charles Tip-
>   ton.
>   845-Melissa Jill Harrell, b. 1959; m., 1982, Jeffrey
>   Tad Wheeler, b. 1956.
>   846-Benjamin Thomas Harrell, b. 1961, m. 1990, Diana
>   Maria Black.

655-JOHN CHARLES THOMAS[8] (477), b. 1946; m. 1968, Audrey
Nell Anhaiser, b, 1947.
>   Issue: (THOMAS)
>   847-Charles Eric Thomas[9], b. 1975.
>   848-Stacey Karen Thomas, b. 1979.

656-PATRICIA FRENCH THOMAS[8] (477), b. 1952, m. 1972,
Richard Dean Hodge, b. 1948.
>   Issue: (HODGE)
>   849-William Thomas Hodge[9], b. 1978, a twin
>   850-David Robert Hodge, b. 1978, a twin
>   851-Jennifer Hodge

661-GEORGE KNAPP SNEDEKER [8] (481), b. 3 Nov. 1942, Ayer,
MA., d. 8 Mar. 1981; m. 2 Mar. 1962, Janice Mae Colquitt, b.
15 May 1942, Columbus, GA.
>   Issue: (SNEDEKER)
>   852-George Knapp Snedeker II [9], b. 11 Dec. 1964,
>   Germany, m. 1991, Susan Elizabeth Erwin.
>   853-Donna Marie Snedeker, b. 22 April 1966, Columbus,

GA.
854-Elizabeth Suzanne Snedeker, b. 29 Sept. 1971,
Orlando, FL., m. Douglas Colon Wiseman, b. 25
May 1971.

664-**MARY JENKINS SNEDEKER**[8] (482), b. 10 July 1954, Princeton, NJ.,m. 27 Aug. 1977, William Kevin Dugan, b. 1946.
Issue:
855-Laura Jenkins Dugan[9], b. 27 May 1979, Burlington,
NJ.
856-Peter William Dugan, b. 21 Feb. 1983, Burlington,
VT.

670-**RUTH AUDLEY BRITTON CONNER**[8] (485), b. 21 Sept. 1946,
Natchez, MS., m. 3 June 1968, at Danville, KY., James Tandy
Coy III, M.D., b. 28 June 1942, s/o James Tandy Coy, Jr. and
wf. Datha Vida Bond.   Ruth and Jim own "Bontura" built in
1851, Natchez, MS.
Issue: (COY)
857-James Tandy Coy, IV[9]. b. 5 Nov. 1973, Lexington,
Fayette Co., KY., m. Elizabeth Nicole Jones.
858-Samuel Coy, b. 1 Nov. 1976, Lexington, KY, m. 7
June 2003, Brooke Russell Shearer.

671-**AYLETTE BUCKNER CONNER**[8] (485), b. 16 Sept. 1947,
Vicksburg, Warren Co., MS., m. Thomas Henry Dickman, b. 26
Oct. 1940, Louisville, Jefferson Co., KY.
Issue: (DICKMAN)
859-Thomas Henry Dickman, Jr.[9], b. 15 May 1970, Tusca-
loosa, AL.

672-**RICHARD ELLIS CONNER, IV**[8] (485), b. 6 Nov. 1951,
Natchez, MS., m. 18 Aug. 1979, at Mobile, AL., Debra Denise
Oliver, b. 17 Oct. 1953, Greenville, Washington Co., MS., d/o
Francis Marion Oliver & wf. Hazel Marie Breazeale.
Issue: (CONNER)
860-Denise Britton Conner[9], b. 7 Mar. 1983, Mobile
861-Courtney Elizabeth Conner, b. 12 Nov. 1985, Mo-
bile, AL.

673-**DENNISON MACRERY CONNER**[8] (485), b. 23 Sept. 1954, Bay
Shore, L. I., NY., m. Clay Graham, div.
Issue: (GRAHAM)
862-Laura Frances Graham[9], b. 6 Mar. 1984, Alpine, TX

674-**ANNE GAILLARD CONNER**[8] (485), b. 18 Aug. 1956,
Natchez, MS., m. 8 June 1996, 'Green Leaves' Natchez, MS., Rex
Allen Wagner, b. 18 Oct. 1956, Cleveland, Bradley Co., TN.
Issue: (WAGNER)
863-Jacob Paul Conner 'Jake' Wagner[9], b. 11 Dec. 1998,
Chattanooga, Hamilton Co., TN.

675-**WILLIAM BELTZHOOVER CONNER**[8] (485), b. 12 May 1961,
Mobile, Mobile Co., AL., m. 31 Dec. 1988, Palm Beach, FL, Mary

Elizabeth, 'Mary Beth' Sineath, d/o Lais Franklin Sineath, III, & wf. Joan Carol Lenderman Sineath.
Issue: (CONNER)
864-William Beltzhoover Conner, Jr.[9], b. 20 Aug. 1999, Lexington, Fayette Co., KY.

676-**GEORGE BELTZHOOVER MORRISON**[8] (486), b. 24 Nov. 1950, Natchez, MS.; m. 13 Sept. 1976, Myra Melissa FARISH, b. 15 July 1960, d/o Andre Farish and wf. Sally.
Issue: (MORRISON)
865-George Wheeler 'Wheeler' Morrison[9], b. 12 July 1977, Natchez, MS.
866-Lowell Langdon Morrison, b. 10 July 1990, Matchez. MS., chr. Trinity Episcopal Church, Natchez

677-**ANN BORODELL MORRISON**[8] (486), b. 12 April 1953, Natchez, MS.; m. 4 June 1972, Oscar Hillman HARTMAN, b. 12 July 1952.
Issue: (HARTMAN)
867-Britton Hillman Hartman[9], b. 24 Nov. 1974; m., 7 April 1997, Holly Hatchel. They have a daughter, Ama Raven Hartman, b. 12 June 1997.
868-Virginia Lee Hartman, b. 19 Dec. 1977

680-**WILLIAM BELTZHOOVER MORRISON**[8] (486), b. 5 Nov. 1968; m., at Trinity Epsicopal Church, 18 Aug. 1990, Kimberly Dawn HINSON, b. 1 Apr. 1968, Bay St. Louis, Hancock Co., MS.
Issue: (MORRISON)
869-Hannah Wheeler Morrison [8], b. 29 Aug. 1994, Monroe, Quachita Parish, LA.
870-Julia Lee Morrison, b. 8 Aug. 1997, Monroe, LA.

685-**CATHERINE TOD BELTZHOOVER**[8] (492), b. 3 Aug. 1911; m. 10 May 1947, Dr. William W. Butzner, Jr. Res. Fredericksburg, VA. In a letter dated 25 July 1983, to Vivian BELTZHOOVER, she stated that she was an only child. That her father died in 1958, George Morris Beltzhoover; that her grandfather, George Morris Beltzhoover was born in Boiling Springs, PA., near Carlisle. Her great-grandfather was Jacob and his wife was Agness. [1] [2]

Catherine Tod Beltzhoover Butzner says, in a letter 12/97 that she was named after her maternal great-grandmother, Catherine Tod, who married Joseph Baker. Catherine Beltzhoover m., 10 May 1947, Charles Towns, Jefferson Co., WV.

William Walker Butzner Jr. Dr., b. 19 Aug. 1911, Frederickstown, VA; d 27 April 1990 (78), at Easton Memorial Hospi-
----

1. Beltzhoover, Vivian (Mrs. George) Wilmington, NC

2. Kamp, Gayle O. research

tal, Easton, MD., g. City Cemetery, Fredericksburg, VA. Funeral services were held at St. George's Episcopal Church in Fredericksburg with Rev. Charles Sydnor, officiating. He was survived by his wife, Catherine Tod Butzner, two daughters, two sisters; Mrs. Byrd S. Leavell, Charlottesville, and Mrs. Baxley T. Tanchard of Franktown. Dr. Butzner was the son of Mr. & Mrs. W. W. Butzner. He graduated from the University of Virginia and the University of Virginia Medical School. He practiced medicine in Fredericksburg for forty years. [1]

Issue: (BUTZNER)

871-Betsy Baker BUTZNER[9], b. 22 Mar. 1948; m. 28 Aug. 1971, at Fredericksburg, VA., James Carson Greene, b. 25 July 1941, West Jefferson, NC., son of Edgar Dudley Greene and wf., Maple Juanata Mast. Res. Annandale, VA. n.i.

872-Anna Moore BUTZNER, b. 16 Oct. 1950, unm.

687-ELSIE MAE MERIDITH[8] (509), b. 28 Nov. 1905, d. 26 Sept 1989, m. 29 Apr. 1925, Cecil Raymond Hicks (1901-1968); s/o Joshua Hicks and wf. Anna Fox Hicks.

Issue:

873-Cecil Raymond Hicks, Jr.[9], b. 19 Feb. 1940.

693-JUANITA LUCILLE MERIDITH[8] (509), b. 26 Feb. 1918; m. 14 Jan 1935 at Carrigan Meth. Church, Ray Everett MILLER, b. 13 May 1913, Grand Prairie, Jefferson Co., IL; d. 25 May 1962, Sandoval, Marion Co., IL.

Ray Everett MILLER was the son of Chester MILLER and wf., Elsie Mae SANDERS

Issue: (MILLER) All children born Marion Co., IL.

874-Joan Marie Miller[9], b. 17 July 1935, Sandoval, Marion Co., IL; m. 11 Sept. 1958, Methodist Church, Sandoval, Murval Andrew Moore

875-Barbara Lucille Miller, b. 1936; m. Kenneth Carpenter

876-Marvin Dale Miller (1938-1976)

877-Paul Dean Miller b. 1939; m. Beth Dodson

878-Wanda Lee Miller, b. 1941; m. Marshall D. Lippert

879-Sandra Kay Miller, b. 1942; m. William Wallace Johnson

880-Betty Jean Miller, b. 1945; m. Joseph Patterson

881-James Chester Miller, b. 24 July 1948, Sandoval, IL.

882-Richard Ray Miller, b. 22 Sept. 1950, Sandoval, IL.; m. Kimberly Marcum

883-Jennifer Lynn Miller, b. 30 June 1958, b. Sandovaal, IL., m. Dennis Gallgher

----

1. The Free Lance-Star, Fredericksburg, VA., Sat. April 18, 1990 Obituary Dr. W. W. Butzner, Jr. Courtesy Mrs. Barbara Willis, Virginia Librarian, Central Rappahannock Regional Library, Fredericksburg, VA. 1997

696-**RUSSELL DARRELL MERIDITH**[8] (509), b. 20 Jan. 1923, Sandoval, IL., d. 28 Nov. 1996, Marion, IL. g. Miners Cem., Royalton, IL.; m./1, 24 Sept. 1944, Kathern Marie Bush, Carbondale, IL., b. (Sept. 1922, d. 30 Dec. 1988, g. Miners Cem., d/o Francis Marion Bush & wf. Lizzie Mae Snider; m./2 Wilma Landford/Langford Jackson. Wilma Jackson had sons (Jackson): Jerry, Murray, Albert (Rip) and Steve.

Issue: (children from first marriage)
> 884-Roger Darrell Meridith[9], b. 9 Dec. 1948, Belleville, IL., m. 25 Jan. 1975, Sandra "Sandy" Kay Gilbert. [1]
> 885-Russell David Meridith, b. 15 May 1954, Belleville, IL., m. 9 Aug. 1981 at Virginia, IL., Linda Maurer.

699-**VIVIAN GERALDINE LEITH**[8] (510), b. 12 Sept. 1923, Midian, KS.; m. 05 April 1942, Wichita, KS., Clarence Braden Shelman, Jr., b. 17 Feb. 1923, Kingman, KS., s/o Clarence Shelman and wf. Bertha Cooley.

Issue:
> 886-Braden Lee Shelman[9], b. 05 June 1945,
> 887-Nieta Carol Shelman, b. 02 May 1948, Wichita, KS.
> 888-Janeen Kay Shelman, b. 06 Oct. 1949, Wichita, KS.

704-**DELORES CORINNE 'DOTTY' BELTZHOOVER**[8] (538), b. 10 June 1929, m. Dale Morrow.

Issue: (MORROW)
> 889-Tom Morrow[9], b 27 May 1952
> 890-Kurt Morrow, b. 23 Jan. 1959

706-**GEORGE EDWARD BELTZHOOVER**[8] (538), b. 22 May 1932; m. 28 August 1954, West Frankfort, IL., Helen Rita Ruscin, b. 9 Dec. 1933, West Frankfort, IL., d/o Michael Steven Ruscin, b. 6 Feb. 1898 (Kosice, Czechoslovakia) and wf. Helen Mary Demchok, b. 23 Oct. 1901 (Albia, IA.).

Issue: (BELTZHOOVER)
> 891-Dirk Edward Beltzhoover[9], b. 19 Sept. 1955, Murray, KY., unm.
> 892-Marianne Beltzhoover, b. 11 July 1957, Murray KY, unm. A son, (in vitro), Jon Ryan Beltzhoover, b. 16 Dec. 2003.
> 893-Eric Richard Beltzhoover, b. 15 Dec. 1958, Clinton, IL, m. Laurie Lambert.
> 894-Carolyn Beltzhoover, b. 14 June 1962, Clinton, IL; m. David Johanson.
> 895-Christine Beltzhoover, b. 14 June 1962, Clinton, IL., m., Gary Greben, div.
> 896-Alex William Beltzhoover, b. 4 Oct. 1964, Joliet, IL: m. Janet CORBETT, b. 14 April 1962.
> 897-Gretchen Beltzhoover, b. 7 Aug. 1970, Joliet,

----

1. Meridith, Roger Darrell (Meridith family information, Jan. 2005)

IL., m. Rolf Troha.

707-**JANICE MARIE BELTZHOOVER**[8] (538), b. 12 Mar. 1934; m. George Waricher (1 child)
    Issue: (WARICHER)
      898-Michael Waricher[9], b. 8 June 1963

708-**KAY LAVONNE BELTZHOOVER**[8] (538), b. 15 Feb. 1937, m. Elwood 'Bud' Kaylor (4 children)
    Issue: (KAYLOR)
      899-Todd Kaylor[9], b. 30 May 1961
      900-Scott Kaylor, b. 14 Aug. 1962
      901-Brett Kaylor, b. 21 Dec. 1965
      902-Kyle Kaylor, b. 21 Dec. 1968

709-**RICHARD LEE BELTZOOVER**[8] (538), b. 3 Feb. 1940, Carlisle, PA., m. June 25 1961, Faye Louise GOODYEAR, b. 23 Aug. 1944, Carlisle, PA. Fay Louise Goodyear Beltzhoover remarried (Schultz).

    Faye Louise GOODYEAR was the daughter of Louis Arlington GOODYEAR, b. 6 April 1912, Carlisle, PA., and wf. Ruby Mae STAVER, b. 5 Mar. 1916, Halstead, Norman Co., MN. Louis GOODYEAR was the son of Alonzo Augustus GOODYEAR, b. 3 Aug. 1883, Mt. Holly Springs, PA., and wf. Floy R. WEHLER, b. 1888. Alonzo GOODYEAR was the son of Milton Samuel GOODYEAR, b. 16 June 1852 and wf. Annie Mary MORRETTE, b. 13 Oct. 1857. [1]
    Issue: (BELTZHOOVER)
      903-George Christopher Beltzhoover[9], b. 23 Nov. 1961, Carlisle, PA.
      904-David Edward Beltzhoover, b. 1 Feb. 1963
      905-Geoffrey Louis Beltzhoover, b. 27 Dec. 1970, m. 25 June 2004, Amy Beck and they res. Steamboat Springs, CO.

710-**CAROLE ANN BELTZHOOVER**[8] (538), b. 23 Oct. 1941, m. Donald Schwartz,
    Issue: (SCHWARTZ)
      906-Josuah Schwartz[9], b. 22 Dec. 1973
      907-Jocelyn Schwartz, b. 11 Dec. 1974

711-**BONITA RAYE BELTZHOOVER**[8] (538), b. 24 Oct. 1943, m. Parker 'Skip' Kuhns.
    Issue: (KUHNS)
      908-Christopher Kuhns[9], b. 16 Dec. 1979
      909-Jonathan Kuhns.b. 24 Dec. 1981, chosen

713-**EMILY IRENE HOOVER**[8] (540), b. 2 Feb. 1899, Cumberland Co., PA., d. 13 Feb. 1972, Shepherdstown, Cumberland Co., PA; m. 9 Oct. 1922 to Harry William Mann, b. 30 July 1899, d. 28

----

1. Ibid., George Beltzhoover, Indianapolis, IN

Feb. 1977. Harry William Mann the son of John Mann and wf. Sarah Peffley.

    Issue: (MANN)
        910-Helen Audrey Mann[9], b. 12 May 1912, Boiling Springs, Cumberland Co., PA.
        911-Harry William Mann, Jr., b. 13 Feb. 1926

714-JOHN HENRY HOOVER[8] (540), b. 12 June 1902, Cumberland Co., PA., d. 24 Dec. 1996, S. Middleton Twp., Cumberland Co., PA., m./1 Elsie Luceta Keesecker, m./2 18 Feb. 1922, Grace M. Boyles, in Boiling Springs, Cumberland Co., PA. John Henry Hoover, christened, d. 24 Dec. 1996, g. Mt. Zion Cem., Monroe Twp., Cumberland Co., PA.

    Issue: (HOOVER) (second marriage)
        912-Freda Hoover[9], b. 10 Sept. 1922, Boiling Springs, Cumberland Co., Pa.,

715-PEARL ELIZBATH HOOVER[8] (540), b 25 Dec. 1904, Cumberland, PA., d. 22 Feb. 1978, Cumberland, PA., m. 24 Sept. 1921, Gordon S. Cullings.

    Issue: (CULLINGS)
        913-Harry M. Cullings[9], b. ca. 1922
        914-Gordon H. Cullings, b. ca. 1926

726-VAUGHN WARDEN LEIDIGH[8] (546), b. 27 Sept. 1897, Mt. Holly Springs, PA., d. 14 Jan. 1987, Camp Hill, PA., m. 21 Jan. 1920, Florence Edna Horning, b. 28 May 1899, Harrisburg, PA., d. 4 Aprl. 1977, Camp Hill, PA. Vaughn was a member of a well know family of butchers and grocers. He opened his first store in 1919 in Carlisle and another, later, in Mt. Holly Springs.

    Issue: (LEIDIGH)
        915-Shirley Mae Leidigh,[9] b. 4 Dec. 1920, Harrisburg, PA.; m. 25 July 1943, John Edgar Kennedy, b. 28 June 1920, Enola PA.

727-BRENDA MAE LEIDIGH[8] (546), b. 21 Dec. 1899, Cumberland Co., PA., d. 20 June 1993, Cumberland Co., PA., m. June 1920, William Brillhart. b. 26 Apr. 1898' d. April 1986.

    Issue: (BRILLHART)
        916-Jean Brillhart[9]. b. 9 Aug. 1921, Cumberland Co., PA.; m. 21 Oct. 1944, Albert Leonard Verdekal, b. 18 Nov. 1913, d, 9 July 1980.
        917-Anna Mae Brillhart, b. 7 April 1923, Cumberland Co.; m. 14 Feb. 1948, Glen Dwight Faught.
        918-Harry Brillhart, b. 28 June 1924, Cumberland Co., PA.; m. 17 Nov. 1943, Alice Franklin, b. 17 Jan. 1925, Stamford, CT.
        919-Brenda Louise Brillhart, b. 20 June 1925, Carlisle; m. 26 June 1948, Howard William Sowers, Jr., b. 22 May 1920, PA., d. 9 May 1996.
        920-Robert E. Brillhart, b. 8 April 1929, Carlisle, d. 26 June 1973, m. Nelda Nailor.

731-**RICHARD OWEN LEIDIGH**[8] (546), b. 27 Dec. 1906, Mt. Holly Springs, PA., d. 16 April 1988, Baltimore, MD., m. 2 Jan. 1930, Williamsburg, Va., Mary Jane Davis, b. 11 Sept. 1905, Carlisle, PA.

They lived in Baltimore more than 50 years. He was a manager, buyer, supervisor of Food Fair Stores. Mary is the daughter of William Durbon Davis and wf. Mary Catherine STONER Davis.
> Issue: (LEIDIGH)
>> 921-Kenneth Leidigh[9], b. 13 May 1933, employed at John Hopkins Applied Physics Laboratory in Baltimore, MD., m./1 Constance --?--, div. m./2 Patricia --?--. div.
>> 922-Mary Louise Leidigh, b. 22 July 1936, d. 22 Feb. 1938
>> 923-Brenda Mae Leidigh, b. 26 June 1939, m. John Du-Rose, b. Nottingham, England, d. 1969

733-**ROBERT IRWIN LEIDIGH**[8] (546), b. 30 Oct. 1911, Carlisle, PA., d. 22 Dec. 1979; m. Mae Elizabeth Kerrigan, b. 15 Oct. 1908, Baltimore, MD., d. 6 June 1988, d/o James J. and Frances M. Yingling Kerrigan.
> Issue: (LEIDIGH)
>> 924-Frances Mae Leidigh[9], b. ca. 1933, Cumberland Co., PA., d.i.
>> 925-Robert Irwin Leidigh, Jr., b. 8 May 1935, Carlisle; m. 23 June 1956, Josephine M. Woutersz, b. 2 May 1936.
>> 926-William Irwin Leidigh, b. 10 Nov. 1937, Harrisburg, PA., m., div.
>> 927-James Harry Leidigh, b. 18 Nov. 1939, Harrisburg, PA., m. 27 Nov. 1965, Sooka JA, b. 3 Apr. 1929
>> 928-Beverly Mae Leidigh, b. 21 July 1945, Harrisburg; m. John G. Tomochik.

738-**PAUL MONROE LEIDIGH**[8] (552). b. 13 Aug. 1909, Mt. Holly Springs, PA., d. 14 Sept. 1976, Carlisle, PA., g Mt. Holly Springs Cem., m. 14 Jan. 1932, Silver Springs, MD., Louise Margaret Thomas, b. 27 July 1912.

As a youth Paul worked as an auto mechanic. He studied music with Nataflusky from the Carlisle Army War College. He played the clarinet and saxophone with several groups. He and Louise moved to Maryland and worked for Glenn L. Martin Airplane Co. He worked on amphibious planes. After the war they went back to Holly Springs.
> Issue: (LEIDIGH)
>> 929-Frances Marie Leidigh[9], b 19 Aug. 1932, Carlisle
>> 930-Carol Ann Leidigh, b 13 Jan 1938, Carlisle, PA; m. David Andrew Wagner.
>> 931-Ronald Thomas Leidigh, b. 18 Nov. 1942, Carlisle, PA; m. Donna Sealover.

747-**EARL L. CASS**[9], (572), (1917-1990), m. Virginia Bunce.
Issue: (CASS)
  932-James Robert Cass[10], b. 17 Nov. 1949, Huntington,
        IN; m. 19 Dec. 1977, Tamra Sue Wheeler. Child-
        ren; Heather Marie Cass, b. 7 June 1982, Ft.
        Wayne, IN.; Austin Cass, b. 23 Nov, 1988, Ft.
        Wayne, IN.

748-**THELMA LOUISA CASS**[9] (572), b. 6 Nov. 1919, Kimball
Co., NE., m. 22 Nov. 1939, Wabash, IN., Gayle O. KAMP, b. 22
June 1916, Normal, IL.
Issue: (KAMP)
  933-Cassandra Lee "Cassie" Kamp[10], b. 30 Aug. 1945,
        Indianapolis, IN., grad. Indiana Univ. ; m. 9
        Mar. 1968, Jerry L. Bradley, b. 15 Sept. 1944,
        grad. Indiana Univ.
  934-Gregory G. Kamp, b. 16 May 1950, Huntington, IN;
        grad. Indiana Univ., grad. Indiana School of
        Denistry, D.D.S.; m. 10 June 1972, Mary Patri-
        cia King, b. 15 June 1949

749-**DOYLEEN KATHRYN CASS**[9] (572), b. 24 Nov. 1932, Huntington, IN., d. 17 Feb. 1987, Ft. Wayne, IN., m. Homer Burnworth.
Issue: (BURNWORTH)
  935-Bryce Burnworth[10]
  936-Brian Burnworth
  937-Todd Burnworth

750-**MARION GRIGGS NIMICK**[9] (580), m. John C. A. Silbert.
Issue:
  938-Kate Spence Silbert[10]
  939-Hannah Jenkins Silbert

751-**FRANCIS BAILEY NIMICK**[9] (580), m. Karen Sue Gillespie.
Issue:
  940-Sarah Christine Nimick[10]
  941-Kathleen Hyeon Nimick

753-**ELEANOR HOWE NIMICK**[9] (580), m. Andy Hay.
Issue:
  942-Christine Nimick Hay[10]

755-**WILLIAM KENNEDY NIMICK**[9] (582), m. Linda Trujillo.
Issue:
  943-Elizabeth Ann Nimick[10]
  944-Stephanie Lynn Nimick
  945-Amanda Marie Nimick

756-**DANIEL SPENCER NIMICK**[9] (582), m. Nancy Reed.
Issue:
  946-Christine Rebecca Nimick[10]

947-Matthew Spencer Nimick

762-**READE BAILEY NIMICK, Jr.**[9] (585), m. Laura Lee Nimick.
Issue:
948-Christopher Reade Nimick[10]
949-Kathryn Elizabeth Nimick

765-**GEORGE GUTHRIE NIMICK, Jr.**[9] (586), m. Alba Yolanda
Salvado Penman.
Issue:
950-George Alexander Nimick[10]
951-Ninotchka Nicole Nimick

766-**ANDREW SUPPLEE NIMICK**[9] (586), m. Daleen Spencer Bixl-
er.
Issue:
952-Stephen Joseph Nimick[10]

769-**CATHLEEN HARWOOD MUTLAND NIMICK**[9] (588), m. Peter
Singleton Austin.
Issue: (AUSTIN)
953-William Childs Austin[10]
954-Natalie Lockhart Austin

780-**SARAH MICHELLE CRAFT**[9] (599), b. 11 Mar. 1974; m. 17
Oct. 1998. John Patrick Draffin.
Issue: (DRAFFIN)
955-Berkeley Miles Draffin[10], b. 14 Aug. 2004

784-**SUZANNE IRENE HALL**[9] (601), b. 24 May 1959, m. 1985-
1986?, Sonnenberg Gardens, Canadaigua, NY., Kenneth Paul Corhan, b. 30 Mar. 1949.
Issue: (CORHAN)
956-Laura Elyse Corhan[10], b. 25 Jan. 1989, CA
957-Chad David Corhan, b. 20 Oct. 1992, CA

785-**SCOTT DAVID HALL**[9] (601), b. 30 April 1962, m. Memorial Art Gallery, Rochester, NY, 1990's?, Michelle Labossiere,
b. 21 Aug. 1967.
Issue: (HALL)
958-Parker David Hall[10], b. 11 Sept. 1997
959-Trevor Scott Hall, n. 12 Jan. 2000

800-**THOMAS MILTON WILSON**[9] (630), b. 1933, m. 1957, Ruth
Anjean Little. b. 1937.
Issue: (WILSON)
960-Cynthia Wilson[10], b. 1958
961-Denise Aline Wilson, b. 1959, m. 1981,   Harold
Loyd Snider, b. 1958.
962-John Milton Wilson, b. 1962
963-Robert Thomas Wilson, b. 1964
964-Paul Nathan Wilson, b. 1966; m. 1987, Ann Carol
Nemmers, b. 1966

801-**MARY EVELYN WILSON**[9] (630), b. 1935; m. 1962, Harold Wayne Kennedy, b. 1930.
    Issue: (KENNEDY)
        965-Mary Louise Kennedy[10], b. 1954; m. Carl Daniel Miller, b. 1954. Ch: (Miller) Laura Beth Miller, b. 1981; Mary Evelyn Miller, b. 1984
        966-Wayne Wilson Kennedy, b. 1957; m./1 1984, Pamela Simpson; m./2 Susan Eirheardt, div.
        967-Carolyn Wynn Kennedy, b. 1959; m/1, 1983, Ronald John Ballman, b. 1957, m./2 Elmaro David, div.
        968-Michael Harold Kennedy, b. 1963; m./1 Angie Kennedy, div.; m./2 Kim Beaty, div.; m./3 1994, Peggy Hier.
802-**DELMA GRACE WILSON**[9] (630) b. 1937; m. 1954, David Joe Kennedy, b. 1934.
    Issue: (KENNEDY)
        969-Harriette Jo Kennedy[10], b. 1962; m/1 Robert Ray Lambert; m./2 David Kendrick Jones.
        970-David Eugene Kennedy, b. 1963; m. 1988, Sherry Lynn Barry, b. 1968.

803-**WALTER HILL THOMAS**[9] (631), (1936-1983), m./1 Mary Ann Poindexter, div.; m./2 1970, Rose Clause; m./3 Doyline Miller, b. 1940.
    Issue: (THOMAS) from the first marriage
        971-Michael Allen Thomas[10], b. 1960
        972-Debroah Ann Thomas, b. 1961
           From the third marriage:
        973-Diane Adair Thomas (1981-1983)

805-**LINDA CHRISTINE THOMAS**[9] (631). b. 1944; m. 1965, David Tucker.
    Issue: (TUCKER)
        974-David Eric Tucker[10], b. 1966
        975-Lynda Katherine Tucker, (1969-1986)

806-**PERRY EDWARD THOMAS**[9] (631), b. 1951; m. 1969, Debbie Henderson.
    Issue: (THOMAS)
        976-Christine Ann Thomas[10], b. 1970
        977-Jennie Marie Thomas, b. 1971

807-**RAYBOURNE EDWIN LYLE**[9] (632), (1934; m. 1954, Bernice Parker, b. 1936.
    Issue: (LYLE)
        978-Susan Annette Lyle[10], b. 1957
        979-Sheila Barbette Lyle, b. 1958
        980-William Lyle, b. 1960

809-**BARBARA ANN SYKES**[9], (634), b. 1940; m. 1959, Glen Brewer, b. 1939.
    Issue: (BREWER)
        981-Marsha Joanne Brewer[10], b. 1960, m. Steven Cox
        982-Jere Clifton Brewer, b. 1962, m. Rochelle --?--,

their daughter, Chelsea Ann Brewer, b. 1990.
        983-Barbara Gayle Brewer, b. 1964
        984-Kyle Glenn Brewer, b. 1972
810-**JANET LOUISE SYKES**[9] (634), b. 1943; m. 1963, Billy Hunt, b. 1941.
    Issue: (HUNT)
        985-Cara Lynn Hunt[10], b. 1966
        986-Anissa Carol Hunt, b. 1968

811-**VELMA MAXINE SYKES**[9] (634), b. 1947; m. 1970, John Robert Brown, b. 1947.
    Issue: (BROWN)
        987-Jason Andrew Brown[10], b. 1974
        988-Alexander Robert Brown, b. 1978
        989-Timothy James Brown, b. 1981

814-**JERRY DEXTER MOORE**[9] (637), b. 1943; m. Dorothy Bailey, div.
    Issue: (MOORE)
        990-Jeff Moore[10], b. 1969

815-**JUDY GERTRUDE MOORE**[9] (637), b. 1949; m. James Fields, div.
    Issue: (FIELDS)
        991-Randy Fields[10], b. 1970
        992-Jody Fields, b. 1974

821-**MARK STEVEN JACKSON**[9] (639), b. 1960, m. 1985, Sandra Sue Keel, b. 1966. Issue: (JACKSON)
        993-Tiffany Nicole Jackson[10], b. 1987, Little Rock, AR
        994-Tyler Steven Jackson, b. 1992, Little Rock, AR

823-**DONNA LYNN SHOFNER**[9] (641), b. 1942; m. 1961, Lonny N. ALLISON, b. 1939.
    Issue: (ALLISON)
        995-Neal Allison[10], b. 1961
        996-Van Shofner Allison, B. 1964
        997-Amy Lynn Allison, b. 1965

824-**DAVID STANTON SHOFNER**[9] (641), b. 1947; m. 1968 Elizabeth BALLARD, div.
    Issue: (SHOFNER)
        998-Brittany Shofner[10], b.

829-**MICHAEL DEAN ECHELBARGER**[9] (643), b. 1945; m. 1966, Kathleen Ann JENKINS, b. 1947, d/o Roscoe Everett Jenkins and wf. Isla L. L. Longstaff.
    Issue: (ECHELBARGER)
        999-Stacie Ann Echelbarger[10], b. 1969, m. 1990, Todd
            Jay Bretz, b. 1990.
        1000-Todd Michael Echelbarger, b. 1973, m. 1995, Cari
            Jane Moser.
        1001-Tyler Jenkins Echelbarger, b. 1979

830-**PATRICK THOMAS ECHELBARGER**[9] (643), b. 1948; m. 1969, Marilyn Lodell MILLER, b. 1948, d/o Guy Harod Miller and wf. Eunice Roseann Kellett.
>   Issue: (ECHELBARGER)
>   1002-Matthew Patrick Echelbarger[10], b. 1975, m. 2001, Shelby Elizabeth Swanberg.
>   1003-Andrew Thomas Echelbarger, b. 1979

831-**LINDSEY LEO ROBINSON ECHELBARGER**[9] (643). b. 1952; m. Carolyn Elizabeth UPDIKE, b. 1949, d/o Robert Earl Updike and wf. Jean Linton.
>   Issue: (ECHELBARGER)
>   1004-James Robert Updike Echelbarger[10], b. 1968
>   1005-Michael Sean Linton Echelbarger, b. 1969
>   1006-Nicholas Lindsey Dean Echelbarger, b. 1981, graduated Cum Laude from Amherst College, BA in History, May 2004.

832-**DEBORAH KAY THOMAS**[9] (645), b. 1948; m/1, 1967, James Ireland, b. 1947: m./2, 1988, James Masters.
>   Issue: (IRELAND)
>   1007-John Patrick Ireland[10], b. 1969.
>   1008-Amy E. Ireland, b. 1974.

833-**KNOX THOMAS III**[9] (645), b. 1951; m. Debbie Lynn Shelton, b. 1956.
>   Issue: (THOMAS)
>   1009-Matthew Bryan Thomas[10], b. 1977
>   1010-Megann Lynn Thomas, b. 1979

835-**SCOTT ALAN THOMAS**[9] (645) (1962-1984), m. 1979, Cynthia Rene Shearon, b. 1962.
>   Issue: (THOMAS)
>   1011-Brittyne L. Thomas[10], b. 1980

836-**WALLACE CARNEY HARRIS II**[9] (648), b. 1953; m./1 1977, Dawn Renee Sloan, div., m./2 1988, Helen Bryan Buck, b. 1954, n.i.
>   Issue: (HARRIS) (first marriage)
>   1012-Maria Dawn Harris[10]. b. 1978
>   1013-Melissa Nicole Harris, b. 1981

837-**JEROLD RODNEY HARRIS**[9] (648) b. 1958: m. 1980, Catherine Ann Johnson, b. 1958.
>   Issue: (HARRIS)
>   1014-Seth Patrick Harris[10], b. 1981
>   1015-Heather Christine Harris, b. 1985
>   1016-Matthew Robert Harris, b. 1989
>   1017-Rebekah Elizabeth Harris, b. 1991

840-**SUSAN PATRICE PATTERSON**[9] (649). b. 1955; m. 1979, George Randall HINSON s/o George Emmett Hinson and wf. Dorothy Ann Nichols.
>   Issue: (HINSON)

1018-William Randall Hinson[10], b. 1980.

841-**LOU ANN ALLISON**[9] (650), b. 1962, m. 1979, Timothy Wayne Bruce.
 Issue: (BRUCE)
  1019-Allison Nannette Bruce[10], b. 1980
  1020-Bobbie Sue Bruce, b. 1983
  1021-Kimberly Mitchell Bruce, b. 1986

842-**STEVEN ERIC BURNETT**[9] (652) b. 1960, m/1, 1978, Joni Carr, b. 1960: m./2, 1986, Sheila Wilson, div. n. i.; m./3, 1998, Jennifer Knight, b. 1971
 Issue: (BURNETT) (marriage one)
  1022-Sara Kathryn Burnett[10], b. 1979, m. Chad Allen Reid.
      (Marriage three)
  1023-Noah Eric Burnett, b. 1998
  1024-Dylan Thomas Burnett, b. 2000

843-**SAUNDRA SUZANNE BURNETT**[9] (652), b. 1964, m. 1993, Paul Michael Kretschmer, b. 1963.
 Issue: (KRETSCHMER)
  1025-Madeline Jane Kretschmer[10], b. 1998.
  1026-Henry Morgan Kretschmer, b. 2000

845-**MELISSA JILL HARRELL**[9] (654), b. 1959; m. 1982, Jeffrey Tad Wheeler, b. 1956.
 Issue: (WHEELER)
  1027-Margaret Jan Wheeler[10], b. 1984
  1028-Steven Edward Wheeler, b. 1986
  1029-Kathleen Grace Wheeler, b. 1988

846-**BENJAMIN THOMAS HARRELL**[9] (654), b. 1961; m. 1990, Diana Marie Black.
 Issue: (HARRELL)
  1030-Emily Harrell[10]
  1031-Elise Harrell

857-**JAMES TANDY COY, III**[9] (670), b. 5 Nov. 1973, Lexington, KY., m. Elizabeth Nicole Jones, b. 1974.
 Issue: (COY)
  1032-Joseph Daniel Jones Coy[10], b. 21 Apr. 1999, Louisville, Jefferson Co., KY.

859-**THOMAS HENRY DICKMAN, Jr.**[9] (671), b. 15 May 1970, Tuscaloosa, AL., m. 28 Dec. 1996, at Green Leaves, Natchez, MS. Melissa Diane Nichols, d/o Perry Augustus Nichols, Jr. and wf. Nancy Beverly Jenkins.
 Issue: (DICKMAN)
  1033-Conner Perry Dickman[10], b. 14 Sept. 2001, Decatur, Morgan Co., AL

867-**BRITTON HILLMAN HARTMAN**[9] (677), b. 24 Nov. 1974, m.

Holly Hatchel. [1]
Issue: (HARTMAN)
1034-Anna Raven Hartman, b. 1997

874-**JOAN MARIE MILLER**[9] (693), b. 17 July 1935, Sandoval, Marion Co., IL; m. 11 Sept. 1958, Methodist Church, Sandoval, Murval Andrew Moore.
Issue: (MOORE)
1035-Thomas Warren Moore[10], b. 18 Dec. 1963; d. 22 Nov. 1966.
1036-Kathryn Marie Moore, b. 7 Aug. 1967.

884-**ROGER DARRELL MERIDITH**[9] (696), b. 9 Dec. 1948, Belleville, IL., m. 25 Jan. 1975, Decatur, IL., Sandy "Sandy" Kay Gilbert.
Issue: (MERIDITH)
1037-Roger David Meridith[10], b. 17 July 1975, Decatur, IL., m. Samantha Nichols.
1038-Russell Dwayne Meridith, b. 7 Nov. 1978, Decatur, IL.

885-**RUSSELL DAVID MERIDITH**[9] (696), b. 15 May 1951, Belleville, IL.; m. 9 Aug. 1981, Virginia, IL., Linda Maurer.
Issue: (MERIDITH)
1039-Diana Lin Meridith[10], b. 13 July 1978., Winter Park, FL.

886-**BRADEN LEE SHELMAN**[9] (699). b. 5 June 1945; m. 2 Sept. 1967, at Andover, KS. Lynda Bernice Norton, b. 11 Mar. 1947, d/o Willie Norton and wf. Berniece.
Issue: (SHELMAN)
1040-Jason Lee Shelman[10], b. 15 Mar. 1976, Wichita, KS.
1041-Justin Troy Shelman, b. 2 May 1979, Wichita, KS.

887-**NIETA CAROL SHELMAN**[9] (699), b. 2 May 1948, Wichita, KS.; m. 4 Nov. 1967, Andover, KS., Jerel Warren Devor, b. 12 Aug. 1948, McPherson, KS., s/o Virgil Devor and wf. Goldie King.
Issue: (DEVOR)
1042-Craig Warren Devor[10], b. 12 Feb. 1970, Wichita, KS. [2]
1043-Bradley Wayne Devor, b. 12 Feb. 1970, Wichita, KS.
1044-Lori Rene Devor, b. 18 May 1973, Wichita, KS.

888-**JANEEN KAY SHELMAN**[9] (699), b. 14 Oct. 1949, Wichita, KS.; m. 24 Oct. 1970, Andover, KS. Kerry Lee Baker, b. 18 Oct. 1949.
Issue: (BAKER)
----

1. Conner, William Beltzhoover, May 2002

2. Devor, Craig Warren (Clarence Norwood Leith family) Jan. 2005

1045-Corey Neil Baker[10], b. 14 Aug. 1972, Wichita, KS.
1046-Aubrie Kay Baker, b. 8 July 1975, Wichita, KS.

893-**ERIC RICHARD BELTZHOOVER**[9] (706), b. 15 Dec. 1958, Clinton, IL., m. Laurie LAMBERT, b. 11 Dec. 1959.
    Issue: (BELTZHOOVER)
       1047-Ryan Michael Beltzhoover[10], b. 6 Aug. 1984
       1048-Rachel Michelle Beltzhoover, b. 14 Sept. 1988

894-**CAROLYN BELTZHOOVER**[9] (706), b. 14 June 1962, Clinton, IL., m. David JOHANSON, b. 11 June 1962.
    Issue: (JOHANSON)
       1049-Christopher David Johanson[10], b. 13 Oct. 1990
       1050-Matthew Steven Johanson, b. 26 Jan. 1992
       1051-Timothy Edward Johanson, b. 28 July 1997
       1052-Sarah Christine Johanson, b. 19 Sept. 2001

895-**CHRISTINE BELTZHOOVER**[9] (706), b. 14 June 1962, Clinton, IL., m., div., Gary GREBEN, b. 9 Nov. 1961.
    Issue: (GREBEN)
       1053-Samantha Beltzhoover Greben[10]. b. 23 July 1990

897-**GRETCHEN BELTZHOOVER**[9] (706), b. 7 Aug. 1970, Joliet, IL., m. Rolf Ugland TROHA, b. 23 June 1966.
    Issue: (TROHA)
       1054-Madeline Beltzhoover Troha[10], b. 12 Mar. 1995
       1055-Lukas Ugland Troha, b. 8 July 1997
       1056-Eric George Troha, b. 7 Oct. 2003

903-**GEORGE CHRISTOPHER BELTZHOOVER**[9] (709), b. 23 Nov. 1961, Carlisle, PA. m. 10 Sept. 1988, Tari Lynn Hinshaw, b. 27 May 1960.
    Issue: (BELTZHOOVER)
       1057-Rachael Christine Beltzhoover[10], b. 5 July 1991

904-**DAVID EDWARD BELTZHOOVER**[9] (709), b. 1 Feb. 1963, m. 1 Oct. 1997, Sheri Leah Hair, b. 22 Aug. 1967.
    Issue: (BELTZHOOVER)
       1058-Hailee Brooke Beltzhoover[10], b. 25 Feb. 1998

910-**HELEN AUDREY MANN**[9] (713), b. 12 May, 1921, Boiling Springs, Cumberland Co., PA., m. 23 Nov. 1941, Edward Replogle Burket, in Shepherdstown, Cumberland Co., PA., b.3 Jan. 1920, son of Edward Burket and wf., Harriet Replogle.

Edward Burket descended as follows: Adam Burkhurdt[1], John Puderbaugh Burket[2], David Benner Burget[3], Adam W. Burkhurdt[4], Edward Stevens Burket[5], Edward Replogle Burket[6].
    Issue: (BURKET)
       1059-Judith Kay Burket[10], b. 13 Oct. 1944, Mechanicsburg, Cumberland Co., PA.
       1060-Lynn Edward Burket, b. 02 Apr. 1947, Mechanicsburg, Cumberland Co., PA., m. 25 Aug. 1968, Kenton, Kent Co., DE., Geraldine Lynn Graham

1061-Brenda Lou Burket, b. 16 May 1950, Mechanicsburg,
            Cumberland Co., PA., m./1, 20 Jul. 1969, Me-
            chanicsburg, PA., Ronald Keith; m./2, 21 May
            1983, Mechanicsburg, PA., James Gerald Smith.

911-**HARRY WILLIAM MANN, Jr.**[9] (713), b. 13 Feb. 1926; m.
Jul. 1946, Jane Louise Sponsler.
    Issue: (MANN)
      1062-Patricia Ann Mann[10], b. 1947
      1063-Susan Mann
      1064-Deborah Mann
      1065-Keith Mann

912-**FREDA HOOVER**[9] (714), b. 10 Sept. 1922, Boiling
Springs, Cumberland Co., PA., m. 05 June 1943, First EUB
Church, Cumberland Co., PA., Francis Blessing.
    Issue: (BLESSING)
      1066-David W. Blessing[10], b. 07 Apr. 1944, Carlisle,
            Cumberland Co., PA.
      1067-Joanna Blessing, b. 08 Dec. 1945, m. 8 Dec. 1945,
            m. 14 Sept. 1968, Timothy Hoff.
      1068-Donald E. Blessing, b. 25 Dec. 1949, Carlisle,
            Cumberland Co., PA.
      1069-Michael D. Blessing, b. 25 Dec. 1949, Carlisle,
            Cumberland Co., PA., m. 23 Apr. 1988, Joanne
            McCartney.

915-**SHIRLEY MAE LEIDIGH**[9] (726), b. 4 Dec. 1920, m. 25
July 1943, Mt. Holly Springs, PA., John Edward Kennedy, b. 28
June 1920, Enola, PA. Jack is the son of Cassius M. and Jo-
sephine L. STEES KENNEDY.
    Issue: (KENNEDY)
      1070-John Edgar Kennedy, Jr.[10], b. 12 Feb. 1945, Car-
            lisle, m. Adele Rosario Capeclatro, b. 7 May
            1947.
      1071-Dianne Lynn Kennedy, b. 10 June 1948, Carlisle, m.
            5 Aug. 1972, Mechanicsburg, PA., Ronald Anthony
            DeGumba, b. 24 Feb. 1947, South River, NJ., s/o
            Gus and Stella FUDNIKOVICH DeGUMBA.

916-**JEAN BRILLHART**[9] (727), b. 9 Aug. 1921, Cumberland
Co., PA., m. 21 Oct. 1944, Albert Leonard Verdekal, b. 18 Nov.
1913, Roaring Creek, PA., d. 9 July 1980. Albert is buried in
St. Patrick's Cem., Carlisle, PA.
    Issue: (VERDEKAL)
      1072-Lois Verdekal[10], m. Leon Littlehale.
      1073-James L. Verdekal, b. 7 July 1946; d. 5 Jan. 2003;
            m. Maria Monachas.

917-**ANNA MAE BRILLHART**[9] (727), b. 7 April 1923, Cumberland Co., PA., m. 14 Feb. 1948, Glen Dwight Faught.
    Issue: (FAUGHT)
      1074-Glen Dwight Faught, Jr.[10], m. Aug. 1994

918-**HARRY BRILLHART**[10] (727), b. 28 June 1924, Cumberland Co., PA., m. 17 Nov. 1943, Alice Franklin, b. 17 Jan. 1925, Stamford, CT.
    Issue: (BRILLHART)
      1075-Janice Brillhart[11]
      1076-Elise Brillhart
      1077-Lauri Brillhart

919-**BRENDA LOUISE BRILLHART**[10] (727), b. 20 Oct. 1925, Carlisle, PA., m. 26 June 1948, Carlisle, PA., Howard William Sowers, Jr., b. 22 May 1920, Philadelphia, PA., d. 9 May 1996, Macon, GA. Howard was the son of Howard William, Sr. and wf. Aleta Minerva Leidigh Sowers. Aleta was a descendant of Johann Michael Leidigh, the sixth child of Leonard Michael and Anna Margaret Leidich/Leidigh.
    Issue: (SOWERS)
      1078-Howard William Sowers, III[11], b. 12 Dec. 1951, Carlisle, m 24 Dec. 1976, Glinda Evans, b. 12 Feb. 1947, Montgomery, AL.
      1079-Jeanette Louise Sowers, b. 4 July 1955, Carlisle, m. Stephen D. Wall, b. 5 Dec. 1957, Warner Robbins, GA.
      1080-Mark Leroy Sowers, b. 29 Nov. 1957, Carlisle, PA., d. 20 June 1975, Warner Robins, CA
      1081-Jack Alan Sowers, b. 29 June 1959, Carlisle, PA, m. 26 Sept. 1981, Cheryl Lynn Henson, b. 26 Oct. 1961, Mobile, AL.

920-**ROBERT E. BRILLHART**[9] (727), b. 8 April 1929, Carlisle, PA., d. 26 June 1973, Mechanicsburg, PA., m. Nelda Nailor.
    Issue: (BRILLHART)
      1082-William E. Brillhart[10], res Shiremanstown, PA.
      1083-Bonnie Brillhart, m. Richard S. Dear, Mechanisburg
      1084-Robert D. Brillhart

923-**BRENDA MAE LEIDIGH**[9] (731), b. 26 June 1939, m./1 John DuRose, b. Nottingham, England, d. 1969, g. New Cathedral Cem., Baltimore, MD. Brenda Leidigh DuRose, m. /2 Patrick Adams, div. 1978; m./3 Charles Emory Crenshaw, m. 8 Mar. 1936, Atlanta, GA. Charles is the son of Emory Lee and Anna Mae CHAPEL CRENSHAW of Atlanta, GA.
    Issue: (DUROSE)
      1085-Mary Margaret DuRose[10], b. 16 Aug. 1970
      (ADAMS) Second marriage
      1086-Heather Michelle Adams, b. 9 May 1976

925-**ROBERT IRWIN LEIDIGH, JR.**[9], (733), b. 8 May 1935, Carlisle, PA., m. 23 June 1956, Harrisburg, PA., Josephine M. Woutersz, b. 2 May 1936. Bob is the manager of Pinehurst Country Club, Pinehurst, NC.

Josephine is the daughter of Clement T. and Kathryn HAHN WOUTERSZ. Her grandfather Bernard Woutersz, emigrated from Ceylon, now Sri Lanka.

Issue: (LEIDIGH)
    1087-Kathleen Elaine Leidigh[10], b. 25 Mar. 1957, Har-
            risburg, m. 26 Dec. 1987, Charles Ledman
            Sweetser, b. 10 Aug. 1961, Harrisburg, PA.
    1088-Stephen Michael Leidigh, b. 10 April 1961, Harris-
            burg, m. 13 May 1989, m. Tracy Ann Heiland, b.
            9 June 1961, div.
    1089-Alan Robert Leidigh, b. 20 May 1963, Harrisburg
    1090-Robert Joseph Leidigh, b. 5 June 1965, Camp Hill,
            PA., m. 4 June 1994, Harrisburg, m. 4 June
            1994, Lisa Renee Haynes, b. 9 Mar. 1965. Lisa
            is the dau. of Harry and Glenda KOHR HAYNES
    1091-Marie Leidigh, b. 24 Feb. 1967, Camp Hill, PA., m.
            30 July 1994, Robert Harry Fox, b. 17 Nov.
            1968, Avis, PA. Robert is the son of Robert
            and Jacqueline Fox.
    1092-Leanne Leidigh, b. 3 Dec. 1970, Camp Hill, PA.

928-**BEVERLY MAE LEIDIGH**[9] (733), b. 21 July 1945, Harrisburg, PA., m. 3 Oct. 1964, John G. Tomochik, b. 11 July 1944.
    Issue: (TOMOCHIK)
    1093-Cynthis Tomochik[10], b. 23 July 1965, m. 24 May
            1986

930-**CAROL ANN LEIDIGH**[9] (738), b. 13 Jan. 1938, Carlisle,
Pa., m. 27 Aug. 1961, Mt. Holly Springs, PA., Ellis Reginald
Wagner, b. 13 April 1937, Carlisle, PA.,
    Issue: (WAGNER)
    1094-David Andrew Wagner[10], b. 28 Oct. 1965, Chamber-
            sburg; m. Eva Christina Reuterskiold.
    1095-Ann Marie Wagner, b. 10 Mar, 1970, Chambersburg

931-**RONALD THOMAS LEIDIGH**[9] (738), b. 18 Nov. 1942, Carlisle, PA., m. 12 Oct. 1963, Donna Sealover, b. 23 June 1944,
Bragtown (now Bermudian), PA.
    Issue: (LEIDIGH)
    1096-Michelle Louise Leidigh[10], b. 15 May 1964, Harris-
            burg, PA., and has a daughter, Nicole Louise
            Leidigh, b. 12 Dec. 1983, Harrisburg, PA.
    1097-Ronald Thomas Leidigh, Jr. b. 7 Dec. 1965; m. Mar-
            yann Gavazzi.
    1098-Scott Allen Leidigh, b. 1 Mar. 1969, Harrisburg,
    1099-Christopher Michael Leidigh, b. 21 Apr. 1976

Tenth Generation

933-**CASSANDRA LEE 'CASSIE' KAMP**[10] (748), b. 30 Aug. 1945,
Indianapolis, IN; m. 9 Mar. 1968, Jerry L. Bradley, b. 15
Sept. 1944.
    Issue: (BRADLEY)
    1100-Matthew Kamp Bradley[11], b. 2 Aug. 1972, Ft. Wayne,
            IN., grad. I. U., MBA, I. U. School of Busi-
            ness; m. 16 Sept. 2000, Indianapolis, IN.,
            Danica Vasilcheck, M.D.

1101-Marla Elizabeth Bradley, b. 19 July 1976, Ft. Wayne, IN., grad. I.U. 1998. Married May 18, 2002, to Brian Mast, grad. Indiana Univ.

934-**GREGORY G. KAMP**[10] (748), b. 16 May 1950, Huntington, IN; grad. I.U., grad. I. U. School of Denistry, D.D.S.; m. 10 June 1972, Mary Patricia King, b. 15 June 1949.
    Issue: (KAMP)
    1102-Ryan Christopher Kamp, M.D.[11], b. 30 Jan. 1976, grad. Suma Cum Laude, Wabash College; grad. I. U. Medical School, Internship Chicago School of Medicine, Chicago, IL., m. 28 Dec. 2002, Anna Nicole Kirincich, M.D.
    1103-Michael Talbott Kamp, b. 4 Nov. 1978, graduate DePauw Univ. 2001., obtained his Masters Degree from Ball State Univ. in 2003.

961-**DENISE ALINE WILSON**[10] (800), b. 1959, m. 1981, Harold Loyd Snider, b. 1958.
    Issue: (SNIDER)
    1104-Kathleen Nicole Snider[11], b. 1983
    1105-Hanna Caroline Snider, b. 1992.

965-**MARY LOUISE KENNEDY**[10] (801), b. 1954; m. 1972, Carl Daniel Miller, b. 1954.
    Issue: (MILLER)
    1106-Laura Beth Miller[11], b. 1981
    1107-Mary Evelyn Miller, b. 1984

967-**CAROLYN WYNNE KENNEDY**[10] (801), b. 1959; m/1 1983, Ronald John Ballman, b. 1957, m./2 Elmaro David, div.
    Issue: (BALLMAN)
    1108-Andrew David Ballman[11], b. 1979

969-**HARRIETTE JO KENNEDY**[10] (802), b. 1962; m/1 Robert Ray Lambert, div.; m./2 1985, David Kendrick Jones, b. 1957.
    Issue: (LAMBERT)
    1109-Justin Ray Lambert[11], b. 1980;
    Child of the second marriage (JONES)
    1110-David DeWayne Jones, b. 1986

970-**DAVID EUGENE KENNEDY**[10] (802), b. 1963; m. 1988, Sherry Lynn Barry, b. 1968.
    Issue: (KENNEDY)
    1111-Zachary David Kennedy[11], b. 1989
    1112-Summer Alexi Kennedy, b. 1994.

981-**MARSHA JOANNE BREWER**[10] (809), b. 1960; m. Steven Cox.
    Issue: (COX)
    1113-Brian Donald Cox[11], b. 1982
    1114-James Robert Cox, b. 1984

982-**JERE CLIFTON BREWER**[10] (809), b. 1962; m. Rochelle --?--.

146

Issue: (BREWER)
  1115-Chelsea Ann Brewer[11]. b. 1990

983-BARBARA GAYLE BREWER[10] (809), b. 1964; m. Cary Funderburg.
  Issue: (FUNDERBURG)
  1116-Brandon Collin Funderburg[11], b. 1983
  1117-Wesley Ryan Funderburg, b. 1986
  1118-Madison Funderburg, b. 1991.

999-STACIE ANN ECHELBARGER[10] (829), b. 1969, m. 1990, Todd Jay Bretz.
  Issue: (BRETZ)
  1119-Thomas Jay Michael Bretz[11], b. 1990
  1120-Tessa Kathleen Bretz, b. 1993
  1121-Sara Kate Bretz, b. 1995

1000-TODD MICHAEL ECHELBARGER[10] (829), b. 1973, m. 1995, Cari Jane Moser.
  Issue: (ECHELBARGER)
  1122-Samuel Will Echelbarger[11], b. 1997
  1123-Hannah Anne Echelbarger, b. 1998, a twin.
  1124-Abigail Grace Echelbarger, b. 1998, a twin.

1002-MATTHEW PATRICK ECHELBARGER[10] (830), b. 1975, m. 2001, Shelby Elizabeth Swanberg.
  Issue: (ECHELBARGER
  1125-Grace Elizabeth Echelbarger[11], b. 2004

1022-SARA KATHRYN BURNETT[10] (842), b. 1979, m. 2001, Chad Alan Reid, b. 1979, s/o Richard Kenneth Reid and wf. Debra Lynn Brazeale.
  Issue: (REID)
  1126-Logan Alexander Reid[11], b. 2002
  1127-Wiley Alan Reid, b. 2004

1037-ROGER DAVID MERIDITH[10] (884), b. 17 July 1975, Decatur, IL.; m. Samantha Nichols. [1]
  Issue: (MERIDITH) Children both born Decatur, IL.
  1128-Zachary David Meridith[11], b. 22 Dec. 1993.
  1129-Alexis Ann Nicole Meridith, b. 31 Jan. 1999.

1042-CRAIG WARREN DEVOR[10] (887), b. 12 Feb. 1970, Wichita, KS, a twin; m. 31 Oct. 1992, Tonganoxie, KS., Joy Lynn Schoemig, b. 17 Aug. 1974, Independence, MO., d/o Gerald Schoemig and wf. Bessie Howland. [2]
  Issue: (DEVOR)
  1130-Austin James Devor[11], b. 12 Oct. 1993.

----

1. Meridith, Roger

2. Devor, Craig Warren

1131-Neil Anthony Devor, b. 29 June 1998
1132-Alec Mason Devor, b. 22 April 2001

1043-**BRADLEY WAYNE DEVOR**[10] (887), b. 12 Feb. 1970, a twin, Wichita, KS.; m. 18 Dec. 1993, Tonganoxie, KS., Emily Leinen, b. 10 Oct. 1975, Long Beach, CA., d/o Frank Leinen & wf. Kathleen Holt.
    Issue: (DEVOR)
      1133-Juan David Devor[11], b. 7 May 1994, Columbia, chosen, Feb. 2005.

1044-**LORI RENE DEVOR**[10] (887), b. 18 May 1973, Wichita, KS.; m. 24 Aug. 1994, Tonganoxie, KS., Scott Roberson, b. 17 Feb. 1971, Manhattan, KS., s/o Roy Roberson & wf. Vicki Anderson.
    Issue: (ROBERSON)
      1134-Kaitlyn Rene Roberson[11], b. 4 Aug. 1997.
      1135-Avery Michele Roberson, B. 6 mAR. 2002.

1045-**COREY NEIL BAKER**[10] (888), b. 14 Aug. 1972, Wichita, KS.; m. in Andover, KS., Danielle --?--.
    Issue: (BAKER)
      1136-Madysen Baker[11], b. 2 Aug. 1999
      1137-Riley Marie Baker, b. 16 April 2003

1046-**AUBRIE KAY BAKER**[10] (888), b. 8 July 1975, Wichita, KS.; m. 29 July 2000, Wichita, KS., Kevin Scott Johnson, b. 15 April 1972.
    Issue: (JOHNSON)
      1138-Colin Scott Johnson[11], b. 28 May 2004

1059-**JUDITH KAY BURKET**[10] (910), b. 13 Oct. 1944, Mechanicsburg, Cumberland Co., PA., m. Dec. 1968, Mechanisburg, PA., Richard Stephen Haller, s/o Loraine Wolford.
    Issue: (HALLER)
      1139-Benjamin Stephen Haller[11], b. 23 Feb. 1976, Harrisburg, Dauphin Co., PA.

1061-**BRENDA LOU BURKET**[10] (910), b. 16 May 1950, Mechanicsburg, Cumberland Co., PA., m./1 20 July 1968, Mechanicsburg, PA., Ronald Keith Loy, s/o Paul Loy and wf., Pauling Patterson; m./2, 21 May 1983, Mechanicsburg, PA., James Gerald Smith.
    Issue: (LOY)
      1140-Christie Ann Loy[11], b. 22 Apr. 1970, Carlisle, PA

1070-**JOHN EDGAR KENNEDY, JR.**[10] (915), b. 12 Feb. 1945, Carlisle, PA., m., 7 June 1967, Madison, NJ., Adele Rosario Capecelatro, b. 7 May 1947, d/o Dr. Achille and Anna Pagano Capecelatro.
    Issue: (KENNEDY)
      1141-Kevin Stees Kennedy[11], b. 30 Oct. 1973, Carlisle, PA
      1142-Allison Faye Kennedy, b. 23 Oct. 1976, Carlisle,

PA.

1072-**LOIS VERDEKAL**[10] (916), m. Leon Littlehale
Issue: (LITTLEHALE)
  1143-Natalie Littlehale[11]
  1144-Albert Littlehale
  1145-Victor Littlehale
  1146-Audra Littlehale

1073-**JAMES L. VERDEKAL**[10] (916), m. Maria Monachas
Issue: (VERDEKAL)
  1147-Sophia Verdekal[11]
  1148-Albert Verdekal

1078-**HOWARD WILLIAM SOWERS, III**[10] (919), b. 12 Dec. 1951, Carlisle, PA., m. 24 Dec. 1976, Atlanta, GA., Glinda Evans, b. 12 Feb. 1947, Montgomery, AL.
Issue: (SOWERS)
  1149-Howard William Sowers, IV[11], b. 26 Nov. 1980
  1150-Evan Brillhart Sowers, b. 24 Nov. 1986

1079-**JEANETTE LOUISE SOWERS**[10] (919), b. 4 July 1955, Carlisle, PA., m. 24 June 1978, Warner Robins, GA., Steven D. Wall, b. 5 Dec. 1957, Warner Robins, GA.
Issue: (WALL)
  1151-Tara Eileen Wall[11], b. 22 Jan. 1979, Atlanta, GA
  1152-Candace Nicole Wall, b. 23 Oct. 1980, Warner Robins, GA
  1153-Alica Jade Wall, b. 4 Sept. 1986, Warner Robins, GA

1081-**JACK ALAN SOWERS**[10] (919), b. 29 June 1959, Carlisle, PA., m. 26 Sept. 1981, Warner Robins, Cheryl Lynn Henson, b. 26 Oct. 1961, Mobile, AL.
Issue: (SOWERS)
  1154-Kristen Michelle Sowers[11], b. 23 Sept. 1982, Warner Robins, GA
  1155-Bridgette Lynne Sowers, b. 10 May 1986, Warner Robins
  1156-Brandon Alan Sowers, b. 14 July 1993, Warner Robins

1087-**KATHLEEN ELAINE LEIDIGH**[10] (925), b. 25 Mar. 1957, Harrisburg, PA., m. 26 Dec.1987, Harrisburg, PA., Charles Ledman Sweetser, b. 10 Aug. 1961, Harrisburg, PA.
Issue: (SWEETSER)
  1157-Charles Anthony Sweetser[11], b. 13 May 1988, Harrisburg, PA.
  1158-Chelsea Lynn Sweetser.b. 1 Apr. 1991, Harrisburg, PA.

1089-**ALAN ROBERT LEIDIGH**[10] (925), b. May 20 1963, Harrisburg. Spouse unknown.
Issue: (LEIDIGH)

1159-Felicia Leidigh[11], b. 7 Aug. 1992, Harrisburg, PA
1160-Brandon Leidigh, b. 8 May 1994, Harrisburg, PA.

1094-DAVID ANDREW WAGNER[10] (930), b. 28 Oct. 1965, Chambersburg, PA., m. 5 Aug. 1989, State College, PA., Eva Christina Reuterskiold, b. 14 Dec. 1957, Stockholm, Sweden.
 Issue: (WAGNER)
  1161-Patrik Ian Andrew Wagner[11], b. 16 July 1990, Lund, Sweden
  1162-Anna Katerina Wagner, b. 31 July 1992, Lund, Sweden

1097-RONALD THOMAS LEIDIGH, Jr.[10] (931), b. 7 Dec. 1965, Carlisle, PA., m. 2 May 1992, Hershey, PA., Maryann Gavazzi. b. 11 Aug. 1966.
 Issue: (LEIDIGH)
  1163-Abigail Marie Leidigh[11], b. 27 Feb. 1995

<u>Eleventh Generation</u>

1100-MATTHEW KAMP BRADLEY[11] (933), b. 2 Aug. 1972, m. 16 Sept. 2000, Danica Vasilcheck, M.D.
 Issue: (BRADLEY)
  1164-Gavin Alexander Bradley[12], b. 17 Dec. 2004, Indianapolis, IN.

1140-CHRISTIE ANN LOY[11] (1061), b. 22 Apr. 1970, Carlisle, PA., m./1, Joseph Lee Chamberlain, s/o Jay Chamberlain and Joyce Myers; m./2 Jonathan Clippinger, 14 Feb. 1987, Mount Holly Springs, Cumberland Co., PA.; m./3, 31 Dec. 1992, Endicott, NY., Allan Ripic.
 Issue: (CHAMBERLAIN)
  1165-Kyle Lee Chamberlain[12], b. 23 Nov. 1990, Carlisle, PA. Christened Nov. 1991, adopted, renamed Jerry Lee Walker.
 Issue: (second marriage) (CLIPPINGER)
  1166-Tiffanie Helen Clippinger[12], b. 08 Aug. 1987, Mount Holly Springs, Cumberland Co., PA.,
 Issue: (third marriage) (RIPIC)
  1167-David John Ripic[12], b. 08 June 1993, Endicott, NY., bpt. 25 Dec. 1994, by Father Robert Tierney at St. Ambrose Church, Endicott, NY. Godfather, Michael Benjamin Ripic; Godmother, Donna Marie Ripic.
  1168-Emily Nicole Ripic, b. 20 Oct. 1995

Other Beltzhoovers'

After years of research there were many Beltzhoovers' that we were unable to prove their place in the families. There were other Beltzhoover families that came to America later and not directly related to our families, to our knowledge.

We have included these 'unable to place' Beltzhoovers' here and in the index in order to help future researchers in their studies.

* * * * * * * * * *

Jesse Beltzhoover, married Louisa Jacobs c. 1828-1829, where?. Jesse or Jacob? There is a record, Jacob Beltzhoover, m. 22 Aug. 1833, Louisa Jacobs of York Co., PA. If this is the Jacob Beltzhoover who died, Williamsport, PA., 25 Mar. 1880 (84-5-0), they were married 47 years. Were there two Louisa Jacobs?

JESSE BELTZHOOVER Is this the son of George of Manchester? No. Jesse m. 1839 too old to be the son of George of Manchester who m. Louisa Jacobs.

* * * * * * * * *

EMMA/CLARA EMMA BELTZHOOVER, d/o George Beltzhoover; m. 1873, Jacob Myers Hertzler, b. 1848, a farmer, son of Christian and Barbara MYERS HERTZLER. [1] [2]

Issue: (see #377, page 83 and #202, pp. 57, 83)
    Barbara R. Hertzler
    James Weir Hertzler
    Emma Laura Hertzler (1878-1942), m. John P. Brindle
        (1879-1937) graves Mt. Zion Cem. Sect L
    Jacob Boyd Hertzler (1884-1961)

* * * * * * * * * *

LOIS BELTZHOOVER on 3 Mar. 1818, on 4 Mar. 1818 and on 13 Jan. 1819, selling town lots Hagerstown, MD. An early lady real estate broker? The information from Index to Hagerstown Newspapers indicates that these properties were owned by other persons.

* * * * * * * * *

ALEXANDER L. BELTZHOOVER, d. 20 Feb. 1909 (61), reported in the Pittsburgh Gazette 23 Feb. 1909, the funeral from the residence of his mother, Mrs. Eliza J. Beltzhoover, Castle Shannon. He m. Emma R. Hargleroad and had dau., Jennie. [3]

* * * * * * * * * *

HARRIET BELTZHOOVER, b. ca. 1817; d. 7 May 1897 (80), Ellsworth Ave., Pittsburgh, PA., mother of John and Harry Beltzhoover. Harriet Beltzhoover resided at 5896 Elsworth

----

1. Ibid., Hist. of Cumberland and Adams Co.'s   pp. 509-510, courtesy Jerri Burket, Langswamp, PA 2/15/00

2. Zion Cemetery, Monroe Twp., Cumberland Co., PA

3. Pittsburgh Gazette Times Feb. 22 1909, Monday

Ave. The 1880 census gives her place of birth was PA and that her father was born in England and her mother was born in PA. Harriet's husband may be, John # 22, p. 20-22. His first wf. Anne? and second wf. Harriet? Issue: [1]

John D. Beltzhoover , b. ca 1842. The 1880 census shows him as single and 38, a foreman at L. Sable. His mother Harriett and brother, John are living with him. Your researchers suspect that this John Beltzhoover is the Mountain Home, TN soldier. The 1910 census shows him as age 68, single, TN.

Harry B. Beltzhoover, b. c. 1856. Union Dale records residence as Dixmont, PA. Newspaper says, 47 Alderson St., Allegheny, PA. The 1880 census shows him living with his single brother, John D., and his mother, Harriett. His occupation is Clerk in Und. T. Ess. [2].

Nathaniel Beltzhoover, b. ca. 1850, d.y.?
****
HITA RODRIQUEZ BELTZHOOVER, b. 22 Sept. 1900; d. 9 Mar. 1985, Guadalupe Valley Hospital, Seguin, TX. Her residence was at 440 Wallace St., Seguin. Funeral Mass was held at ST. James Catholic Church, g. Sacred Heart Catholic Cemetery, Floresville, TX. Survivors were a sister, Zulia Spelman of Seguin and one brother, J. M.? Rodriquez of San Antonio. The name of her deceased husband, **John Beltzhoover**, d. 1953, g. Sacred Heart Cem. There is no mention of any children. The family relationship is not known. [3]
****
ANNA BELTZHOOVER ss 494-09-8056, b. 16 Nov. 1887; d. Dec. 1978, IL., 62882, Sandoval, Marion Co., IL.
MARY/MAIZE BELTZHOOVER died same zip 62882, Sandoval, Marion Co., IL., b. 15 June 1891, d. Feb. 1977. Both, Anna & Mary, d/o's of Jacob W. & Josephine G. Beltzhoover. See Nos. 504, 505, pp. 96-97.
****
MARY S. BELTZHOOVER From Library of Congress Records, A song, "Cling to the Rock" published in 1862 by Henry S. Revd and dedicated to Miss Mary S. Beltzhoover. Deanna has a Mary, dau. of George and Elizabeth Kuntz Beltzhoover, but doesn't know if this is the right one.
****
FREDERICK W. BELTZHOOVER d., 28 Oct. 1868, Notice in Cincinnati Commerical, p. 5 1 Nov. 1868 (28 years old). See

----

1. Pittsburgh Gazette May 8, 10 1897 reported the death of Harriet B. as May 7, 1897,, Courtesy Norman Schwotzer

2. Pittsburgh Gazette Death Notices Feb. 13. 1895; Harry B. died 12 Feb. 1895 Courtesy Norman Schwotzer

3. Obituary Seguin Gazette Enterprise , Seguin, TX. 10 Mar. 1985

#152, p. 44.

****

McMAHON, Thomas (9-7-07 to 8-29-75) husband of Florence Moeller, s/o Bernard and Hattie Beltzhoover McMahon, g. Oak Hill Cemetery, Springfield Twp. Cemeteries, Hamilton Co., OH

****

ELLEN BELTZHOOVER, b. 30 Dec. 1911, d. 10 Mar. 1952, daughter of David and Harriet Beltzhoover, g. Mt. Washington Cemetery, Anderson Twp., Hamilton Co., OH. Her last residence was Washington, D. C. bur. section 11, lot ?

****

GEORGE SINDORF BELTZHOOVER, b. 12 July 1885 (not known where he was born), d. 4 Nov. 1953, Los Angeles, CA., son of John Beltzhoover and wife Ella Sindorf Beltzhoover. Ella S. Beltzhoover, age 75 (born PA) on the 1930 California census and her son, George S. Beltzhoover, age 44, in the same household. Ella applied for a CW widow's pension on Jan 10, 1891. John Beltzhoover was a Sgt. Co. C., G., 1st Regiment Maryland Calvary file # M 388 Roll 1. Then, John was found in the 1890 Federal Census Wisc. Veterans Schedule and it shows him living at the NW Branch National Home in 1890. Ella filed again for something in CA June 1, 1932. There was a John Beltzhoover who enlisted in MD 25 Aug. 1861. There also was a John H. Beltzhoover who enlisted in PA on 21 July 1864. [1]

****

ADDIE KLINE BELTZHOOVER, b. 22 July 1857, PA., d. 17 Jan. 1950, Los Angeles, d/o --?-- Kline and wf., --?-- Baker Kline.

****

NANCY BELTZHOOVER, Mrs, m. 3 Dec. 1871, St. Louis, MO., Thomas McSpiritt. She was the widow of a Beltzhoover?

****

JANE BELTZHOOVER, Mrs., d. 2 Feb. 1888, pp. 10,24,26 [2]

****

MARIA BELTZHOOVER, b. c. 1875, in 1920 Census, Santa Monica Twp., Los Angeles, CA., b. Stelermark, Syria, age 45

****

MRS. BELTZHOOVER, Peters Twp. Washington Co., PA., Dr. Hugh Thompson, res. near Thompsonville, and was a large land owner and Dr. in Canonsburg, PA. His son Robert "Doctor Bob" took over his father's practice for several years then removed to Bridgeville, which is about 12 miles SW of Pittsburgh, where he married a Mrs. Beltzhoover and died there. [3]

Dr. Robert Thompson was a Trustee of Peter's Creek Presbyterian Church, and J.P. on July 15, 1781, he was famous for his horsemanship. He had a son, Robert, also an M.D. who went

----

1. Oklepek, Deanna 5/5/03

2. Death Notices 1786-1900 Microfilm Carnegie Library, Mrs. Jane Beltzhoover. Courtesy Norman Schwotzer

3. History of Washington Co., PA. Peter's Twp. pp. 887, 899

to Wash. Co., OH; served in the State Senate from Guernsey Co., OH.; and then lived in Columbus, OH., where he died 18 Aug. 1886. The Samuel McMillan Manuscript p. 196 lists several of the Thompson family. These may be death dates: Dr. H. B. Thompson 19 May 1845 (87); Esther Thompson 17 Mar. 1836 (74); Robert 27 Mar. 1857 (95); Louiza wf. of John P. C., 17 Aug 1865 (34) all "Oak Spring" Cemetery?

****

BARNABAS HUGHES married Miss Beltzhoover of Hagerstown, MD.

****

ELIZA J. LONG, wf. of Samuel B. #46, where son, George G. was omitted in error. Ch: (1810), Alexander, Rheuben, Catherine, George, Ella (Mary Ellen), Tillie (Matilda). In 1900, Eliza is with dau. Catherine Wilson and g-dau. Fannie Wilson. In 1910, she is second household from Richard Hicks, whose dau., Margaret was married to a Beltzhoover also.

****

BALDWIN BELTZHOOVER, in the 1870 census, age 12, b. 1857, FL., Key West, Monroe Co., FL. no further informaton.

****

Mrs. A. L. BELTZHOOVER TANZY\TANZEY, (Mary Ann Bausman, b. 1852) d/o Allen L. Tanzey & wf. Henrietta Clawson Bausman.

****

SARAH BELTZHOOVER, m. John AIRES, 14 Aug. 1800, Washington Co., MD.--Hagerstown? [1]

****

Census 1840 7th Ward Baltimore Co., MD., **George Beltzhoover**; 1840 census Washington Co., MD., Clear Spring Twp.; **Milly Beltzhoover**; 1860 census Washington Co., MD., Funkstown, **Sarah Beltzhoover**; 1819 Census Washinton Co., MD., **George Beltzhoover**; 1860 census Washington Co., MD., Hagerstown, **Amelia Beltzhoover**. [2]

****

Annie E. Mumfres/Mumper **Beltzhoover** b. ca. 1855, age 25, a widow, b. ca. 1855, PA. in the household of her parents in 1880 Census Carroll, York Co., PA. Her parents are shown as Michael B. Mumfres/Mumper, b. c. 1813, PA (67) and wf. Eliza J. Mumfres, b. c. 1820 (60), PA. Annie E. m/2, age 37, 12 Apr. 1892, Dillsburg, PA., by Rev. Barr, George W. Koch of Dillsburg. In the 1870 census, Carroll, York Co., Michael and Eliza Mumper had children Susie 15, John M., 12, Alverda 11. Is Susie 15 really Annie E.? [3]

****

H. Beltzhoover, single, female age 30, 1880, b. ca. 1850,

----

1. Maryland Marriages 1667-1899

2. Maryland Census 1772-1890

3. York Co., Marriage License Book K. p. 311, D. Oklepek

a cousin of the Munpher's household, and her parents both born in PA. Also in the household H. L. Beltzhoover, a cousin, male, b. c. 1857, PA. (23), both parents born in PA. Head of household, Barree, Huntingdon Co., PA., J. W. Munpher, iron manuf., b. c. 1855, PA. and wf. Lula Munpher, b. c. 1855. Lula Munpher indicates that her father was born in S.C. and her mother in PA. Also in the household, a widow, M. A. Munpher, mother, b. ca. 1835, (45) PA. and her mother and father were both born in PA. M. A. looks to be the mother of J. W. Munpher. How are the Beltzhoover's related and who are they?

Mary Ann **BELTZHOOVER**, d/o Christian Herman Beltzhoover and wf. Rebecca R. Wolford, grandaughter of Col. John Wolford, widow of Abraham Mumper? Mary Ann Wolford m. Abram Mumper?

****

ELIZABETH (RACHEL\ELIZABETH) BELTZHOOVER[4] (20), b. 4 Mar. 1794; d. 31 May 1878 (78-2-27), g., Silver Spring Cemeteries, Silver Spring Twp., Cumberland Co., PA.; d/o George and (Rachel LEIDIGH) Belzhoover/Beltzhoover. Rachel\Elizabeth married 25 June 1818-1819, John Herman, b. 19 May 1796; christened 10 June 1796, New Kingston; d. 16 Sept. 1859 (63-3-27)). He died after an illness of three days from lock jaw as a result of stepping on a nail. John Herman was the son of Christian Herman and wf. Elizabeth Bowers. [1] [2] [3]

John Herman was born on the homestead and passed his early life on the farm. He bought his father's farm and acquired land adjacent to the homestead, it was called "Maple Hill." He was a member of the Lutheran Church and was a Deacon and an Elder for many years.

John and Rachel\Elizabeth Beltzhoover Herman had ten children:
Issue: (Herman)
  (1)-Christian Herman
  (2)-Rachel A. Herman, m. George Leidigh
  (3)-Henrietta Herman
  (4)-Manasseh Herman, b. 1829, went west and returned and in 1859 married Mary E. Meily, d/o Jacob and Mary (Fry) Meily of Cumberland Co., To them children were: Warren Serenus, A. Lorena, Mary E. Rachel A. G., Manasseh H. Jr.
  (5)-George T. B. Herman
  (6)-John E. A. Herman, b. Mar. 1836; m./1 1859, Eliza J. Fought, d. 1868, d/o Daniel Fought, and there were two children: Mary E. and Bertha J. John E. A. m./2, 13 Mar. 1873, Lizzie A. Zeigler, d/o Abraham and Elizabeth (Horner)

---

1. Bates, Samuel P. History of Pennsylvania Part I p. 539 D Oklepeck

2. American Volunteer, Carlisle, PA. Thursday Mar. 11, 1819 D. Oklepeck

3. Beers, History of Cumberland Co., PA. , p. 539

Zeigler, of this county. Mr. & Mrs. Herman are members of the Lutheran Church. He was a man of excellent business habits, energentic and upright. In politics he was a Democrat. [1]

(7)-Margaret Herman

(8)-Maria Elizabeth Herman, (Beer's History p. 516 states that Thomas Ulric Williamson, Monroe Twp., near Allen, in 1855, marrying Marie Elizabeth, daughter of John and Elizabeth (Beltzhoover) Herman. Thomas Ulric Williamson, farmer, son of James & Mary (ULRIC) Williamson. (Monroe Township, Cumberland and Adams Co.'s PA. History p. 516)

Mr. & Mrs. T. U. Williamson celebrated their 50th Anniversay 25 January 1903 at their residence, one mile northeast of Churchtown. Guests included, viz: G. T. B. Herman and wife, John E. A. Herman and wife, James Williamson and family, Mrs. William Williamson and daughter, Mrs. Josephl L. Herman, Edward Quigley and sister, Alfred Baker and wife, G. W. Strock and family, Manasseh Myers and family, Lemouel Fought and wife, H. A. Walter and wife, Miss Retta Bowman, Mrs. J. W. Herman, H. T. Herman and family, W. W. Wonderly and family, E. W. Herman and family, Robert C. Jerman and wife, Edward Smyser and family, Christian Humrich and sister. [2]

Issue:

Mary E. Williamson
Thomas U. Williamson
James W. Williamson
Jennie L. Williamson
C. Herman Williamson
Cora M. Williamson
Lillie G. Williamson
Linda F. Williamson

(9) Joseph L. Herman, b. 4 Mar. 1813; d. 23 July (30-1-19)

(10) Benjamin F. Herman, b. 1 June 1806; ds. 17 Sept. 1830 (21-0-7).

****

HERMAN FAMILY (HERMAN/HERMANN/HARMAN)

The Beers History of Cumberland Co., (PA)on p. 539 states, "Cumberland Valley has no name of more antiquity and honor than that of Herman, and among the sons are men of high

----

1. History of Cumberland and Adams Co.'s, Biographical Sketches p. 539 Silver Spring Twp.,

2. Carlisle Sentinel 25 January 1905.

rank and great ability".

The Herman family originated in Germany. Martin Herman, b. Germany (1732-1804), immigrated to Philadelphia, landing July 2, 1752 and in 1754, then to Lancaster Co., PA., where he married Anna Dorothea Boerst (1738-1824) (87). On the 15th of April 1771 he purchased a tract of land called "St. Martin's" in Silver Spring Twp., Cumberland Co., PA., where he died in 1804 (72) g. Longsdorf Cemetery. [1] [2] [3]

Martin and Anna Dorothea Boerst Herman had children: John Herman, the eldest who married Rachel\Elizabeth Beltzhoover and Christian Herman (1761-1829, b. 20 Oct. 1761; m., who married Elizabeth Bauer/Bower(s). [4]

John (1796-1859), m. 1818, Rachel\Elizabeth Beltzhoover, d/o George and Rachel Leidigh Beltzhoover. (See under Elizabeth Beltzhoover)

Christian Herman, b. 20 Oct. 1761; d. 23 Oct. 1829. was a grandson of Martin Herman the immigrant. He married in 1799, Elizabeth Bowers/Bower/Bauer, d/o John and Elizabeth Bower (York Co., PA will L. 4, Huntingdon Twp. (now Adams Co.). Elizabeth was b. 21 Apr. 1773 at Gardner's near York Springs, York Co., PA.; d. 18 Feb. 1848 (74-9-27). Both are buried in Longsdorf Cem., Cumberland Co., PA. They were members of the New Kingstown Lutheran Church and their graves are in Longsdorf Cem. At one time he owned 610 acres of land. Christian served as a Private in Capt. Roodelph Stodler's (Rudolph Statler's) Company, First Battalion, Lancaster Co., Militia. [5]

Christian and Elizabeth Bower Herman had eleven children (the Cumberland History says ten), nine are named in his will. All baptisms in New Kingstown Lutheran Church.

Issue: (HERMAN)

(1) Martin Herman, b. 31 Jan. 1795; d. 10 Feb. 1799; m. Elizabeth Wolford (1802-1842); children were Margaret, Margery A., Mary J., P. Wolford, Martin C., David B.

(2) Johannes (John) Herman, b. 19 May 1796; d. 16 Sept. 1860, m. Rachel\Elizabeth Beltzhoover. Cemetery records for Silver Spring Cem., Silver Spring Twp., Cumberland Co., PA., show a John Herman, b. 14 May 1796; d. 16 Sept. 1859 age 63-3-27 and alongside is Elizabeth Herman, b. 4 Mar. 1794; d. 31 May 1878 age 78-2-27.

----

1. Lawson, Jane Lyle May 2003

2. Zeamer, Jere Courtesy Jane L. Lawson

3. Beers & Co., History of Cumberland and Adams Co.'s PA 1886 p. 380

4. Ibid., SAR Rachel Beltzhoover Herman

5. Penn. Archives, Series 5, Vol.7, p. 509

(3) (Mary) Anna Maria Herman, b. 11 Nov. 1799; d. 30 May
        1871; m. Michael G. Belhoover of Cumberland
        Co., PA.
(4) Jacob, b. 3 June 1798; d. 11 Aug. 1864; m. Elizabeth
        --?--who was b. 10 Nov. 1799; d. 31 Mar. 1882.
        They had a dau. Angeline Harman Morrett; d. 16
        May 1864 (23-3-2), d/o Jacob and Elizabeth
        Harman and wf. of Hez. Morrett. Angeline and
        Hez. Morrett had a dau. d. 10 Aug. 1863 (26
        days).
(5) Anna Dorothea Herman, b. 4 Feb. 1805; m. Dr. Jacob
        Bosler, Mechanicsburg physician and drug store
        operator, before moving to Ohio.
(6) Elizabeth Herman, b. 30 Sept. 1810; m. 20 Feb. 1830,
        Abraham Bosler of Cumberland Co., PA., They
        were married by Rev. James Williamson, pastor
        of Silver Spring Presbyterian Church.
(7) Martin Christian Herman, b. 10 July 1801; d. 22 May
        1872; m. Feb. 1827, Elizabeth Wolford, b. 1802,
        York Co., PA., d. 30 July 1852 d/o Hon. Peter
        and Elizabeth ALBERT Wolford. They had six
        children: Margaret, wf. of Ezra Myers of Adams
        Co.; Margert A. wf.of Rev. A. W. Lilly of York;
        Mary Jane, wf. of Crawford Fleming of Carlisle,
        PA.; Peter Wolford Herman, Martin C. Herman
        (Judge); David B., (1844-1876), killed by
        Indians on a cattle ranch;
(8) Christian Bower Herman; b. 1802; d. 1863; m. 1850,
        Mary Armstrong.
(9) David Herman, b. 28 Feb. 1807
(10) Benjamin F. Herman, b. 31 Aug. 1809; d. 17 Sept.
        1830 (21-0-7), g. New Kingston.
(11) Joseph L. Herman, b. 6 Mar. 1813; d. 25 July 1833
        (30-1-19), g. New Kingston

* * * * * * * * * *

INDEX

Gayle O. Kamp
2006

162

163

Mary Maria, 41
Mary Paulina, 51
Mary Roane, 27, 51
Mary S., 152
Mary/Anna Maria HERMAN, 158
Mary/Maria, 22
Mary/Mary S.?, 61
Mary/Mazie, 152
Matilda, 22
Matilda (Tillie), 154
Matilda Long, 43
Mayme, 83
Mazie, 99
Melcheor, 1, 3
Melchior, 13, 14, 18, 20, 38, 50
Melchior (1810-1850), 21, 22, 38,
   40, 41
Melchior Roch (1892-1945), 75, 96
Melchior Roch III, 112
Melchior Roch Jr., 96
Melchior Roch Jr. (1918-2002), 111
Melchior Stewart, 47, 48, 52, 75
Melchior Stewart Capt.
   (1868-1918), 74
Melchior Wallace Capt., 26
Melchior Wallace Capt.
   (1815-1879), 47, 48, 75
Melchor, 4, 67, 91
Melchor Bailey, 68
Melchor M. (1837-1907), 67
Melchor Mason, 40
Mesha, 22
Michael, 34, 61, 62, 79
Michael (1773-1843), 4, 5
Michael (1792-   ), 60
Michael (1809-   ), 34, 60
Michael (1824-1883), 82
Michael B., 54
Michael C.?\G.? (1860-1914), 82
Michael G., 76, 158
Michael G. (1792-1873), 31, 52, 53
Milly, 154
Minerva, 60
Monroe C./G., 85
Moris/Morris, 54
Mrs., 153
Myra T. Anna DALE, 92
Myrtle, 71
Myrtle M. TOMLINSON, 107
Myrtle May TOMLINSON, 93
Nancy, 21, 22, 44
Nancy H. FITCH MCSPIRIT, 45
Nancy Mrs., 153
Nathaniel, 152
Nellie M., 103, 117
Nola, 83
Olive, 72

Peal KENT, 104
Pearl KENT, 87
Phyllis Eileen, 116
Rachel, 32, 58
Rachel Christine, 142
Rachel Elizabeth, 83, 100, 157
Rachel LEIDIGH, 155, 157
Rachel Michelle, 142
Rachel WATTS
   Mrs. THOMPSON, 82, 83
Rachel/Elizabeth, 52
Reba Pauline, 102, 115, 116
Rebecca, 82
Rebecca LEIDIGH, 55, 56
Rebecca Margaret KUNTZ, 62, 63
Rebecca R. WOLFORD, 76, 155
Regina, 29, 30
Reuben Henry, 43
Rhea Grace, 94
Rhea Grace WELLER, 94
Rhea Jeanne, 94, 108, 122
Richard Lee, 116, 132
Rita RUSCIN, 116
Robert Edward, 84
Robert Henry, 92
Ruben, 154
Ruth Ann, 106, 121
Ruth Audley Britton, 96, 112
Ruth Audley Britton WHEELER, 96
Ryan Michael, 142
S. P., 69
S. Pryor, 91
Sallie, 47
Samuel, 3, 7, 14, 15, 16, 61
Samuel (1785-1817/1819), 10, 22
Samuel (1803-1836), 34, 58
Samuel (1823-1890), 21
Samuel (Dr. Sam) (1823-1890), 22
Samuel Dr., 69
Samuel G. (1838-1869), 45
Samuel M.D. (1823-1890), 43
Samuel S. (1818-1851), 23
Sanuel Blackmore, 43
Sarah, 16, 36, 61, 154
Sarah (Sally), 32, 34, 58
Sarah (Sister Agatha), 51
Sarah/Sarahan, 60
Shatto/Shotto, 76
Sheri Leah HAIR, 142
Sherry French GARDNER, 112
Silas Pryer II (1905-1957), 105
Silas Pryor, 2, 42, 70, 107
Silas Pryor (1847-1915), 43, 68
Silas Pryor (1905-1957), 92
Susan Mae, 84, 101
Susan RHERER, 58, 59
Susan/Annie?, 61

Susannah/Susan, 56
Tari Lynn HINSHAW, 142
Thomas, 13, 92
Thomas H., 91
Thomas Hessler, 92
Thomas Husler (1892-1975), 70
Thomas Skiles (1863-1916), 84, 100
Virginia Lee, 96, 112
Virginia Lee KOONTZ, 48, 74
Virginia Roane, 75, 96
Vivian, 129
Vivian Louise KRECKER, 92, 106
William, 3, 7, 17, 20, 24, 59
William (1844-1935), 86, 87
William (c.1811-c.1867), 21, 22,
   39, 40
William (ca.1785-   ), 10
William (Willie), 50
William N., 68
William S., 116
William Smith, 101
William Smith (1879-1959), 84
Wm., 25
Wunderlich, 76
Zara, 26, 47, 48
Zara Miss, 27, 28
BELTZHOVER
Kate M. Mrs., 27
BELTZHUBER,

   see BELTZHOOVER
Anna Maria, 1, 2, 4, 12
Anna Maria (Mary), 2
Anna Maria (Mary/Polly)
   GROSS, 29
Anna Maria GROSS, 30
Catherina, 5
Catherine (Regina) MICHAELS, 28
Chistena Sophia ZINN, 11
Christian Melchior/Melchor
   (1713-1760), 1
Christina, 10, 35
Conrad, 64
Daniel, 4, 30, 31
Elizabeth, 5, 12
Elizabeth relic, 7
Elizabeth SHUNK, 7
Eva, 11
Eva GROSS, 33
George, 10, 30
George (Conrad) Conrad
   (1741-1815), 10
George Conrad, 3, 4, 11
George Peter (1768-1846), 11
George Peter Sr. (1768-1846),
   28, 29
Harri Etta, 38

172

176

178

184

189

Printed in the United States
57054LVS00002B/253